Birds of Oregon

Status an

D0732247

Editors

Jeff Gilligan

Dennis Rogers

Mark Smith

Alan Contreras

Illustrations

Ramiel Papish

Technical Consultant

Owen Schmidt

Contributing Authors

David Anderson

Jim Carlson

Tom Crabtree

Dan Gleason

Steve Gordon

Tad Finnel

Dave Irons

George Jobanek

Mark Koninendyke

C.D. Littlefield

Alan McGie

Terry Morgan

Harry Nehls

James Olson

Eleanor Pugh

Owen Schmidt

Brian Sharp

Richard Smith

Tye Steinbach

Steve Summers

Bill Thackaberry

Clarice Watson

Herb Wisner

Cinclus Publications

McMinnville, Oregon

Birds of Oregon: status and distribution
/ editors, Jeff Gilligan, [et. al] ;
illustrations, Ramiel Papish ; technical
consultant, Owen Schmidt. -- McMinnville, Or.
: Cinclus Publications, ©1994.

p. : ill. ; cm.

Includes bibliographical references (p.)
and index.
ISBN 0-9637765-1-7

1. Birds--Oregon--Geographical
distribution. 2. Bird populations--Oregon.
I. Gilligan, Jeff.

QL684.07B   598.2'9795 dc20
                                          00-

Cinclus Publications
Box 284
McMinnville, OR, 97128
U.S.A.

Table of Contents

List of Maps

Introduction

This book is intended to provide both the knowledgeable field ornithologist and the beginner interested in Oregon's birds a single convenient reference regarding the *status* and *distribution* of the state's birds. By status we mean information about whether each species breeds in, migrates through, or winters in the state, as well as any changes in these patterns that have become apparent. A brief summary of records of birds that have occurred in Oregon only a few times, usually called "vagrants," is also included.

Regarding distribution, we have tried to describe accurately *where* in the state each species occurs at different times of year or under varying conditions. The ranges of distinct subspecies are discussed in a few cases when we thought such a detailed review might be of interest to most readers.

This book does not provide information on bird identification except in a few cases; there are many fine field guides and references available for that purpose. We recommend the National Geographic Society's *Field Guide to North American Birds*.

For a good overview of what birds you are likely to find in a particular location we recommend *A Birder's Guide to Oregon* by Joe Evanich or *Birding Oregon* by Fred Ramsey. Both are available at many bookstores and can be ordered if not on the shelf. Evanich covers many more areas; Ramsey generally provides more detailed coverage, but is somewhat out of date.

In order to understand Oregon's avifauna it is necessary to understand the state's geography, vegetation, and even weather patterns. We have provided an overview of these topics; for more information we recommend the following books: *Natural Vegetation of Oregon and Washington* (1975) by Franklin and Dyrness, available from OSU Press; *Mammals and Life Zones of Oregon* (1936) by Vernon Bailey (out of print but sometimes available through used book dealers), *Atlas of the Pacific Northwest* (1985, seventh edition) by A. Jon Kimerling and Philip L. Jackson, available from OSU Press, or the *Atlas of Oregon* (1976) by Loy et al. (out of print but easy to find at used book stores).

We hope that this book proves useful to anyone interested in Oregon's birds. Since any effort involving so many people, so much data, and so much time cannot help but contain errors or incomplete presentation of information, we encourage anyone to send corrections, changes, or thoughts about Oregon's birds to Jeff Gilligan.

Enjoy Oregon's birds!

Jeff Gilligan
Mark Smith
Alan Contreras
Dennis Rogers
July, 1994

Acknowledgments

There is no such thing as a bird distribution book written by one person or even a few people. The nature of a book on the distributive ornithology of a large region is such that hundreds of people contribute to it in one way or another. There is no perfect way to acknowledge these contributions, but we have attempted to do so here by thanking the many people who offered general or special expertise to this large undertaking. We have made every effort to acknowledge everyone who contributed to the book, but if we left someone out, it was an oversight.

The help provided by the Portland, Salem and Siskiyou Audubon Societies is gratefully acknowledged. Staff of the Nature Conservancy, Oregon Department of Fish and Wildlife, the U.S. Fish and Wildlife Service, the U.S. Forest Service and the Bureau of Land Management contributed considerable information to this book, as did staff from the Oregon State University Wildlife Research Unit.

The following people read preliminary versions or portions of the manuscript and provided helpful comments: David Bailey, Craig Corder, Tom Crabtree, David Fix, Matt Hunter, Nick Lethaby, Donna Lustoff, Jim Johnson, Craig Miller, Mark Stern, and Steve Summers.

Thanks are due to:

Ann & Merle Archie, Ben Arndt, David Bailey, Bob Barnes, Range Bayer, Barb Bellin, Marshall Beretta, Tim Bickler, Diana Bradshaw, M. Ralph Browning, John Biewerer, Christy Brindle, Terry Bryan, Dan Bump, Wilson Cady, Dawn Campbell, Judy Carlson, Barbara Combs, Romain Cooper, Craig Corder, Marion Corder, Cathy Crabtree, Fred Craig, John Crowell, Dave DeSante, Colin Dillingham, Steve Dowlan, Elsie Eltzroth, Merlin E. Eltzroth, Richard Erickson, Joe Evanich, Ben Fawver, Darrel Faxon, Hugh Feiss, Rob Fergus, Shawneen Finnegan, David Fix, Cecil Gagnon, John Gatchet, Roy Gerig, Greg Gillson, Rebecca Goggans, Sayre Greenfield, Barbara Griffin, Omar Halverson, Steve Heinl, Hendrik Herlyn, Steve Herman, David Herr, Lynn Herring, Barbara Hill,

W.E. Hoffman, Mike Houck, Rich Hoyer Sr., Rich Hoyer Jr., Bob Hudson, Tom Hunt, Matt Hunter, Kamal Islam, Steve Jaggers, Tim Janzen, Bonnie Jakubos, Jim Johnson, Meredith Jones, Sheran Jones, Durrel Kapan, Jan Kapan, Karen & Jerald Kearney, George Keister, John Kempe, Bob Kindschy, Ken Knittle, Harriet Kofalk, Jan & Rick Krabbe, Kit Larsen, Paul Lehman, Nick Lethaby, Gerard Lillie, Robert Loehning, Doug Lorain, Tom Love, Roy Lowe, Robert Lucas, Tom Lund, Mike Lundstrom, Donna Lusthoff, Don MacDonald, Ron Maertz, David Marshall, Larry McQueen, Kathy Merrifield, Tom & Allison Mickel, Craig Miller, Marjorie Moore, Charles Morrow, Pat Muller, Don Munson, Harry Nehls, S. Kim Nelson, Bob Olson, Bob O'Brian, Tom O'Neil, Carrie Osborne, Richard Palmer, Alice Parker, Mike Patterson, Dennis Paulson, Alice Pfand, Phil Pickering, Robert Pittman, Steve Powell, Eric Pozzo, Dorothy Pratt, Al Prigge, Claire Puchy, Bill Pyle, Fred Ramsey, Paul Reed, Craig Roberts, Jim Rogers, Skip Russel, Jon Sadowski, Martha Sawyer, Iris & John Schaumburg, Jerr Scoville, Guy Sheeter, Tim Shelmerdine, Paul Sherrel, Jamie Simmons, Gerald Smith, Elmer Specht, Kevin Spencer, Tom Staudt, Dave Stejskal, Mark Stern, Bill & Zanah Stotz, Paul Sullivan, Pricilla Summers, Otis Swisher, Shoaib Tareen, Verda Teale, Larry Thornburgh, Lyn Topits, Charles Trost, Bill Tweit, Dan van den Broek, Dennis Vroman, Teri Waldron, Ann Ward, Tom Winters, Linda Weiland, Bob Wilson, Tom Winters, and Bing Wong.

The editors are responsible for any incorrect use of data provided by the many people who helped produce this book.

Oregon Field Ornithologists

Oregon Field Ornithologists is the principal statewide birding organization. It publishes the quarterly *Oregon Birds*, which carries articles on distribution, behavior, and population trends mostly written by amateurs. Field notes detailing sightings from around the states are a mainstay. Members can also submit their personal lists for Oregon and its counties at the end of year for publication and comparison.

A number of other publications as well as T-shirts etc. are for sale. A complete listing can be found in each issue of *Oregon Birds*.

The group also holds annual meetings and weekend conferences at various birding localities around the state. For membership information write: Oregon Field Ornithologists, Box 10373, Eugene, OR, 97440.

Oregon Field Ornithologists sponsors the Oregon Bird Records Committee. It reviews records of species defined as rarities within the state. Most of the species on its review list are those defined as "vagrant" in the text of this book, generally those recorded fewer than four times per year in the state. The committee archives written reports, photographs, sound recordings, etc. that it reviews. It also establishes the official OFO list of Oregon birds. Records can be submitted to: Harry Nehls, Secretary, OBRC, 2736 SE 20th Ave., Portland, OR, 97202.

A Brief History of Oregon Ornithology

Oregon bird lists date from 1814, when the Paul Allen edition of Lewis and Clark's expedition report appeared, with brief mention of birds seen. Each decade thereafter witnessed explorers' reports, observations of military men, and records by early residents of the birds around their settlements. The first state list, however, did not appear until just before the end of the nineteenth century.

In three numbers of the *Oregon Naturalist*, from 1895 into 1896, Arthur L. Pope published "A List of the Birds of Oregon." Pope was then president of the Northwestern Ornithological Association, a group he had founded the year before, and prepared his list as an association project with members' assistance. It lists 252 species, most without annotation. There are several dubious records, such as Greater Prairie-Chicken, Sooty Tern, and Brown Noddy, that are not now accepted as valid. Ira Gabrielson and Stanley Jewett, in *Birds of Oregon*, either overlooked or disregarded Pope's list. However, it was a significant and historical contribution to an understanding of the state's birdlife.

In 1901, William R. Lord privately published a slim volume, *A First Book upon the Birds of Oregon and Washington*. He listed 106 species, and illustrated the book with photographs of mounted specimens. Shortly after the book's appearance, the Oregon Text Book Commission selected it to be used in the public schools. Lord began an immediate revision, which appeared in 1902. This second edition listed 142 species, and replaced all but one of the illustrations with more attractive photographs. Furthermore, to facilitate its use in the schools, Lord added a chapter outlining "a course of study upon birds for schools and bird-students." In a short section, he discussed the early bird literature of the two states. Lord reprinted the book in 1913 in an edition identical to that of 1902 except for the addition of three regional lists.

At the same time as Lord's second edition, Arthur R. Woodcock published his "Annotated List of the Birds of Oregon." Woodcock prepared this as a thesis for the Master of Science degree from Oregon Agricultural College (as Oregon State University was then known). It lists 274 species, and includes observations of 23 persons from 40 locations in 19 counties, following the model of Lyman Belding's 1890 publication, "Land Birds of the Pacific District." Gabrielson and Jewett described Woodcock's list as "the first real list of the birds of the State," but added that Woodcock was "somewhat unfortunate in the selection of his observers and accepted many statements that, to say the least, are dubious." These dubious records include species such as Ashy Storm-Petrel, American Oystercatcher, Gull-billed Tern, and Japanese Murrelet.

In the 1920s, two works appeared that dealt with Oregon birds within a larger regional context. Willard A. Eliot published *Birds of the Pacific Coast* in 1923. The main text omitted many major groups, such as the ducks and geese and almost all shorebirds. A "List of the Birds Found in British Columbia, Washington, Oregon and California" credited Oregon with 329 species. Joseph Grinnell found several inaccuracies and complained in a review that despite the apparent regional focus implied by the title, "the whole book breathes of *Oregon*, but Oregon is only one of a series of 'Pacific Coast' states."

In 1927, Ralph Hoffmann published *Birds of the Pacific States*. This again treated Oregon as part of a region, but in a more accurate and comprehensive fashion than Eliot. Hoffmann based the Oregon distributional and abundance descriptions on the notes of Stanley Jewett. Hoffmann's perceptive observations of behavior make this book still highly readable, useful, and enjoyable 65 years after its publication.

Ira Gabrielson and Stanley Jewett are remembered by recent generations of birders as the authors of *Birds of Oregon*, published in 1940 by Oregon Agricultural College (reprinted in 1970 by Dover Publications as *Birds of the Pacific Northwest*). Written by Gabrielson, but with the notes and assistance of Jewett, the book lists 333 species for Oregon, with an additional 24 species included in an hypothetical list. The species accounts carefully delineate distribution and abundance, and are significant historical records.

Although numerous short articles appeared in the thirty years following *Birds of Oregon*, another statewide publication did not appear until Gerald A. Bertrand's and J. Michael Scott's "Check-list of the Birds of Oregon," in 1971. This listed 364 species for Oregon, with 24 hypothetical species, and defined distribution and abundance in five geographical zones within the state. The authors republished the list with only slight changes in 1973. In 1979, Merlin S. Eltzroth and Fred L. Ramsey revamped both the zonal definitions and the distributional and abundance annotations in a third edition; Eltzroth republished in 1987.

Other state lists, appeared in the 1970s and 1980s. Larry McQueen and Sue Motsinger began circulating a state list in the mid-1970s. George Jobanek revised this list and published a preliminary copy in *SWOC Talk* in 1976, requesting reader input prior to final publication. A final draft was never published, however. Tom Crabtree and Harry Nehls published "A Checklist of the Birds of Oregon" in *Western Birds* in 1981, and in 1986, the Oregon Bird Records Committee published in *Oregon Birds* "The Official Checklist of Oregon Birds." Field checking cards listing the birds of Oregon, often ephemeral in duration, have circulated within the birding community periodically.

Familiar Birds of Northwest Forests, Fields and Gardens, by David B. Marshall (1973), and *Familiar Birds of Northwest Shores and Waters*, by Harry B. Nehls (1975) are informative and useful. They are also regional works without a specific focus on Oregon. The same is true of the more inclusive *Birds of the Pacific Northwest: Washington, Oregon, Idaho and British Columbia*, by Earl J. Larrison (1981). Both *Birding Oregon*, by Fred L. Ramsey (1981) and *The Birder's Guide to Oregon*, by Joseph E. Evanich, Jr. (1990) include state lists supplemental to their site guides.

Oregon's Geography and Habitats

The varied topography of Oregon contributes to its variety of avifauna. Four geologically separate mountain ranges and several intermontane valleys are the most significant features, while the high plateau of the Great Basin also covers a significant portion of the state's area. The impact of the Pacific Ocean on the climate of Oregon reaches beyond the immediate coastal area.

Coastal headlands with second-growth Sitka spruce and lodgepole pine forest, Lincoln County.

The near-shore Pacific is generally a rich habitat for birdlife, becoming somewhat less so beyond the edge of the continental shelf a few miles off the coast. Boat trips well offshore usually produce a good variety of species not readily seen from land, but this aspect of Oregon's ornithology is not as well known, especially in the more inclement seasons.

The Pacific coastline varies from rugged headlands to sandy beaches at different parts of its 300-mile reach. With the exception of the Columbia, Umpqua, and Rogue Rivers and their valleys, most of the west side of the Coast Range is drained by short rivers and creeks that empty directly into the ocean or the larger bays. In a few places the topography has allowed the formation of tidal estuaries which are of special interest as stopping points for migrating waterbirds.

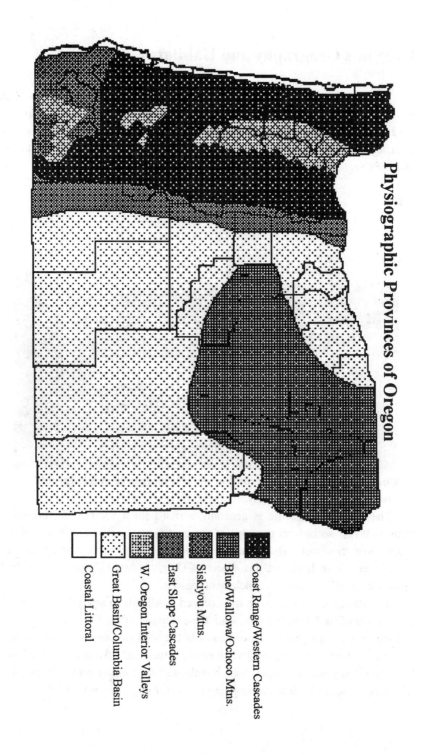

Physiographic Provinces of Oregon

Coast Range/Western Cascades

Blue/Wallowa/Ochoco Mtns.

Siskiyou Mtns.

East Slope Cascades

W. Oregon Interior Valleys

Great Basin/Columbia Basin

Coastal Littoral

Important bays and estuaries include the mouth of the Columbia River, Nehalem Bay, Tillamook Bay, Siletz Bay, Yaquina Bay, the estuary of the Siuslaw River, Winchester Bay, Coos Bay, the estuary of the Coquille River, and the mouth of the Rogue River. For the most part these are shallow bays that vary a great deal in size depending on the tide, at low tide exposing large areas of good foraging habitat for migrant and wintering shorebirds.

Tidal estuary with mud flats covered. Siletz Bay, Lincoln County

The forests in the immediate influence of salt water are primarily dominated by Sitka spruce, Douglas-fir, Western hemlock, and the coastal form of the Lodgepole pine, known locally as shore pine. Few untouched examples of this habitat remain, as most have been logged sometime in the last 50-80 years, and many areas have been converted to residential development, pasture or cranberry bogs. Understory is generally heavy with various species of woody plants and ferns, and brush quickly re-colonizes cleared areas. This habitat is not distinct enough to have localized birds, though the Wrentit is a characteristic species whose range ends abruptly at the Columbia River.

The Coast Range from the Columbia south to northern Coos County is characterized by heavy rainfall, often as much as 150 inches per year, and lush forests of Douglas fir, western hemlock, and western red cedar. Habitat is consistent up to the tops of the highest peaks at nearly 5,000 feet. Virtually all of the coast range is in various stages of regrowth following heavy logging in the last

50 years. Characteristic birds of the second-growth forests here are Hermit Warbler, Winter Wren, Swainson's Thrush, and Varied Thrush.

Further south and extending inland through Josephine and southern Jackson Counties, the Siskiyou range is geologically older than the Coast Range and supports many plants with Californian affinities. At lower elevations, its forests are similar to those of the Coast Range but above about 3,000 ft. dry forest types become prevalent. These are dominated by Douglas-fir, sugar and western white pines, Port Orford and incense cedars, and tanoak. Mesic shrubs including various *ceanothus* and *manzanita* species and tanoak dominate large areas of natural clearings and improperly reforested clearcuts, providing habitat for a legion of MacGillivray's Warblers. At the highest areas of these mountains, some over 5,000 ft., much of the ground is untimbered. This area supports a number of unusual plants, including an endemic tree, the Brewer's spruce. Birds of this area are more typical of eastern Oregon, including Mountain Chickadee, Rock Wren, and Green-tailed Towhee nesting within 30 miles of the coast.

Inland, the great interior valleys can be divided into two groups. The Willamette River and its tributaries drain much of the Coast Range and the west side of the Cascades, forming a great broad valley. These rich soils were settled early and converted to agriculture almost in their entirety, but areas of regrowth

Typical scene from the Willamette valley, with grain fields, pastures, and Christmas tree plantations. Yamhill County.

provide habitat for many adaptable birds, and wintering geese utilize the fields in great numbers. Further south, the valleys of the Umpqua and Rogue Rivers are drier and not so agriculturally productive, but still are mostly altered. Oak forest mixed with Douglas-fir or the local Jeffrey pine is more typical, especially of the Rogue Valley, which supports habitat for several birds not found widely elsewhere in Oregon. California Towhee, Plain Titmouse and especially Blue-gray Gnatcatcher are primarily associated with the *ceanothus* chaparral that forms thick fields of brush in some areas.

The outstanding geological feature of the state is the Cascade Range, a string of dormant and extinct volcanoes with several peaks above 10,000 feet. The range of altitudes and rainfall regimens means that the Cascades support a variety of habitats. Mostly the lower elevations of the west slope are similar to the Coast Range, though the predominance of public ownership in some areas means that more old-growth remains untouched. Some of the last remaining strongholds of the Northern Spotted Owl are here.

High-elevation forest dominated by *Abies* firs and Lodgepole pine, short and sparse near timberline. Deschutes County.

Higher, the forests are dominated by *Abies* firs, Mountain hemlock, and Lodgepole pine. The low commercial value of the timber here means that large areas are for the most part intact, and several wilderness areas have been established. Oregon's only National Park, Crater Lake, protects a large area of this alpine forest type. Many birds typical of more northerly climes inhabit this zone, such as Three-toed Woodpecker, Boreal Owl, and Gray Jay.

The rain shadow effect means that the east slope of the Cascades Range is much dryer, and it is dominated by Ponderosa and Lodgepole pines in a regime requiring regular fires for regeneration. Fifty years of successful fire suppression in the name of forest protection have altered this habitat in some areas, as has logging of the valuable Ponderosa, so that in many areas White fir has become a major component. The open pine forests, often with a knee-high understory of Antelope bitterbrush, have many interesting birds including White-headed Woodpecker, Williamson's Sapsucker, Pygmy Nuthatch, and Clark's Nutcracker.

Stretching east into Idaho and Nevada, the high deserts of the Great Basin occupy nearly a third of the state. Large areas here are without any outlet to the sea and drain into lakes or large marshes where the water is fresh enough to

Sagebrush desert typical of the Great Basin, with isolated mountains supporting a few trees at higher elevations. Deschutes County.

allow marsh vegetation, such as in the Malheur National Wildlife Refuge. Several lakes, such as Harney, Summer, and Abert, are too alkaline to support anything but brine shrimp, though these feed large populations of American Avocet and Wilson's Phalarope and provide refuge for a few Snowy Plovers.

Vast areas of the Great Basin are covered with sagebrush, with some influx of junipers depending on grazing pressure and moisture. Typical birds of this habitat include Sage Sparrow, Loggerhead Shrike, and Brewer's Sparrow. Several isolated mountain ranges of considerable size, such as Steens Mountain and Hart Mountain, break the monotony of the desert. The higher elevations capture enough moisture to support forests similar to the east slope of the Cascades, with similar birdlife.

Isolated oases in this desert concentrate migrants and have produced many of the sightings of vagrants in Oregon. Malheur National Wildlife Refuge Headquarters and the town of Fields in Harney County figure prominently in any listing of the rare birds of Oregon.

North of the Great Basin, the Deschutes and John Day Rivers flow north towards the Columbia through canyons of their own making and forests related to the east side of the Cascades. Nearer the Columbia is a large area of rolling plains that was once sage desert and grassland but has mostly been converted to dryland wheat production, with the original habitat restricted to canyons too steep for agriculture. Oases here also offer potential for vagrants.

In Northeast Oregon, the Blue and Wallowa Mountains are old ranges with connections to the Rocky Mountains. Birdlife includes typical Rocky mountain species like Spruce Grouse and Pine Grosbeak. Forests here are similar to interior types, and have suffered a great deal due to fire control. In many areas, pines have been replaced by disease- and insect-prone Grand fir and large areas of timber are dying, much to the benefit of the local woodpecker population. Riparian zones in these mountains have several birds of more eastern affinities not regular elsewhere in Oregon, including Gray Catbird, Veery, and American Redstart.

Most areas of Oregon will fall within one of these definitions, though transitional climes of course exist. The birdlife of any location will reflect its position among the biological diversity of Oregon.

Oregon
Counties

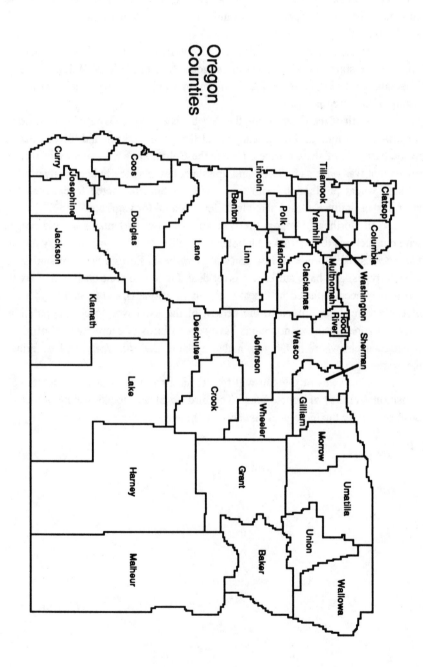

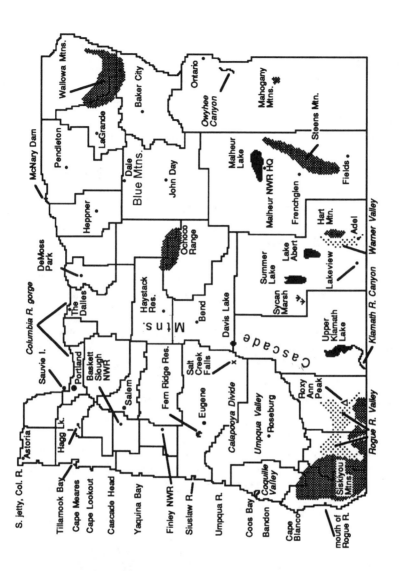

Frequently
Mentioned
Locations

Definitions:

Summer Resident: A breeding species normally found within the described range in summer.

Visitant: A species that is found within a particular area at the described season, but does not breed.

Transient: A species that migrates through a particular area, but does not either spend the winter or summer there.

Migrant: A species that migrates. It may be a transient, or a species that moves into and out of an area to spend part of the year.

Erratic: A species whose movements are not predictable.

The terms of relative abundance cannot be precisely defined. In descending order of abundance the terms used range from Abundant, Very Common, Common, Fairly Common, Uncommon, Very Uncommon, Rare, Very Rare, to Vagrant. At the extremes, Abundant species are present in truly large and conspicuous numbers, while Common species are present in good numbers considering the habitat and special requirements of the species, usually filling the available habitat. Rare birds are present in only small numbers, and generally fall short of filling the available habitat that would appear suitable.

The terms of relative abundance are not numerically comparable from one species to another. The habitat, food, and spacial requirements of the particular species must be taken into consideration. A raptor that might be described as uncommon may need several square miles of territory, while there may be several dozen vireos of a species also described as uncommon in the same area.

Key to common map features

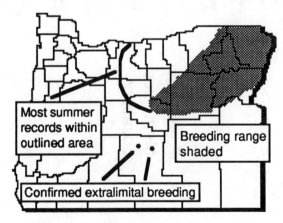

xvi

Species

Accounts

Order GAVIIFORMES
Family Gaviidae

Red-throated Loon. *Gavia stellata.*

Common transient, uncommon winter visitant, and rare summer visitant along the coast. Rare winter visitant and an uncommon spring visitant along the lower Columbia R. Rare to very uncommon transient and winter visitant inland in western Oregon and along the Columbia R. east to Sherman Co. Rare elsewhere in eastern Oregon.

The Red-throated Loon is a common transient along the coast. The first fall influx arrives in late August and numbers gradually build to a peak in late October and November, then decrease through December. It remains as an uncommon to locally fairly common winter visitant, especially on estuaries and more sheltered inshore ocean waters. The earliest signs of the spring migration are in late March, but it is usually not until late April that a large movement begins. An example of migrant numbers is 40 per hour passing the mouth of the Columbia R. on May 1, 1976. The spring migration continues through May, and transients are sometimes noted into June. This loon remains as a rare non-breeding summer visitant along the coast.

The Red-throated Loon is a rare to uncommon winter visitant in inland western Oregon. It is most regularly recorded on large bodies of water such as Fern Ridge Res., Lane Co., Henry Hagg L., Washington Co., and along the Columbia R. from Sherman Co. to the ocean. It is an uncommon to fairly common spring visitant along the lower Columbia R. from Multnomah Co. to the ocean from late February to early April, especially when large numbers of smelt are in the river. In eastern Oregon away from the Columbia, it is a rare visitant to large bodies of water. Most such records are from fall.

The Red-throated Loon migrates over the ocean within sight of land, often in the company of other loon species. It utilizes the ocean near shore, estuaries, and to a lesser extent, fresh water for feeding and resting.

Pacific Loon. *Gavia pacifica.*

An abundant transient along the coast, uncommon winter and summer visitant. Rare transient and winter visitant to inland western Oregon. Rare east of the Cascade Mts.

The Pacific Loon is primarily a coastal species in Oregon. Huge numbers migrate over the ocean within sight of land in both spring and fall. It is an uncommon winter visitant along the coast, being far less numerous than either the Common Loon or the Red-throated Loon. It is also an uncommon non-breeding summer visitant along the coast.

The southward movement starts in mid-August and peaks in late October and early November. Very large numbers are often observed during this period. The spring migration occurs from mid-April to late June and is often spectacular. As many as 2,500 per hour have been seen passing coastal locations in early May, and a small but steady northward flight has been observed as late as the last week of June. Resting flocks of several thousand have been observed on the ocean as late as early June.

Along the coast the Pacific Loon prefers the ocean near shore, but also utilizes estuaries and occasionally freshwater lakes. This species is a rare transient and winter visitant inland west of the Cascades, where it is usually recorded on large reservoirs, lakes, and along the Columbia R. It is a rare transient at larger bodies of water east of the Cascades, mostly in fall and early winter.

Common Loon. *Gavia immer.*

Common winter visitant and transient along the coast. Uncommon to rare winter visitant and transient inland. Uncommon summer visitant along the coast. Very rare summer visitant inland.

The Common Loon is common along the coast from late August into May. It remains common throughout the winter, but is most numerous during the fall and spring migrations. Along the coast it utilizes the open ocean within about a half-mile of shore, estuaries, the larger rivers, and freshwater lakes. A few non-breeding birds summer along the coast, at that season the species is uncommon to very uncommon.

It occurs almost anywhere inland as a winter visitant and transient where large, reasonably deep bodies of water exist. The Columbia R., parts of the Willamette R., and larger lakes and reservoirs are utilized. Inland the species is generally uncommon to rare at some localities. An exceptional record was 438 on Wickiup Res., Deschutes Co. on April 15, 1993. Inland migrants are generally not noted in fall until October. The Common Loon is very rare inland during the summer months. Although it has summered at mountain lakes, and its mating calls have been heard at some of these locations, there is no evidence of nesting.

Yellow-billed Loon. *Gavia adamsii.*

Very rare transient and visitant along the coast. Vagrant inland.

The Yellow-billed Loon is a very rare winter visitant, mostly to the larger estuaries of the coast. Most records are from late September to April, but there are records from every month. There are four inland sightings. One was seen at Fern Ridge Res., Lane Co., Dec. 31, 1989-Jan. 3, 1990; one was at Timothy Lake, Clackamas Co., from May 15 to June 6, 1988; one was at the mouth of the Hood R., Hood River Co., in February 1990; and one was on the Klamath R., Klamath Co., on April 29, 1993.

Order PODICIPEDIFORMES
Family Podicipedidae

Pied-billed Grebe. *Podilymbus podiceps.*

Fairly common summer resident throughout Oregon. In winter, common in western Oregon and variably in low numbers east of the Cascades.

The Pied-billed Grebe is a fairly common summer resident on marsh-edged bodies of fresh water throughout Oregon. It breeds from sea level to over 5,000 ft., and is most abundant on the large marshes of Klamath, Lake, and Harney Cos.

3

Breeders are very secretive, but in other seasons the species occurs primarily on open water.

Migrants from north of the state arrive throughout Oregon in September and October. In western Oregon Pied-billeds are common to uncommon on open fresh water from October through March. Migrants depart in March and early April, leaving smaller numbers that breed locally. The species is very uncommon on estuaries in winter.

East of the Cascades most migrants and local birds depart by December and, depending on the availability of unfrozen water, are very uncommon to absent in winter. Breeders and transients return in late March and early April.

Horned Grebe. *Podiceps auritus.*

Very local and irregular summer resident east of the Cascades. Very rare else-where in summer. Common winter visitant on the coast and uncommon in interior valleys. Uncommon during migration and rare in winter east of the Cascades.

The Horned Grebe has bred intermittently at Malheur N.W.R. since 1958; in recent years a few pairs have usually nested on the refuge. Nesting has also occurred at Downy L., Wallowa Co., and Sycan Marsh, Lake Co., where at least five pairs nested in 1981. Breeding may also occur irregularly on Upper Klamath L., where as many as 10 birds have been observed in summer.

Horned Grebes are common winter visitants to the coast, first arriving from late August and early September. They depart in late March and April, with a few present into mid-May. The greatest numbers occur during migratory peaks in late September and October, and late March and April. Some coastal CBCs regularly tally over 100 individuals. Non-breeders are very rare on the coast in summer.

In the interior valleys of western Oregon and along the Columbia R., the Horned Grebe is uncommon (common along parts of the Columbia R.) from September through early May, and very rare at other times. East of the Cascades it is very rare away from breeding areas in summer. It is rare east of the Cascades (away from the Columbia R.) in winter, and uncommon during migration from late August through early November, and from late March into May.

4

Breeders inhabit marshes and non-breeders occur on estuaries, the ocean near shore, and open bodies of fresh water.

Red-necked Grebe. *Podiceps grisegena.*

Breeds on Upper Klamath L. Locally fairly common to rare migrant and winter visitant on the coast. Rare inland throughout the year.

The Red-necked Grebe has bred in small numbers at Rocky Point, Upper Klamath L., since the late 1950s. In recent years five to 10 pairs have nested. Summer residents return in early April and depart in September. Other Oregon breeding sites include Howard Prairie Res., Jackson Co., where one pair bred successfully in 1965 and 1969; and Malheur N.W.R. where it was observed breeding for the first time in 1993.

On the Oregon coast the Red-necked Grebe is an uncommon to rare winter visitant, arriving from late August (exceptionally by mid-August) through October and departing in late March and April, with a few records as late as early June. During the migratory peaks in late September, October, and November, and March and April, it may be locally fairly common.

Inland, Red-necked Grebes are rare in fall, winter, and spring on large bodies of water throughout the state. Aside from breeders, there are three inland summer records: one collected at Diamond L., Douglas Co., on Aug. 5, 1931; a pair at Howard Prairie Res., Jackson Co., on July 4, 1976; and one at Malheur N.W.R, in June and July, 1980.

Eared Grebe. *Podiceps nigricollis.*

East of the Cascades, locally common summer resident, fairly common to abundant in migration, and rare in winter. Very uncommon on the coast and rare in the interior valleys from September through early May; rare in summer west of the Cascades.

The Eared Grebe is a locally common summer resident in marshes east of the Cascades. The greatest numbers inhabit the vast marshes of Harney, Lake, and Klamath Cos., but sizable colonies also exist on the intermountain lakes of Deschutes Co., where nesting occurs to 5,000 ft. or more. Breeding Eared Grebes prefer larger marshes and marsh-edged lakes. Breeding habitat is limited, and colonies are local away from these areas of concentration. Colony establishment is largely dependent on water conditions, and colonies move from year to year.

Summer residents and transients usually arrive in late March and early April, at which time they are fairly common on many lakes. Thousands of transients stage at Malheur N.W.R., in April and early May. Lake Abert, Lake Co., also supports large numbers, with an estimated 30,000 on April 28, 1994. By mid-May most transients east of the Cascades have moved north. In fall southbound transients peak east of the Cascades in late August, September, and early October, and many linger into November. During the fall migratory peak, thousands stage on Lake Abert, where they feed on abundant brine shrimp. Eared Grebes are absent during most winters east of the Cascades, though a few can be seen around John Day Dam in Sherman and Wasco Cos.

On the coast the Eared Grebe is very uncommon on estuaries and freshwater from September through early May, and in the interior valleys of western Oregon it is rare during this period. Slightly greater numbers are detected during September, October, November, March, and April, the peak months of migration. There are two summer records for western Oregon, one observed Aug. 11, 1970, at Finley N.W.R., Benton Co., and one at Warrenton, Clatsop Co., on July 26, 1980.

Western Grebe. *Aechmophorus occidentalis.*

Locally common summer resident east of the Cascade Mts. In winter, common along the coast and locally common to rare inland.

The Western Grebe is a locally common summer resident east of the Cascades in the large marshes and marsh-edged lakes of Harney, Lake, Klamath, Deschutes, Morrow, and Umatilla Cos. Colony location varies from year to year in response to water conditions, and occasionally colonies arise in other counties. Considerable numbers sometimes breed at Malheur N.W.R. where in the last two decades the nesting population has ranged from none to nearly 3,000 pairs. Numbers are

6

greatly affected by water levels, and also by other factors, such as the use of Rotenone to control carp in Malheur L.

Away from the nesting areas, non-breeders are uncommon on large bodies of water east of the Cascades in summer, occurring to over 5,000 ft. Breeders and transients usually arrive east of the Cascades during the latter half of March, but have been recorded as early as Feb. 22, at Malheur N.W.R. Transients are fairly common on large bodies of water in April and early May, and in September and early October. The fall migration begins in late August, peaks in mid-September, and nearly all have departed by early November. During winter, Western Grebes are uncommon to common on parts of the Columbia R., very uncommon in the Klamath Basin, and rare to absent elsewhere east of the Cascades, depending on winter severity.

In Western Oregon during winter, Western Grebes are common on the coast in estuaries and on the ocean near shore, generally uncommon on large bodies of water in the Willamette Valley and on the Columbia R. below The Dalles, and locally uncommon in the interior valleys of southwestern Oregon. During the migrations from late March to early May and from Mid-September through October, they are very common on the coast and uncommon in the interior valleys. In summer non-breeders are rare in the interior and uncommon on the coast, where concentrations of 100 or more occasionally are observed. A pair of Western Grebes was seen with young on July 17, 1992 at Fern Ridge Res., Lane Co., and nesting was recorded the following year as well.

Clark's Grebe. *Aechmophorus clarkii.*

Locally common summer resident east of the Cascade Mts. Rare fall transient and very rare in winter west of the Cascades.

Clark's Grebe is a common breeder in the extensive marshlands of Klamath and most of Lake Co. In Klamath Co. it is approximately equal in number to its close relative the Western Grebe, with which it was considered conspecific until recently. At Goose L., Lake Co., it is the most common large grebe. In Harney Co. it is far less numerous than the Western Grebe, and is only an uncommon summer resident. A few probably breed in Malheur Co. along the Snake R. and at

7

a few large reservoirs. Arrival on the breeding lakes is in early to mid-March; most are gone by late November with occasional birds remaining to winter on Upper Klamath L.

West of the Cascades, the Clark's Grebe is a rare fall and winter visitant; it has summered at Fern Ridge Res. Its status is still not totally clear as virtually no records pre-date the split from Western Grebe. It has been recorded the length of the coast, but most records are for Coos Bay south. There are several winter records for the Columbia R. near Portland and east as far as John Day Dam. One was in the Cascades at Oakridge, Lane Co., on Sept. 28, 1991.

Order PROCELLARIIFORMES
Family Diomedeidae

Short-tailed Albatross. *Diomedea albatrus.*

Extremely rare. Only one recent record.

At the turn of the century the Short-tailed Albatross was fairly common over the entire north Pacific. Remains of this giant bird have been found in excavations of Native American dwelling sites from the Aleutian Is. to the California coast, corroborating the findings of early naturalists that the species was more common near shore than other albatrosses. In 1889 over 100,000 birds were estimated nesting on Torishima I., which hosted the largest colony of the nine breeding islands scattered south of Japan. By 1933, when the Japanese government banned the taking of albatrosses on Torishima, Japanese fowlers seeking oil and feathers for quilts had reduced the population to 30-50 birds (Hasegawa and DeGange 1982). Since 1950, at which time a few nests were rediscovered, the population has been building and now includes over 250 individuals (Hasegawa and DeGange 1982).

The Short-tailed Albatross apparently still roams its traditional north Pacific range. It is extremely rare and since 1940 there have been only a few valid records for the west coast south of Alaska. Most of these records fall between April and August, one is for February. The only Oregon records are an immature photographed Dec. 11, 1961, about 30 miles west of Yachats, Lincoln Co. (Condor 65:103, (1963)), and two sight records, an immature 20 miles southwest of

8

the Columbia R. bar in June 1978 (Oregon Birds 15:264 (1989)) and one 20 miles off Depoe Bay, Lincoln Co., on Sept. 19, 1989 (OB 16:181 (1990)). Sightings off California and Washington in the last five years indicate that part of the very small population is still using the northeast Pacific. Anyone reporting this species should be aware of the identification problem caused by very worn-plumaged or old Black-footed Albatrosses.

Black-footed Albatross. *Diomedea nigripes.*

Fairly common beyond 10 miles offshore from April through October, and typically very uncommon in winter. Rare nearer to land.

The Black-footed Albatross is a fairly common visitant to Oregon from April through October, occurring from about 10 miles offshore (the 450 ft. depth contour) to the edge of the continental shelf. It may be attracted to shelf waters by the abundant food provided by fishing vessels active in the area (Wahl 1975). Beyond the shelf, numbers are reduced, although it does occur in deep water across the north Pacific. Full-day pelagic boat excursions during summer usually view from 10-25 Black-foots, but near large fishing vessels 50 or more are regularly seen. Breeding occurs during autumn and winter on Pacific islands, the most important of which are members of the Hawaiian chain. Most birds apparently withdraw from our offshore waters around mid-October, but small numbers, probably non-breeding immatures, remain in our area. Ocean temperature may affect the numbers wintering in a particular year.

Black-footed Albatrosses are primarily solitary fliers, but they will gather together in loafing flocks, sometimes of a dozen or more individuals. They are attracted to boats of all sizes, and frequently accompany ships for long distances, readily feeding on discards. Occasionally individuals occur within three miles of land, and have on very rare occasions been seen from shore. On June 23, 1980, three were observed in Yaquina Bay during a period of calm weather.

Laysan Albatross. *Diomedea immutabilis.*

Uncommon beyond the continental shelf from late August to April and rare in summer. Rare in winter over the shelf and very rare in summer.

From late August through April the Laysan Albatross is uncommon from the edge of the continental shelf (approximately 75 miles offshore) seaward and rare over the shelf. The species prefers colder waters, which extend nearer to shore in winter. In summer the Laysan Albatross moves northward and is extremely rare off Oregon, although it does occur in small numbers far at sea. Unusual numbers were seen over the continental shelf during the winter of 1992-1993, which coincided with an El Niño occurrence. There is a single June record for Oregon shelf waters and a mid-July record of a dead bird found on the beach.

Family Procellariidae

Northern Fulmar. *Fulmarus glacialis.*

Common offshore in winter, variably rare to uncommon in spring and summer, and usually uncommon from late July through October.

The Northern Fulmar is an uncommon to common offshore visitant to Oregon from late summer through winter. Following breeding in Alaska, Fulmars disperse southward, with numbers off Oregon beginning to increase around mid-July. There is a great deal of fluctuation from year to year. From late July through October full-day pelagic cruises venturing over five miles from shore usually view between five and 10 individuals, but near fishing vessels hundreds may congregate to feed on discarded waste. From April through June they are typically rare, with offshore excursions seldom viewing more than a few if any.

Fulmars are not confined to the continental shelf and slope. They regularly occur hundreds of miles at sea. They are common beyond 10 miles from shore during winter, and westerly gales intermittently drive large numbers within sight of land. Many are often found dead on beaches, and every few years large die-offs occur following severe or prolonged winter storms. At these times dozens may be found in a single mile of beach.

Fulmars are usually solitary but will concentrate at a food source. At least 95 percent of the birds observed in Oregon are dark phase, indicating that most originate from the breeding colonies along the Aleutian Is. and in south Alaska where this form predominates. Following strong westerly gales, Fulmars have on a few occasions been found in bays. The only inland record is a bird found at Steamboat, Douglas Co., on Feb. 9, 1983, following fierce gales. Several dead birds that have been found along the Willamette R. at Portland almost certainly arrived on ships.

Dark-rumped Petrel. *Pterodroma phaeopygia*

Vagrant.

There is one sight record of this species in Oregon waters, one bird seen Oct. 19, 1986 about 270 nautical miles off Cape Arago, Coos Co. This is technically not in Oregon waters, but scattered records in the North Pacific suggest the possibility of regular occurrence within 100 miles of the North American mainland (Pyle *et. al.* 1993).

Mottled Petrel. *Pterodroma inexpectata.*

Rare but regular offshore visitant.

The Mottled Petrel breeds on a few small islands off the coast of New Zealand. This petrel is probably regular far offshore despite the limited number of confirmed records. Most records have been in the winter when observer presence in deep water is negligible. The several beached birds and a few sightings have all been from the winter months, except for a record of one found dead near Alsea Bay, Lincoln Co. on July 25, 1959. The species is recorded most frequently during periods in which Northern Fulmars are particularly numerous, perhaps indicating a preference for colder water.

Murphy's Petrel. *Pterodroma ultima.*

Vagrant.

A Murphy's Petrel was found dead on the beach near Newport, Lincoln Co., on June 15, 1981. This constituted the first specimen record for North America. Additionally, on May 20, 1981, several dark *Pterodroma* petrels were observed by a researcher 50-60 miles off southern Oregon.

11

Pink-footed Shearwater. *Puffinus creatopus.*

Fairly common offshore from late April through mid-August and common off-shore from late August through mid-October.

The Pink-footed Shearwater is fairly common during summer from six miles off-shore, the 220 ft. depth contour, seaward to about 75 miles offshore where waters deepen to over 5,500 ft. (Wahl 1975). It breeds on islands off Chile and migrates north in spring, reaching Oregon in late April. From late April through mid-August it is fairly common, with full-day pelagic excursions typically viewing at least 20. From mid-August through early October greater numbers are observed, pelagic excursions often tallying over 50 and occasionally several hundred. Fewer are observed in late October, and there are only three November records, the latest November 21. Although probably absent during most winters, it was common offshore during the winter of 1992-1993, a period of unusual water temperatures due to the El Niño phenomenon.

Pink-footed Shearwaters are less gregarious than Sooty Shearwaters, usually occurring singly or in groups of less than a dozen, although hundreds may be attracted to large fishing vessels. Unlike Sootys, Pink-footeds are infrequently observed from shore, most land-based sightings consisting of individuals mixed among the vast flocks of Sootys.

Flesh-footed Shearwater. *Puffinus carneipes.*

Rare offshore from May through October.

The Flesh-footed Shearwater is rare offshore. The records extend from April 28 to October 17 and all have been since 1973. Despite the paucity of Oregon sightings, California and Washington observations leave no doubt that the species is a regular, rare summer visitant from early May through October, and possibly later. There is some variability in abundance from year to year, perhaps correlated to water temperature. It prefers the warmer waters typically found well offshore.

Buller's Shearwater. *Puffinus bulleri.*

Uncommon offshore from late July through October.

The Buller's Shearwater is an uncommon late summer and autumn visitant in waters over five miles off the Oregon coast. There are a few sightings of this species from shore, when it has been seen among large flocks of Sooty Shearwaters.

This species breeds during our winter on small islands off the north coast of New Zealand, migrating northward toward Japan in spring, apparently following the trade winds eastward during summer to the west coast of North America. It arrives on the Oregon coast in small numbers during late July and early August.

The species is highly variable in numbers from year to year. The greatest numbers are typically seen from late August through mid-October, when boat trips sometimes record over a hundred individuals, but sometimes find none. There are a few November sightings, and one December record off Coos Bay.

Sooty Shearwater. *Puffinus griseus.*

Common to abundant offshore from May through September. Very uncommon to rare in winter.

The Sooty Shearwater is common to abundant over the continental shelf from May through September, however its seasonal abundance fluctuates widely from year to year. During the summer it is by far the most common species offshore. On the north coast, the greatest numbers generally occur within three miles of land. Beyond the shelf, numbers are much reduced. A significant crash of food organisms during the El Niño of 1993 resulted in very low numbers.

During winter it is very uncommon offshore, but occurs in increased numbers during El Niño periods when the water is abnormally warm. In March and April the population builds as the species returns from South Pacific breeding grounds. Numbers decline gradually during October and November. Flocks totaling tens of thousands of birds are sometimes seen from shore from early July through mid-September, especially from Tillamook Head to the mouth of the Columbia R. Sooty Shearwaters also occur singly and in small groups.

Flocks or individuals occasionally enter large estuaries, especially that of the Columbia R. Records of dead birds from Portland are almost certainly of birds that have been brought up river on ships.

Short-tailed Shearwater. *Puffinus tenuirostris.*

Uncommon fall and winter offshore migrant. Very rare offshore in other seasons.

The Short-tailed Shearwater is typically a fairly common to uncommon late fall and winter migrant offshore. Upon departing their Australian breeding islands during our spring, a portion of the population embarks on a vast migration around the Pacific. Most spend the northern summer in the Bering Sea and Arctic Ocean, migrating south in autumn along the West Coast of North America.

Off Oregon and Washington during some years very small numbers are noted from mid-August through September, but usually they are not observed until October, while November and December appear to be the peak periods with a few sighted into January. The species has also been recorded in at least some years into early May, when it may be of regular occurrence. The greatest numbers are seen following westerly gales during November and December, when hundreds are occasionally observed from shore and many sometimes wash up dead onto beaches. Throughout summer Short-tailed Shearwaters are extremely rare offshore visitants.

Short-tailed Shearwaters occur individually or in flocks, which may number in the thousands. There is some evidence that they generally migrate farther offshore than the similar Sooty Shearwater, preferring areas near the continental shelf approximately 75 miles offshore, where they often are attracted to the discards of fishing vessels. Short-tailed Shearwaters occur in small numbers close to shore, and are sometimes seen from land. There are no records for coastal bays, estuaries, or inland.

Black-vented Shearwater. *Puffinus opisthomelas.*

Vagrant.

Small shearwaters of indeterminate species have been seen several times in Oregon, but specimens or diagnostic photographs have not been obtained. Most of these records are from shore: one at Oceanside, Tillamook Co., on Sept. 17, 1977; one at Gearhart, Clatsop Co., on Sept. 12, 1979; and one at Boiler Bay, Lincoln Co., on Nov. 3, 1979. One at Bandon, Coos Co., on Nov. 22, 1992, was identified as Black-vented.

The Manx Shearwater has recently been split into a number of species, including the Black-vented Shearwater, the form found most regularly on the West Coast. White-vented Manx-type shearwaters of unknown origin have occurred on the West Coast, including a Sept. 10, 1977 sighting off Coos Bay.

Family Hydrobatidae

Wilson's Storm-Petrel. *Oceanites oceanicus.*

Vagrant.

The Wilson's Storm-Petrel has been observed in Oregon only once, a bird seen very close to the S. Jetty of the Columbia R., Clatsop Co., on May 31, 1976. This date followed several days of strong southwest winds, and dozens of Fork-tailed and Leach's Storm-Petrels were also present at the time.

Fork-tailed Storm-Petrel. *Oceanodroma furcata.*

Breeds in small numbers on offshore rocks. Rare to locally uncommon throughout the year over the continental shelf beyond 10 miles from shore. Very rare near shore in all seasons but occasionally seen from land following storms. Very uncommon beyond the continental shelf.

Fewer than 1,000 pairs of Fork-tailed Storm-Petrels are estimated to breed in Oregon as of 1988 (Lowe pers. com.), but censusing is difficult because the species is nocturnal on land and nests in burrows and crevices among large offshore colonies of Leach's Storm-Petrels. Small breeding populations are known to exist on Goat and Hunters Is., Curry Co., and Haystack Rock, Tillamook Co., and at least three other colonies are suspected including one at Haystack Rock, Clatsop Co., and one at Three Arch Rocks, Tillamook Co., where they historically nested (Varoujean and Pitman 1979).

Fork-tailed Storm-Petrels are rarely seen near their colonies because adults leave and return to the nest at night. They prefer colder waters than Leach's Storm-Petrels, and are rare to locally uncommon over the continental shelf beyond 10 miles from shore during April through October. During this summer period temperatures are cooler over the shelf than beyond. Wahl (1975) found in offshore transects that numbers decrease as sea surface temperatures increase. The species is rare within 10 miles of shore however, and its abundance varies widely with ocean conditions. Many of the birds in Oregon waters may be non-breeders from more northern populations. Beyond the continental shelf it is very uncommon throughout the year, perhaps numbers being slightly reduced in winter (Sanger 1970). The winter status over shelf waters is poorly understood, but beach wash-ups and birds occasionally driven to shore by gales indicate it is regular offshore in winter.

Fork-tailed Storm-Petrels are usually observed singly but also occur in small flocks, some numbering 20 or more birds. They are attracted to fishing vessels which discard oil and wastes small enough to eat.

Gales have blown Fork-taileds to shore in all seasons. During these storms they may be seen from jetties and capes, and rarely in estuaries. Unlike the Leach's Storm-Petrel, the Fork-tailed is not forced inland by gales, and there are no inland records. In late August of 1983, when ocean temperatures along the Pacific Coast reached record highs and the coolest waters were to be found near shore, numerous Fork-tails were seen from shore and between jetties from Newport south. The spring of 1985 also saw large numbers onshore.

Leach's Storm-Petrel. *Oceanodroma leucorhoa.*

Nests on coastal offshore rocks. Very uncommon year-round over continental shelf and fairly common beyond shelf. Extremely rare inland.

The Leach's Storm-Petrel nests on offshore rocks the length of the Oregon coast. Lowe (pers. com.) estimated in 1988 that 435,000 pairs nest on about 15 offshore rocks in the state, and of this number Goat and Hunters Is., Curry Co., host the largest colonies. The Goat I. colony constitutes the largest in the Pacific south of Alaska. with about 105,000 birds. Colonies of about 4,000 pairs also occur on Crook Point Rocks, Saddle Rock, and the eastern Whalehead I., all in Curry Co. Fewer than 1,000 pairs nest along the northern two-thirds of the coast, the largest colony being 500 pairs on Haystack Rock, Tillamook Co.

Although thousands of Leach's Storm-Petrels nest in Oregon, shore and boat observers see very few. This is due to the their habit of returning to island colonies primarily at night, thus avoiding predation by gulls. This species appears to prefer warmer water temperatures than the more frequently seen Fork-tailed Storm-Petrel, and most breeders fly to or past the continental shelf edge about 75 miles from shore. Occasionally a strong gale may force large numbers to within sight of land-based observers. This most often happens in the autumn, but has also occurred in April and May. Exceptional storms have even driven birds far inland, such as the storm of Nov. 10, 1975 when hundreds of birds were blown into the valleys of western Oregon. An individual that was probably ship-assisted was seen along the Willamette R. at Portland for an entire day on June 30, 1987. Another was seen following a storm at Salem on May 26, 1989. Several dead individuals have been found along the Portland waterfront that were probably brought up river, either alive or dead, by ocean-going ships.

There is evidence of a general southward shift in autumn and in winter. The species is less abundant in winter than summer. Birds off the Oregon coast in winter may originate from populations to the north. Small numbers of wash-ups appear on beaches throughout the winter. In late April, small scattered groups have been noted moving steadily north beyond the continental shelf off southern Washington. Breeders return to the Oregon colonies in late April and May. This species is usually observed in small groups or singly, and it is occasionally attracted to bright lights at night.

Black Storm-Petrel. *Oceanodroma melania.*

Vagrant.

The only record of the Black Storm-Petrel for Oregon is of a flock of 10, some of which were photographed, at the estuary of the Necanicum R., Clatsop Co., on Sept. 8, 1983. Several birds that were possibly this species were also seen at the estuary of the Umpqua R. in that month. These sightings occurred during a very strong El Niño warming of the Pacific, which caused other unusual seabird occurrences.

Order PELECANIFORMES
Family Phaethontidae

Red-billed Tropicbird. *Phaethon aethereus.*

Vagrant.

The Red-billed Tropicbird has been recorded three times off Oregon: one was observed 460 miles west of Cape Blanco, Curry Co., on Sept. 7, 1945; one was seen 10 miles west of Coos Bay, Coos Co. during the second week of July, 1978; and one was 10 miles off Tillamook, Tillamook Co., on April 23, 1992. No records have been submitted to the Oregon Bird Records Committee.

Family Pelicanidae

American White Pelican. *Pelecanus erythrorhynchos.*

Breeds at Upper Klamath L., in the Warner Basin, and occasionally at Malheur N.W.R. Locally common in Klamath, Lake, and Harney Cos. in all seasons but winter, when rare. Very rare in all seasons throughout the remainder of the state.

In Oregon the White Pelican currently breeds only at Upper Klamath L., Klamath Co., and in the Warner Basin, Lake Co. Breeding colonies fluctuate widely both in size and location from year to year, the result in part of varying water levels and island availability. Early in this century tule mats and islands in Malheur L., Harney Co., were utilized for nesting. In 1932, following years of drought, there were no known colonies in the state. At Malheur N.W.R. breeding was sporadic from 1938 to 1960, the nesting population ranging from 50 to 450 pairs, and in many years no nesting occurred. White pelicans did not nest at the refuge from 1960 to 1984. A few young were produced on islands in Harney L. in 1985. This population grew to 1,500 pairs in 1988, but falling water levels since have made the lake unsuitable for breeding. Small colonies also inhabit the Warner Basin. The Upper Klamath L. colony has supported 100 to 200 pairs since 1976, but had up to 600 pairs in the decades prior to that.

White Pelicans first arrive in the Klamath Basin in early March and in the Harney and Warner Basins in late March and early April. Occasionally birds are noted in late February. In March, April, and May, and to a lesser extent throughout the summer, small numbers of migrants and wandering non-breeders occur widely east of the Cascades. Small flocks irregularly summer along the Columbia R. Breeders from the Oregon colonies and from colonies at Clear L. and Lower Klamath N.W.R., in California, in addition to non-breeders, forage on many lakes and reservoirs in the Klamath Basin and Great Basin. Bodies of water utilized regularly include Summer L. (northern marshes), Thompson Res., Goose L., Dog L., Drews Res., and Sycan Marsh, all Lake Co., and Swan L., Gerber Res., and along the Klamath R. in Klamath Co. Howard Prarie Res. and Hyatt L. in Jackson Co. also support regular non-breeding visitants. Post-breeding visitants are common along the Columbia R. in Umatilla Co. Breeding White Pelicans are known to travel more than 50 miles to foraging sites that have suitable shallow water and fish abundance.

The Harney Basin population builds throughout the summer. It is thought that carp, which have been introduced to the Basin, attract the great numbers that stage there in autumn. The population peaks early in October, often at more than 5,000; and over 10,000 have been recorded. In years when Rotenone is used to poison carp, fewer pelicans gather in the Basin. Banding and color marking studies indicate that some Harney birds come from colonies in Nevada, California, and the Warner and Klamath Basins.

Most White Pelicans have left Oregon by November, after which they are extremely rare. During the September and October migration small numbers may appear anywhere east of the Cascades. There are three winter records for Malheur N.W.R. and a few for Upper Klamath L.

West of the Cascades there are many records for the interior valleys and about five for the coast, all in areas from Yaquina Bay south. Most western Oregon records are of single birds, but occasionally small flocks occur. The periods from March to May and from August to December are when most are observed, but there are also mid-summer and mid-winter records. During the 1940s White Pelicans were regular summer visitants to Fern Ridge Res., Lane Co., and although over 100 occasionally were observed, nesting was never confirmed.

Brown Pelican. *Pelecanus occidentalis.*

Common visitant along the coast mid-spring to November.

The Brown Pelican, which nests on islands off the coast of southern California and western Mexico, moves northward along the Pacific coast after the breeding season. Most of Oregon's birds probably originate in Mexico.

Before 1980 few arrived along the Oregon coast before June. Since the early 1980s the species has been arriving earlier in the spring. A few now reach the northern coast by late April. An immature at Yaquina Head, Lincoln Co., on Feb. 20, 1992, could have been either an early or late migrant.

Peak numbers occur in late August and throughout October, when in recent years 300 or more have been present in and around some large estuaries. Through October and early November there is a gradual decline as birds move south, with the last usually recorded in late November. With the general increase in numbers, there have been more December and January records.

During the late 1960s and early 1970s a drastic decline occurred in the number of Brown Pelicans reaching Oregon each summer and fall. This decline resulted from the reproduction failure of the southern California and northern Baja California colonies, where nesting adults were producing thin-shelled eggs which broke during incubation. The thinning was caused by high concentrations of DDT released into the Pacific with agricultural runoff and concentrated in anchovies, the pelicans' principal food. Since 1972, when the domestic use of DDT was outlawed, Brown Pelicans have made a steady and remarkable recovery and are again common along Oregon's coast.

Great Blue Heron

Family Phalacrocoracidae

Double-crested Cormorant. *Phalacrocorax auritus.*

Fairly common year-round on the coast. Uncommon in summer and fairly common in winter on the Lower Columbia R. and near Portland. Rare to uncommon year round in the Willamette, Rogue, and Umpqua Valleys. East of the Cascades, common in summer at breeding colonies, sporadic elsewhere, and rare in winter.

On the Oregon coast the Double-crested Cormorant nests on the sod crowns and slopes of headlands and offshore rocks. Varoujean and Pitman (1979) located 14 coastal colonies and estimated 850 pairs breed on the coast, while Lowe (pers. com) found 6,000 pairs in 1988. The coastal population varies little in abundance during the year, although there is some evidence that inland birds move toward the coast in fall. Double-cresteds are fairly common in estuaries and on the ocean within two miles of land, but rarely occur farther from shore.

Inland the Double-crested Cormorant frequents large rivers, lakes, and reservoirs. Along the lower Columbia R. (from The Dalles west) and the northern Willamette R. near Portland, it is generally fairly common in winter. It is very uncommon in summer and nests occasionally in the same areas. The autumn influx begins in July and August and migrants depart in March. Elsewhere in the Willamette Valley it is rare to very uncommon in all seasons but late summer and fall, when it is uncommon. In the Rogue and Umpqua Valleys it is rare throughout the year.

East of the Cascades breeding colonies are widely scattered in the southern basins and south Cascades, and their locations often change in response to fluctuating water conditions. In this region colonies occur on islands, in trees, and on mats of emergent vegetation.

Oregon's Klamath Basin summer population is close to 2,000 birds. In recent years 100-300 pairs have nested there, primarily on Upper Klamath Marsh. At Malheur N.W.R. the population has fluctuated widely in this century. In recent years usually between 50 and 200 pairs have nested on the Refuge. Banding data indicate that Malheur birds disperse both south and northwest. Smaller colonies are located in the Warner Valley, Lake Co., at Crane Prairie Res., Deschutes Co., and at other lakes and reservoirs in the region. Small numbers also nest on pilings, trees, and islands along the Columbia R., and in this area the species is generally fairly common in all seasons but winter. Small numbers of non-breeders may occur in summer on bodies of water anywhere in the Cascades and eastward, even at elevations of 6,000 ft. or more, such as at Crater Lake, Klamath Co. In Union and Wallowa Cos. in northeastern Oregon it is noted only in spring and fall, when it is very uncommon.

The last migrants depart areas east of the Cascades in October and November and return as early as February to the Klamath Basin and early March to Malheur N.W.R. In winter it is rare to uncommon along the Columbia R. and in the Klamath Basin, where a few usually occur on Lake Ewauna in Klamath Co. Elsewhere east of the Cascades there are few winter records. In mild years small numbers occasionally winter at Malheur N.W.R.

Brandt's Cormorant. *Phalacrocorax penicillatus.*

Locally common breeder and fairly common throughout the year along the coast.

The Brandt's Cormorant is locally common at breeding colonies in spring and summer, and fairly common elsewhere throughout the year over the length of the Oregon coast. It is by far the most abundant cormorant nesting on the coast, with 11,500 pairs estimated breeding in the state (Lowe pers. com.). There are about 60 known Oregon colonies, located on the tops and slopes of headlands and rocky islands, often in association with Common Murres. Most of these colonies support fewer than 100 pairs, but several are much larger, including the colony at Sea Lion Caves, Lane Co., with 2,250 pairs (Varoujean and Pitman 1979).

Brandt's Cormorants feed primarily on or near the bottom over both sandy and rocky substrates, and thus are more uniformly distributed over the inshore waters than the rock-favoring Pelagic Cormorant (Ainley *et al.* 1981). Rarely do they occur more than three miles from shore, and they are generally uncommon in estuaries.

Beginning in July and continuing through early September, there is movement of Brandt's Cormorants north along Oregon's coast. Banding records indicate that at least some of these post-breeding migrants originate from colonies in California. The autumn southward migration occurs primarily in October and November. Many, probably local stock and perhaps birds from north of Oregon, remain through the winter. At that time it is the least common cormorant on the Oregon coast.

Pelagic Cormorant. *Phalacrocorax pelagicus.*

Fairly common in all seasons along the Oregon coast.

The Pelagic Cormorant is fairly common throughout the year along the entire Oregon coast. It breeds on rocky islands and headlands, where nests are placed upon ledges on steep rock faces. The population was estimated at 11,000 birds in 1988 (Lowe pers. com).

Despite its name, the Pelagic Cormorant is not encountered in deep water areas. It is the least gregarious of Oregon's cormorants, being most often encountered singly and otherwise in flocks of fewer than 10. In autumn there appears to be a slight southward movement into and perhaps through the state, and northern nesting birds may winter on the Oregon coast. It occurs very sparingly on coastal lakes and occasionally ascends a short distance up coastal rivers. There are no records east of the Coast Range.

Family Fregatidae

Magnificent Frigatebird. *Fregata magnificens.*

Vagrant.

This conspicuous seabird has been found several times along the coast and once inland. The first record was an apparent immature found dead at the Tillamook Lighthouse, Tillamook Co., on Feb. 18, 1935. Since then it has been seen on the coast at Gold Beach, Curry Co., on July 24, 1979; Big Creek, Lane Co., on March 4, 1987; Charleston, Coos Co., on March 7-11, 1987; Yachats, Lincoln Co., on July 12, 1986; Newport, Lincoln Co., on Aug. 18, 1987; Cape Arago, Coos Co., on Feb. 1, 1992; and Newport, Lincoln Co., and Florence, Lane Co., on July 29, 1983. The last two sightings are presumed to pertain to the same bird. One was inland at Portland, Multnomah Co., on June 4, 1987.

Additionally, an unidentified frigatebird (likely *magnificens*) was observed by a fisherman on Aug. 2, 1981, approximately 50 miles west of Cascade Head, Lincoln Co. An immature Magnificent Frigatebird was photographed July 1, 1975, over the Washington side of the Columbia R. at Umatilla N.W.R.

Order CICONIIFORMES
Family Ardeidae

American Bittern. *Botaurus lentiginosus.*

Fairly common summer resident throughout most of Oregon. Rare in winter west of the Cascades; very rare east of the Cascades.

The American Bittern is locally a fairly common summer resident and spring and fall transient throughout much of the state, where suitable fresh and brackish water habitat exists. Such habitat is scarce in many areas, such as most of southwestern Oregon. The largest numbers occur in the vast marshes of Harney, Lake, and Klamath Cos.

The peak of the spring migration is in April. At Malheur N.W.R. migrants first arrive in late March to mid-April. The fall migration extends from late August through October. It is uncommon in winter west of the Cascades in the inland valleys and along the coast. The American Bittern is very rare in winter east of the Cascades; where it has been recorded in Harney, Klamath, Lake, and Umatilla Cos.

Least Bittern. *Ixobrychus exilis.*

Rare summer resident in Klamath, Harney, and probably Lake Cos. Vagrant elsewhere.

The Least Bittern is a rare summer resident at Malheur N.W.R., Harney Co., and at Upper Klamath L., Klamath Co. These populations are apparently small and perhaps irregular, although no systematic effort has been made to census the species at either location. It may be absent or in extremely small numbers at Malheur N.W.R. during periods when the marshes are greatly reduced in size due to flooding or prolonged drought. Recent records from Upper Klamath L. have been from the Rocky Point area along the canoe trail, where it may be uncommon.

There are several records for Klamath Marsh N.W.R., and the Least Bittern may also occur in other marshes of Klamath and Lake Cos. Individuals have been recorded as early as April 29 and as late as Sept. 8 at Malheur N.W.R.

Western Oregon records include a specimen collected near Prospect, Jackson Co., Aug. 10, 1959, and well-substantiated sightings of individuals at Fern Ridge Res., Lane Co., June 14, 1968; Baskett Slough N.W.R., Polk Co., May 20, 1970; and Salem, Marion Co., July 19, 1975. Some additional reports from western Oregon may pertain to young Green Herons.

Great Blue Heron. *Ardea herodias.*

Common west of the Cascade Mts. throughout the year. Uncommon to locally common east of the Cascades in summer; uncommon to locally fairly common most winters.

The Great Blue Heron breeds at widely scattered sites throughout Oregon. The total state breeding population probably exceeds 2,500 pairs, and most sources conclude that the population is stable. The greatest number occur west of the Cascades. On the coast Great Blue Herons are very common throughout the year, and from a single vantage dozens may often be viewed in the shallows of estuaries. In the Willamette, Rogue and Umpqua Valleys they are common year round, and during summer regularly ascend the tributaries into the mountains. A recent survey of active nests in the Willamette Valley located 722 nests in 31 colonies. Single nests and a few small colonies also occur in the Rogue and Umpqua Valleys. Birds from north of Oregon may migrate into western Oregon in fall, and as a result possibly more occur during winter than in summer. East of the Cascades, Great Blue Herons are uncommon to locally common during the summer. Colonies are widespread, but the greatest number of birds nest in the Klamath and Harney Basins. Elsewhere east of the Cascades, small colonies, usually of fewer than 30 pairs, occur near large lakes and rivers. Most birds migrate south out of the region during fall, chiefly in September and October. They are usually very uncommon during the winter, except in the Klamath Basin, the Harney Basin, and along the Columbia R., where in mild winters they may be fairly common. During severe winters they are rare in most areas, and many may die of exposure and starvation.

Great Blue Herons frequent estuaries, marshes, lakes, ponds, and watercourses of all dimensions. They often capture small rodents in flooded as well as dry fields, especially during winter. They may nest singly, but typically nest in colonies, which occasionally exceed 100 pairs. A variety of nest sites are utilized. Trees, especially cottonwoods that border watercourses or are situated on islands, but also large conifers within forests, are most frequently selected for nesting. Colonies are sometimes located near urban centers; one is situated near downtown Portland on Ross I.

Great Egret. *Casmerodius albus.*

Locally common summer resident and rare during winter in Harney, Lake, and Klamath Cos.; rare elsewhere east of the Cascade Mts. from spring to fall. West of the Cascades, rare from May to mid-July; in late summer and fall fairly common on the south coast and rare to locally fairly common elsewhere (irregular); rare to locally common in winter.

The Great Egret is common during summer in the three regions where it breeds, the Harney Basin, the lakes of Lake Co., and the Klamath Basin. The largest breeding population occurs in the Harney Basin where in most years about five colonies exist on Malheur N.W.R. and adjacent private lands. The Malheur population has grown gradually from near extirpation by plume hunters at the turn of the century to 520 pairs by 1984. In the Klamath Basin 100 to 200 pairs nest in colonies on Upper Klamath L. In the Warner Basin about 20 pairs annually nest on islands in Pelican L. and colonies occasionally occur north to Summer L. Elsewhere east of the Cascades, Great Egrets are rare in spring, summer, and fall, occurring most frequently in the southern counties and after the post-breeding dispersal in mid-July. Individuals occasionally wander to forested lakes at over 6,000 ft. Most migrants depart the breeding areas in September but many remain through October. Birds have wintered on a few occasions at Malheur and there are several winter records for the Klamath Basin. Migrants generally return to areas east of the Cascades in late March and April.

West of the Cascades, Great Egret observations began to increase markedly in the early 1970s. Breeding occurred in 1980, 1988, and 1989, when it nested within a Great Blue Heron colony on the North Spit of Coos Bay, Coos Co. In May, June and early July Great Egrets are rare on the coast of Coos and Curry Cos. and very rare elsewhere in western Oregon.

Following post-breeding dispersal in mid-July, numbers increase dramatically west of the Cascades. On the coast they become fairly common, less so north of the Siuslaw R. estuary. Most years they are common at Fern Ridge Res., Lane Co., along the Rogue and Umpqua Rivers, and at other favored sites. Elsewhere they are rare to irregularly fairly common. During November and December most leave the region. The greatest wintering concentrations occur in Coos Co. Most wintering birds depart in April.

Snowy Egret. *Egretta thula.*

Uncommon summer resident in the Harney Basin and locally in southern Lake Co. Rare to uncommon from spring to fall in the Klamath Basin. Vagrant spring to fall elsewhere east of the Cascade Mts. Rare from April to October in the Rogue Valley and rare from late July to April on the south coast. Vagrant elsewhere in western Oregon.

The Snowy Egret is uncommon in summer in the Harney Basin, where Oregon's main breeding population exists on Malheur Lake. The Malheur population was exterminated early in this century, but became re-established during the 1940s. In the 1970s the population ranged between 40 and 140 pairs, and in 1984, 108 nests were located in two colonies. At Crump L. in the Warner Basin, Lake Co., a colony of about 100 pairs persisted until the late 1960s. Currently in the Warner Basin, Snowy Egrets are uncommon from spring to fall, and recently a small colony has become established at Summer L., in southern Lake Co. In the Klamath Basin, colonies are confined to California; in Oregon individuals are rare in spring and summer, and uncommon during the post-breeding dispersal from late July through September. An occasional bird or two seen in Malheur Co. are probably wandering Idaho birds. Elsewhere east of the Cascades, vagrants have appeared between May and September in Baker, Crook, Deschutes, Malheur, and Union Cos.

Migrants arrive at Malheur N.W.R. in late April and early May; the earliest sighting is April 11. Most depart in September, with the latest observation on Oct. 25.

West of the Cascades, Snowy Egrets only began to appear regularly in the late 1970s. From April to October they are very rare in the Rogue Valley, where in recent years there have usually been several sightings annually. More than 24 seen there in August, 1992. Elsewhere west of the Cascades they are vagrants in the interior valleys and along the central and northern coast, with approximately 20 records between late July and early November.

On the coast from Douglas Co. south they are rare during this period. The northernmost coastal locale of regular occurrence is the estuary of the Umpqua R., where one to several sometimes occur in the autumn. One wintered at Coos Bay, Coos Co., in 1976-77 for the first western Oregon winter record. Since 1976 up to 12 birds have wintered annually around Coos Bay; these typically depart in April. Winterers have also occurred at Bandon, Coos Co., Gardiner, Douglas Co., and Florence, Lane Co.

There are only three spring records for northwestern Oregon, one at Finley N.W.R., Benton Co., May 8, 1972; at Finley April 16, 1983; and one at Yaquina Bay, Lincoln Co., May 24, 1973. There is also a single spring record for the Cascades, a bird at the Diamond L. sewage ponds May 26, 1988.

Little Blue Heron. *Egretta caerulea.*

Vagrant.

There are two records of adult Little Blue Herons along the Willamette River and two of immatures from the coast. One was photographed near the Buena Vista Ferry in Marion and Polk Cos. on May 16-18, 1985; one was at Milwaukie, Clackamas Co., on June 18, 1987; another was at Brownsmead, Clatsop Co., from Jan. 20 to March 11, 1990; and one was at Yaquina Bay, Lincoln Co., on Aug. 29-30, 1991.

Tricolored Heron. *Egretta tricolor.*

Vagrant.

There are three records of the Tricolored Heron for Oregon: a male in first fall plumage was collected at Malheur N.W.R. on Oct. 31, 1943; one was at Finley N.W.R., Benton Co., from May 12-31, 1976; and one was at Ona Beach State Park, Lincoln Co., from Nov. 7-13, 1993.

Cattle Egret. *Bubulcus ibis.*

Uncommon to rare from November to February on the coast and very rare during this period in interior western Oregon valleys. East of the Cascade Mts., a few pairs have bred in the Harney Basin in recent years, and it is a rare spring and summer visitant to the Klamath Basin, Klamath Co.; vagrant elsewhere.

The Cattle Egret first appeared in the U.S. in Florida during the early 1940s. Its range expanded rapidly and an individual was first reported in Oregon from Sauvie I., Multnomah Co., on Nov. 29, 1965. By the mid-1970s it was a fairly regular visitant to the state.

In recent years the Cattle Egret has become a locally uncommon post-breeding visitant from late November to early February in pasturelands along the Oregon coast. Favored counties with large areas of pasture are Curry, Coos and Tillamook. During this same period Cattle Egrets are very rare in the interior valleys of western Oregon, appearing most frequently in the Willamette Valley. Generally, they occur in small flocks of 5 or fewer, but solitary individuals and larger flocks numbering up to 31 birds are also observed. They usually arrive in western Oregon in late November but occasionally appear as early as October. Most disappear by early February, but there are a few March records and one was at Coos Bay, Coos Co., April 3, 1979. One near Forest Grove, Washington Co., on June 27, 1984 is the only summer record for western Oregon.

The first Cattle Egret recorded east of the Cascades was an individual at Malheur N.W.R., Harney Co., on Aug. 13, 1974; this bird remained into September. Single birds were also observed at Malheur July 16, 1976 and from April 30 to May 7, 1977. There were additional observations at Malheur in the early 1980s with as many as 18 together at Malheur N.W.R. In 1983 and 1984 at least two pairs nested in a large colony of egrets and herons north of Malheur L. near Lawen. Nesting has been confirmed almost annually somewhere in that county since then. As many as 18 were seen together at Malheur N.W.R. in May, 1994. In the Klamath Basin a few Cattle Egrets have been observed in May, June and July most years since 1979. Elsewhere east of the Cascades there are scattered sightings, mostly in the fall.

Green Heron. *Butorides virescens.*

Uncommon summer resident and rare in winter in western Oregon. East of the Cascade Mts. generally rare but locally very uncommon in summer, with one winter record.

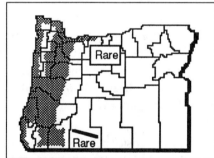

The Green Heron is an uncommon summer resident in the interior valleys of western Oregon and along the coast. Greatest numbers are found along the Rogue and Umpqua Rivers. Its numbers have increased markedly over the last few decades. In winter it is rare to locally uncommon in western Oregon. Migration occurs primarily in April and October. It inhabits freshwater and brackish marshes and the vegetated banks of estuaries, ponds and lakes.

East of the Cascades it is a very uncommon, local summer resident and probable breeder (no nesting records) in Klamath Co. Elsewhere east of the Cascades there are about 20 records, all between late May and October, including several Lake Co. records, a few in Harney Co., and records for Deschutes, Jefferson, Malheur, Umatilla, Union, and Wasco Cos. A sub-adult observed in Klamath Falls, Klamath Co., Dec. 2-4, 1978, is the only winter record east of the Cascades.

Black-crowned Night-Heron. *Nycticorax nycticorax.*

East of the Cascades locally fairly common near breeding colonies and rare else-where in summer and migration. Winters in Klamath Falls, Klamath Co. Rare year-round in western Oregon, wintering locally.

The Black-crowned Night-Heron is a locally fairly common summer resident at large wetlands east of the Cascades, and non-breeders are rare in summer throughout the region. Colonies are located in dense marshes, in trees and in bushes on islands. Colony size and location vary markedly from year to year. The largest Oregon colony exists on Malheur L., Harney Co., where the population has dropped from 1,000 pairs in 1974 to approximately 500 in the late 1980s. DDT residues ingested during migration and on the wintering grounds are impli-cated in this reduction, though there is considerable year-to-year fluctuation. Sig-nificant numbers also breed in Lake and Klamath Cos. Small colonies are scattered elsewhere in eastern Oregon where suitable habitat exists.

In late July and August when breeders and young disperse and through the Sep-tember peak of migration Black-crowned Night-Herons are observed more widely east of the Cascades. Three thousand or more may gather at Malheur N.W.R. in September, most departing by early November. About 100 birds usu-ally winter in the Klamath Basin, Klamath Co., most along the Link R. in Kla-math Falls. Birds have also wintered at Malheur and Umatilla N.W.R.s and at Summer L. Spring migrants return in late March and April.

Early in this century a colony of as many as 200 pairs existed near Portland but in recent decades nesting has not been recorded west of the Cascades, although small numbers are observed regularly during summer around Coos Bay, Coos Co., Roseburg, Douglas Co., Medford, Jackson Co., and rarely elsewhere. Most summer sightings west of the Cascades occur after mid-July when dispersal from breeding areas begins. Through fall, winter, and spring they are rare in the inte-rior valleys and absent from the coast except in the Coos Bay area and along the lower Rogue and Chetco Rivers, Curry Co., and near Tillamook Bay where in recent years a few have wintered. Currently winter communal roosts of up to 28 birds each exist in Portland; Roseburg, Douglas Co.; Grants Pass, Josephine Co.; and Medford, Jackson Co; and Myrtle Point, Coos Co. There are a few additional scattered winter records for the interior valleys.

Family Threskiornithidae

White-faced Ibis. *Plegadis chihi.*

Fairly common summer resident at Malheur N.W.R. Expanding into rest of south-central and southeastern Oregon and a vagrant elsewhere.

In Oregon the White-faced Ibis has its center of abundance at Malheur N.W.R., where nesting has occurred at least since the 1870s. The size of the Malheur population fluctuates widely in response to water conditions there and at colony sites in Nevada. In the late 1960s about 20 pairs nested. By the late 1970s there were 150 pairs, and in 1984 880 pairs were counted in three colonies, two on Malheur L. and one on adjacent Harney L. Numbers reached 4,600 pairs in 1987. By 1987 a few pairs also were nesting at Silver L., Lake Co., and a colony was established at nearby Summer L. Substantial numbers from colonies in the California portion of the Klamath Basin were seen in Oregon in the spring of 1993. Most migrants depart Malheur in early and mid-September, but there are November and January records, the only winter records east of the Cascades. Migrants generally return to Malheur in May with the earliest arrival date April 9. During the spring and fall migrations and the late July and August post-breeding dispersal period, ibises regularly appear at other wetlands of south-central and southeastern Oregon, including the Klamath Basin, Klamath Co., the Alvord Basin, Harney Co., Goose Lake, Lake Co., and generally in the Warner Valley, Lake Co. Population increases have resulted in scattered reports elsewhere in eastern Oregon, mostly in May.

West of the Cascades there are about 20 records of the White-faced Ibis. There are several coastal records, mostly from spring but including one at Tillamook, Tillamook Co., on Dec. 15, 1979, the first winter record in western Oregon. Four also wintered once at Sauvie I. Virtually all the remaining western Oregon reports come from the Willamette Valley in May.

Order ANSERIFORMES
Family Anatidae
Subfamily Anserinae

Fulvous Whistling-Duck. *Dendrocygna bicolor.*

Vagrant.

A flock of 11 was in the dune lakes north of Coos Bay, Coos Co., from Feb. 14-24, 1970. One was collected and photographs of the flock were taken.

Tundra Swan. *Cygnus columbianus.*

Fairly common and locally abundant transient statewide. Uncommon to locally common in winter.

The Tundra Swan is a fairly common transient throughout much of Oregon. The number of birds in the Pacific flyway has been increasing at a rate of about 1,200 birds per year. From 1970 to 1980 the average Pacific flyway population has been estimated at 58,000. Many of these birds pass through Oregon en route between their Arctic nesting grounds and primary wintering areas in California. Fall migrants typically begin to arrive in Oregon in early November, and rarely by early October. Transient movements continue through December. The greatest migratory concentrations occur in the large lakes of Klamath, Lake, and Harney Cos., on Sauvie I., and along the lower Columbia R. in Clatsop and Columbia Cos. Smaller numbers occur widely throughout the state.

Mid-winter waterfowl surveys in early January have in recent years reported 5,000-6,000 birds wintering in the state. Most are in western Oregon, with concentrations at Sauvie I., the lower Columbia R., the Willamette Valley, and along the coast. Important coastal wintering locations include the Siuslaw and Umpqua R. estuaries, and the dune lakes north of Coos Bay, Coos Co. East of the Cascade Mts. about 1,500 birds regularly winter in the Klamath Basin, and small numbers are also found at widely scattered locations during mild winters. An average of 1,000 use Summer L., though 10,000 wintered in Lake Co. during the mild winter of 1980-81.

Spring migration begins early. Numbers in the Klamath Basin peak in February and almost all have gone north by mid-March. Peak numbers pass through Malheur N.W.R. in mid-March and are usually gone by early April. At Sauvie I. the peak is in late February; almost all are usually gone by mid-March, although a few have been recorded into early May. As during the fall migration, many other lakes, marshes, and estuaries also host transients. Single birds, perhaps crippled or sick, on occasion summer in Oregon.

The Tundra Swan utilizes shallow lakes, estuaries, marshes, and flooded fields. It is especially attracted to marshes east of the Cascades that have sago pondweed.

The Asian race, *C. c. bewickii,* or Bewick's Swan has recently been lumped with Whistling Swan, *C. c. columbianus,* to form the Tundra Swan. Single Bewick's Swans (perhaps the same bird) were seen in 1974, 1975, 1979, 1980, and 1981 at Lower Klamath N.W.R. or Miller Island Refuge, Klamath Co. Three probable hybrid Whistling X Bewick's Swans were seen in the Klamath Basin in February, 1979. A Bewick's Swan was at Sauvie I., Multnomah Co., in January, 1982. Another was seen near Nehalem, Tillamook Co., on Feb. 28, 1982.

Whooper Swan. *Cygnus cygnus.*

An individual of this species spent much of two winters on the California side of the Lower Klamath N.W.R., and was seen briefly just over the state line on the Oregon side on Dec. 13, 1991.

Trumpeter Swan. *Cygnus buccinator.*

Uncommon permanent resident in Harney Co. (introduced). Rare winter visitant to northwestern Oregon; very rare in winter east of the Cascades away from Harney Co.

During the 1800s several observers noted this species in winter along the lower Columbia R., in the Willamette Valley, and east of the Cascades. The only specimen that Gabrielson and Jewett (1940) could locate was that of a bird collected along the Columbia R., near Portland, Multnomah Co., on April 8, 1881. They reported a sighting of a possible Trumpeter Swan at Davis L., Klamath Co., on Sept. 7, 1929.

35

During recent winters small numbers have sometimes occurred in the vicinity of the lower Columbia R. in Multnomah, Columbia, and Clatsop Cos. They have usually arrived in December, but sometimes as early as late October or early November, and have departed in February or March. The most regular winter location in western Oregon is in western Polk Co., where a small flock has occurred since the mid-1980s.

It is unclear whether the Trumpeter Swan was originally a breeding bird east of the Cascade Mts. Both Bendire and Prill found them at Malheur L. during the breeding season. Between 1939 and 1958 a total of 137 adults and cygnets were transplanted from Red Rock Lakes N.W.R. in Montana to Malheur N.W.R. Trumpeter Swans are now established on various small ponds and warm springs within the refuge, most commonly along the Blitzen R., and rarely on Malheur L., Despite declines in numbers in recent years, they have pioneered in small numbers into surrounding Harney Co. Birds at Malheur N.W.R. typically remain on the refuge through the winter. Trumpeter Swans are very rare elsewhere east of the Cascades in winter.

Mute Swan. *Cygnus olor.*

Introduced; generally not self-sustaining despite continuing introductions.

On several occasions Mute Swans have escaped or have been introduced to the wild in Oregon. A breeding population was established at Siletz Bay and Devil's L., Lincoln Co., in the 1920s, and small numbers were still present in January and February, 1966, four to six birds in 1969-70, and one to two birds in the mid-1970s (Bayer and Booth 1977). Other localities where introductions have been made include Rockaway, Tillamook Co.; the Willamette Valley near Woodburn, Marion Co., where two cygnets were banded in 1959; Buchanan, Harney Co.; and Bend, Deschutes Co., where four hand-reared flying birds were banded and released in 1968.

Introduced populations in Oregon seem to breed and increase in numbers for a few years before dwindling away. The Bend colony peaked at nine birds in 1972 and declined to three birds in 1980. Seven Mute Swans appeared on the Snake R. in Baker Co. in March, 1974.

Greater White-fronted Goose. *Anser albifrons.*

Common transient; rare to locally uncommon in winter.

Two subspecies of Greater White-fronted Goose are found in Oregon, the common "Pacific White-fronted Goose" (*A. a. frontalis*) and the rare "Tule White-fronted Goose" (*A. a. gambelli*), the breeding grounds of which were recently discovered near Cook Inlet, Alaska. "Tule White-fronts" can be identified in the field by their larger size, chocolate-brown heads, and blackish backs.

The Greater White-fronted Goose is a common fall transient in many parts of the state on both sides of the Cascade Mts. Flocks begin to arrive in Oregon in late August, rarely early August, after a transoceanic (or possibly coastal) flight of 2,000 miles from Alaska to the mouth of the Columbia R. Small numbers move down the coast and as many as 200 have been seen at Tillamook Bay. Most migrate up the Columbia to Sauvie I. (where up to 3,500 have been found in early October), and the Willamette Valley, then over the Cascades to the Klamath Basin and Summer L. area. Few are found west of the Cascades after early November.

At least 2,000 birds stop at Summer L., arriving at the end of August and departing by October 1. One hundred to 200 birds are usually recorded at Umatilla N.W.R., and 3,000 at Malheur N.W.R. (possibly entering Oregon from Idaho and eastern Washington). In the Klamath Basin (including the California portion), average fall populations are currently about 100,000, having declined from around 500,000 birds in 1966-68 (O'Neill 1979). Eskimo subsistence harvest in Alaska and sport harvest (mostly in California) are believed to have combined to deplete breeding stocks despite the species consistently high productivity (36% young in the fall population) (Bellrose 1976).

By December most Greater White-fronted Geese have moved into the Central Valley of California. They are rare to locally uncommon in Oregon in winter, and individuals have wintered on the coast. An increasing number (up to 7,000) have wintered annually in the Klamath Basin, including the California portion.

Birds begin leaving the Central Valley of California and appearing in the Klamath Basin and at Sauvie I. in February. Large numbers of spring transients use

37

the Klamath Basin. Significant flocks stop at Summer L. and in the Warner Valley of Lake Co. The high count at Malheur N.W.R. in 1980 was 3,700 in early April. Over 2,000 at one time have been recorded at Conley L., Union Co., from late February to late March. The refuges of Umatilla and Morrow Cos. also are regular stopover areas.

Up to 3,500 have been recorded at Sauvie I. in March and early April, but such numbers are far greater than the typically small flocks seen there at that season. Lesser numbers are occasionally seen elsewhere in the state. Flocks of several hundred are sometimes noted in flight along the northern coast in April and early May. The last transients are typically gone by mid-May, though late transients have been seen in early June. There are rare examples of White-fronts summering, often with domestic waterfowl.

Snow Goose. *Chen caerulescens.*

Uncommon but locally abundant transient. Rare but locally uncommon to common winter visitant.

The information given by Gabrielson and Jewett (1940) regarding the occurrence of the Snow Goose in Oregon is still accurate for the most part. Recent banding recoveries have demonstrated that Oregon Snow Geese come from distinct breeding populations in the western Canadian Arctic and on Wrangel Island in Siberia. Both populations have undergone marked changes in numbers, not always in synchrony, due to the vagaries of Arctic weather.

The Canadian birds, joined in the American Arctic by part of the Siberian population, arrive in eastern Oregon via Freezeout L., Montana (Bellrose 1976). Numerous Canadian-banded birds have been recovered from mid-October to mid-November (some late November, early December) at Summer L., Lake Co., Harney Basin, Warner Basin, Harney Co., Klamath Basin, and a scattering of other eastern Oregon locations such as the Crooked R., Crook Co. A large number of Russian-banded geese have been recovered at Summer L. Peak fall populations at Malheur N.W.R. recently have had about 3,000 birds, at Summer L. about 100,000, and Klamath Basin from 160,000 to 240,000 (primarily in the California portion of the Basin). Between 25 and 100 birds stray to Umatilla and

Cold Springs N.W.R.s, Morrow and Umatilla Cos. There are also a few fall recoveries of Canadian-banded birds in the Willamette Valley.

The remainder of the Wrangel I. population migrates directly across the ocean from Alaska, some to the Skagit Flats in Washington (where they winter) and some to the mouth of the Columbia R. A few hundred birds are recorded at Lewis and Clark N.W.R., Clatsop Co., in the fall, and Russian color-marked birds have been seen at Sauvie I. Most of this western Oregon contingent eventually join the birds using the eastern migratory route at Summer L. and the Klamath Basin.

Most Snow Geese move south to winter in California. However scattered flocks or individuals can be found in winter on the Lower Columbia R., Sauvie I. (up to about 2,000 birds some winters), Umatilla and Cold Springs N.W.R.s, the Willamette Valley, rarely along the coast, and in the Malheur and Klamath Basins in some winters. Overwintering populations in the Klamath Basin some winters have exceeded 10,000 birds.

The return movement in spring into the Klamath and Harney Basins begins in early February, most birds having moved northeast by mid-April. Peak numbers moving through Malheur N.W.R. are 4,000 birds. Probable late migrants were 16 birds banded in the Klamath Basin in the fourth week of May 1937. Two birds were banded in the Warner Valley in June 1954 and July 1956, and an immature Snow Goose was seen at Sauvie I., Multnomah Co., June 3, 1967. Two flightless immatures were with a flightless adult at Malheur N.W.R. July 8, 1960, and nesting was believed to have occurred. A few individuals occasionally summer in the Klamath Basin.

The blue phase of the Snow Goose has been recorded rarely at Sauvie I., Cold Springs and Malheur N.W.R.s, Summer L., and in the Klamath Basin in fall, winter, and spring. The proportion of blue to white phase birds is in the order of 1 in 10,000. Some central Arctic Snow Geese (where the blue phase is more common) are apparently migrating into the Pacific Flyway (Dzubin 1979).

Ross' Goose. *Chen rossii.*

Common spring and fall transient in southeastern and south-central Oregon. Vagrant elsewhere.

"Known only as a straggler" to Gabrielson and Jewett, Ross' Geese are now common during both spring and fall migration in south-central and southeastern Oregon. Considered rare in the 1900s, and estimated at 2,000 birds in the 1950s, the population is now over 100,000, having increased at an average rate of 7 percent per year from 1964 to 1979 (McLandress 1979). Better field surveys probably account for some of the increase. The end of market hunting, restricted bag limits, association with Snow Geese, and a shift in food utilization from natural grasses to irrigated grasses and grains, are some of the possible causes of the increase in numbers. A high percentage of the world population of this species moves through Oregon annually.

Ross' Geese arrive in southeast Oregon in mid-October. The greatest numbers pass through in November, and they occasionally have been noted into early December. A few birds sometimes winter in the California portion of the Klamath Basin.

In spring, Ross' Geese return to the Klamath Basin in late February and early March, and remain into late April. Up to 10,000 may be present at one time at the Miller I. W.M.A., Klamath Co., in April. From there the population migrates northeast. Summer L. is also a regular spring stopping place. The average date of arrival at Malheur N.W.R. is March 13, with flock sizes similar in size to those at Miller I. Small flocks at Malheur N.W.R. are sometimes noted into the first days of May. It is a rare spring and fall transient through Baker, Union, and Wallowa Cos. An occasional bird or two sometimes summers in the Klamath Basin.

The Ross' Goose is very rare away from Malheur, Harney, Lake, Klamath, Baker, Union, and Wallowa Cos. It is very rare in fall, winter, and spring along the northern coast, on Sauvie I., and in the Willamette Valley, and has also occurred in central Oregon (Deschutes Co.) in spring.

Single blue morphs (or hybrids with blue phase Snow Geese) are seen regularly at Miller I. and rarely elsewhere. A Snow/Ross' hybrid banded at Perry R., Canada, in August 1967, was shot at Summer L. on Nov. 21, 1970.

Emperor Goose. *Chen canagica.*

Rare visitant in fall, winter, and spring.

There are more than 30 records of the Emperor Goose in Oregon, mostly of single birds or small groups, probably families. Records are fairly evenly divided between coastal and inland locations, mainly October through March (earliest is October 3). Inland, Emperor Geese have been seen most regularly at Sauvie I., the Klamath Basin, and various locations in the Willamette Valley.

The largest group (17) as well as the latest spring record (May 8) was from Gold Beach, Curry Co. (Murrelet 24:29). An adult, which had arrived in immature plumage the previous fall, was still present near Nehalem, Tillamook Co., on June 9, 1979, with domestic geese (originally having associated with Canadas and White-fronts). While in the state, Emperor Geese seem to be equally at home in salt or fresh environments, feeding either on eelgrass, sea lettuce, and barnacles, or sedges and grasses.

Brant. *Branta bernicla.*

Common transient and locally common winter visitant along the coast. Rare transient and winter visitant inland.

In the fall migration the greater part of the Pacific flyway Brant population misses the Oregon coast, flying directly from Alaska or Siberia over the ocean to California or Mexico. Transient and wintering Brant typically arrive on the Oregon coast in mid-November, with the major influx occurring in December.

The 1,000 to 2,500 Brant that winter in Oregon estuaries constitute approximately one percent of the Pacific flyway population. Flocks regularly winter in Tillamook Bay, Netarts Bay, Tillamook Co., and in Yaquina Bay, Lincoln Co., (up to 760 birds). Smaller numbers sometimes winter at other locations, such as Coos Bay.

The northward migratory movement along the coast begins in late February, the main passage occurring in March and the first half of April, with small flocks lingering into early May. Over 500 birds per hour are sometimes seen in early April from coastal promontories as the birds fly northward over the ocean a short distance from land.

41

Individuals or small flocks regularly summer in coastal estuaries. A high percentage of these birds are probably crippled or sick.

The Brant is a rare vagrant inland, occurring most frequently during the fall migration, but also in mid-winter and during the spring migration. Most inland occurrences have been reported from the Willamette Valley or Sauvie I., but there are also records from the Umpqua Valley, Douglas Co., the Warner Valley and Summer L., Lake Co., Sisters, Deschutes Co., Cold Springs N.W.R., Umatilla Co., and in the Klamath Basin.

The normally-occurring race in Oregon is *B. b. nigricans*, formerly considered a separate species, the "Black" Brant. The light-bellied *B. b. hrota*, formerly referred to as a separate species called the "Atlantic" Brant, has twice been collected on Tillamook Bay, Tillamook Co., and once was photographed in May at the mouth of the Columbia R., Clatsop Co. Two were seen on Sauvie I. Oct. 28+, 1984. An intergrade between these two races spent the summer and fall of 1973 on Yaquina Bay, Lincoln Co., (Hoffman and Elliot 1974). Another intergrade, banded at Melville I., Canada, was recovered at Coos Bay.

Winter population levels of Brant have declined somewhat in Oregon, and it is thought that the habitat should support slightly larger populations. While in the State, Brant are usually found feeding on eelgrass and algae (sea lettuce) in bays and estuaries. They also rest offshore, probably in response to disturbance on the bays. Inland vagrants have been found on lakes and grazing with other geese in fields.

Canada Goose. *Branta canadensis.*

Locally common permanent resident. Common transient and winter visitant.

Eight subspecies of Canada Geese are found in Oregon, most of which can be identified by differences in size, color, range, and season of occurrence. The two largest subspecies (*moffitti* and *maxima*) breed, the two smallest (*minima*, which is abundant, and *leucopareia*, which is endangered) are migrants wintering primarily in the central valley of California, and four (*taverneri, occidentalis, parvi-*

pes, and *fulva*) winter. *Parvipes* and *fulva* cannot be distinguished in the field from *taverneri* and *occidentalis*, respectively, and are relatively uncommon in Oregon.

The Great Basin Canada Goose, Western Canada Goose (*B. c. moffitti*), is more or less resident throughout the western states. This is the large (8-10 lb.) light-bellied goose that nests commonly east of the Cascades, and in lower but increasing numbers in the Willamette Valley and along the coast. The total breeding population east of the Cascades of about 4,000 pairs includes 1,400 in Harney Basin, 1,100 elsewhere in the Great Basin, 100 on the Snake River islands, and since 1900, 250 on upper Columbia River islands. The latter population was apparently suppressed by the formerly high Indian population along the river. Dams, flooding of islands, recreational boating, and heptachlor poisoning have reduced productivity of these geese recently. Large numbers of recoveries of banded birds have demonstrated that those *moffitti* that breed in eastern Oregon also winter east of the Cascades, with some scattering throughout the Great Basin. There are a few recoveries of *moffitti* in western Oregon from Montana bandings. Small flocks of large pale Canadas of this or the following subspecies are seen in the Willamette Valley, Sauvie I., and on the coast in early fall. An adult *moffitti* banded at Malheur N.W.R. July 1942 was recovered in October 1963 after having lived at least 22 years.

The Giant Canada Goose (*B. c. maxima*) was introduced from the Midwest in 1938 near Knappa, Clatsop Co., and the nesting population now numbers 300 birds. Giant Canadas resemble Great Basin Canadas, but are somewhat larger and heavier (11-12 lbs. or more), and often have a white patch on the forehead instead of the usual black head of other subspecies. They are presumably resident.

In fall, six other subspecies of Canada Geese arrive in Oregon. Cackling Geese or "cacklers" (*B. c. minima*), distinguished by voice, extremely small size (3 lbs.), stubby necks, and short bill, arrive at the mouth of the Columbia R. in mid-October and migrate up river and down the Willamette Valley to congregate in Klamath and Lake Cos. There are a few band recoveries from northeast Oregon. Peak populations in November in the Klamath Basin (mostly on the California side of the border, but there is movement back and forth during the fall) have recently declined to less than 100,000 from 3-400,000 in the mid-1960s. Most cacklers have moved into California by early December, but a few winter at the Willamette Valley refuges, in the Klamath Basin (up to 12,000 in some winters on both sides of the border), and occasional individuals on the coast. The return flight to breeding grounds on the Yukon-Kuskokwim Delta, Alaska, apparently follows a route west of the Cascades as flocks of cacklers do not appear at Malheur N.W.R. in spring.

Endangered Aleutian Canada Geese (*B. c. leucopareia*), which nest in the easternmost Aleutian Islands, are rare transients, and local winter visitants, along the coast.

In winter two subspecies of Canada Geese are abundant in Oregon. Lesser or Taverner's Canada Geese (*B. c. taverneri*, the *B. c. leucopareia* of Gabrielson and Jewett), which can be identified as medium-sized (5-6 lbs.), light-colored geese, winter both east and west of the Cascades. *Taverneri* from breeding grounds in northern Alaska begin to arrive in the upper Columbia Basin in October. Numbers build throughout the winter, peaking at 90,000 birds at Umatilla (some on the Washington side of the Columbia), Cold Springs N.W.R., and McKay Creek N.W.R. in December and January. Some birds move south to winter in Harney, Lake, and Klamath Cos. and in California. In spring these birds begin to move out in February and are gone by mid-April. Western Oregon Lesser Canadas derive from western Alaska breeding grounds and appear somewhat later, arriving first at the mouth of the Columbia R. in early November, then to Sauvie I. (peak numbers 24,000 in November) and the Willamette Valley, where they winter. Wintering *taverneri* populations have increased in recent years to 51,000. Mixed in with these birds are approximately 2,000 *B. c. parvipes* (also called "Lesser Canadas" and similar in appearance), primarily at Baskett Slough N.W.R., Polk Co.

Dusky Canada Geese (*B. c. occidentalis*), which nest only on the Copper River Delta in south-central Alaska arrive in western Oregon in October. They are identified by their overall dark coloration, including the belly, and large size (8-10 lbs.). Their wintering populations have also increased in the Willamette Valley since the establishment of the valley refuges. There are now close to 40,000 birds in the fall flight, and their winter range has expanded to include Sauvie I. and the lower Columbia R. Flocks of up to 150 Dusky Canadas also winter on coastal bays, pastures, and offshore rocks as far south as Curry Co., apparently less commonly than in the early part of the century. Of nearly 2,500 bands recovered from birds banded at the Copper River Delta, only one was from east of the Cascades.

44

Dusky and Lesser Canada Geese leave the Willamette Valley in April, perhaps by a reverse of their fall routes, i.e., along the coast for Duskies, and via interior valleys of British Columbia for Lessers, though their spring migration movements are poorly understood.

The winter picture is somewhat complicated by the presence of *B. c. fulva*, which is mainly resident in southeast Alaska and coastal British Columbia. It has been reported at the mouth of the Columbia, where there are sightings of birds neck-collared on Vancouver Island, B.C., and in the Willamette Valley. In addition, a flock of less than 200 birds with characteristics intermediate between Lesser and Aleutian Canadas has recently been discovered wintering at Haystack Rock near Pacific City, Tillamook Co. Some of these birds were banded at Semidi Island in the Aleutians.

Subfamily Anatinae

Wood Duck. *Aix sponsa.*

Fairly common summer resident and transient, and an uncommon to rare winter visitant west of the Cascade Mts. East of the Cascades an uncommon to rare transient and summer resident, and a rare winter visitant.

The Wood Duck is a fairly common transient and summer resident in the valleys and coastal lowlands west of the Cascade Mts., extending into the Cascades where there is appropriate habitat. It is generally an uncommon to rare but locally common winter resident west of the Cascades. It is rare or absent from many localities in winter along the northern coast that support summering populations, but is a locally common winterer in coastal Coos and Curry Cos.

East of the Cascades the Wood Duck is an uncommon resident of northern Morrow and Umatilla Cos. in the Columbia R. lowlands and other riparian areas. It is also a fairly common summer resident in the Klamath Basin and along the lower Owyhee R. and along stretches of the Snake R. in Malheur Co. This species is regularly noted and may be a local summer resident in Hood River Co. and northern Wasco Co. Elsewhere east of the Cascades it is unevenly distributed as an uncommon to rare summer resident. It is rare in summer at Malheur N.W.R. Transients occur more widely than summer birds, but are generally more common in the areas that also support summer populations. In winter the Wood Duck is mostly rare or absent east of the Cascades, except in the Klamath Basin and near Bend, Deschutes Co., where it is uncommon.

Wood Ducks utilize a variety of fresh water habitats including slow-moving rivers, lakes, ponds, and sewage lagoons, especially where they are bordered by deciduous trees such as cottonwoods, willow, or oaks. Birds foraging for acorns are sometimes encountered away from water. Either large trees with natural cavities or artificial nest boxes are necessary for breeding.

Green-winged Teal. *Anas crecca.*

East of the Cascade Mts., a very uncommon summer resident, common transient, and uncommon winterer. West of the Cascades, very rare breeder and non-breeding summerer, common transient and winter visitant.

The Green-winged Teal is a very uncommon summer resident east of the Cascades, where breeding has been confirmed in Harney, Lake, Klamath, and Umatilla Cos. Although not reported, breeding is probable elsewhere east of the Cascades, as the species is occasionally noted in suitable nesting habitat. It is a common transient and an uncommon to fairly common winterer where water remains open east of the Cascades.

In western Oregon the Green-winged Teal is a very rare breeder and non-breeding summerer. Nesting has been reported from Sauvie I., near Portland, and Tillamook Co. It is a common transient and winter visitant west of the Cascades.

The Green-winged Teal utilizes a variety of shallow fresh and salt water habitats. The normally occurring race in Oregon is *A. c. carolinensis*. The "Common" Teal, formerly considered a distinct species, is recorded in small numbers more or less annually as a transient and winter visitant. Both the Aleutian form *A. c. nimia* and the Eurasian form *A. c. crecca* have been collected in Oregon.

Baikal Teal. *Anas formosa.*

Vagrant.

46

The only record of this Asian species for Oregon is a male shot on Jan. 12, 1974, near Finley N.W.R., Benton Co.

American Black Duck. *Anas rubripes.*

Vagrant.

There are at least five specimen records of the American Black Duck for Oregon: Nov. 12, 1950, at Summer L., Lake Co.; Nov. 25, 1969, Sauvie I.; Jan. 1950, Ontario, Malheur Co.; Feb. 9, 1963, Sauvie I.; and Mar. 1950, Ontario. In addition, three were seen at Daley L., Tillamook Co., on Feb. 2, 1976, and one was at Malheur N.W.R., May 5, 1977. Some of these records may refer to birds escaped from captivity, but the species occurs sparingly as far west as Alberta, and waterfowl are capable of occurring far out of their regular range.

Mallard. *Anas platyrhynchos.*

Common permanent resident throughout the state.

The Mallard is a common permanent resident throughout Oregon. Large numbers breed in the great marshes of southeastern and south-central Oregon. It nests in every county, but is scarce at higher elevations in the Cascades, Blue, and Wallowa Mts. A variety of habitats are suitable for nesting, including marshes, lake shores, and stream margins. It has even been found to nest as high as 10 feet above ground in a bigleaf maple.

Large numbers occur in migration. The fall migration of birds from north of the state begins in July, but the greatest movement occurs in October and November. The Mallard remains common throughout the state in winter wherever open water is available. Large numbers winter in Klamath Co., and at Umatilla N.W.R. where the waters of the Columbia R. usually remain open and there is ready access to vast grain fields. Fifty thousand at Umatilla N.W.R. on Jan. 27, 1980, is not unusual for that area. Other significant wintering areas include Sauvie I., the Willamette Valley N.W.R.s, and Fern Ridge Res.

During the winter the Mallard uses a variety of freshwater habitats and coastal estuaries. They often feed on waste grain or in other types of fields. The main spring movement is in February and March. Free-ranging domestic birds are common in city parks, near farms, and elsewhere.

Northern Pintail. *Anas acuta.*

East of the Cascade Mts. a common summer resident and transient, and uncommon to rare winterer. West of the Cascades a common transient and winter visitant; rare non-breeding summerer.

The Northern Pintail is a common summer resident in the marshes of Harney, Lake, and Klamath Cos. Lesser numbers breed elsewhere east of the Cascades. It is a rare non-breeder in western Oregon in June.

The Pintail is a common transient on both sides of the Cascades. Banding records indicate that the first migrants from the north appear in late June. By August it is fairly common in western Oregon, especially on the larger estuaries.

Numbers east of the Cascades also increase dramatically by August. During fall migration some birds may use high Cascade lakes as rest areas. The peak numbers east of the Cascades are typically noted in October, while the peak west of the Cascades is usually in November. It remains common throughout winter in western Oregon. East of the Cascades it is generally an uncommon winter bird, but is typically common in the Klamath Basin. The spring migration extends from late February through mid-May, with the greatest numbers in March and early April. As is the case with most waterfowl, the species has declined in numbers in recent decades.

Garganey. *Anas querquedula*

Vagrant.

There are two records of this Eurasian teal for Oregon, both from Tillamook Co: one in eclipse plumage Sept. 17-24, 1988 at the Nehalem sewage ponds, and a breeding plumage drake May 9-13, 1992 at the Bay City sewage ponds.

Blue-winged Teal. *Anas discors.*

Uncommon transient and summer resident east of the Cascades. Uncommon transient, very uncommon breeder, and rare in winter west of the Cascades.

The Blue-winged Teal is an uncommon transient and summer resident east of the Cascades. The greatest numbers occur in the marsh regions of Harney, Lake, and Klamath Cos. This species is a very uncommon summer resident west of the Cascades. Breeding has been confirmed in the Willamette Valley, the Rogue Valley, and along the coast in Tillamook, Coos, and Clatsop Cos. West of the Cascades the Blue-winged Teal is generally an uncommon transient, but as many as 300 have been seen together in late September on Sauvie I. and a flock of 32 has been recorded in Clatsop Co. in late May.

The spring migration on both sides of the Cascades typically begins in late April or early May, and may continue into early June along the coast. Fall migrants are noted from early August through mid-October, and occasionally into early November. The Blue-winged Teal is a rare to very rare winterer west of the Cascades. It utilizes a variety of other shallow freshwater habitats, with transients occasionally noted on coastal estuaries.

Cinnamon Teal. *Anas cyanoptera.*

Common to fairly common summer resident and transient throughout the state. Very rare in winter west of the Cascade Mts.

The Cinnamon Teal is a common transient and summer resident throughout Oregon. It is more common as a breeder east of the Cascades, but is also fairly common in the coastal lowlands and interior valleys of western Oregon. The greatest numbers occur in the extensive marshes of Harney, Lake, and Klamath Cos. In at least some years it is the most numerous breeding duck at Malheur N.W.R., where as many as 17,000 young are produced in optimum years.

The spring migration commences in mid-February, but the bulk of the migration is in March through mid-April. The greatest part of the fall migration is in August and September, and by November this species is rare. It remains as a very rare winterer along the coast and in the inland valleys of western Oregon, but goes unreported some years.

The Cinnamon Teal nests in marsh habitats. Transients and winterers utilize a variety of freshwater habitats, including lakes, flooded fields, and sewage ponds.

Northern Shoveler. *Anas clypeata.*

Locally fairly common summer resident and fairly common to common transient east of the Cascade Mts. Fairly common transient and uncommon winter visitant west of the Cascades. Very uncommon in winter east of the Cascades. Very rare in western Oregon in summer.

The Northern Shoveler is a fairly common summer resident in the large marshes of Harney, Klamath, and Lake Cos. In the Malheur-Harney Basin (including Malheur N.W.R.) approximately 1,000 pairs have bred in some years. Upper Klamath N.W.R., Klamath Co., supports up to 500 breeding pairs. The remaining breeders occupy numerous smaller marshes east of the Cascade Mts. In western Oregon, Shovelers are very rare during summer. The only certain breeding record for western Oregon is of a female with ten young at Fort Stevens, Clatsop Co., on May 3, 1989.

The fall migration begins earlier east of the Cascades than west, with small numbers first arriving in mid-August. The migration peaks from late September to mid-October. In the 1950s and 1960s Malheur N.W.R. and Upper Klamath N.W.R. each supported up to 200,000 migrants during good years, but numbers have decreased greatly.

Most western Oregon migrants come from post-breeding areas in coastal Alaska, where open water is often available into early winter. Although migrants are first

50

noted in mid-August and increase gradually through September, the peak of the western Oregon migration occurs in November.

During winter in western Oregon, shovelers are uncommon on coastal bays and estuaries, locally common on sewage ponds, and uncommon on suitable shallow water in the interior valleys. A location of special concentration is the Sheridan sewage lagoons, Yamhill Co., where as many as 500 sometimes winter. East of the Cascades where numbers fluctuate greatly with winter severity, shovelers are local and uncommon winter visitants. However, at Upper Klamath L. they are sometimes fairly common. During some years a few thousand may winter at Umatilla N.W.R. Elsewhere east of the Cascades they are very uncommon but may occur on almost any open body of water.

The spring migration is relatively late, usually peaking in the latter half of April, although a slight influx of migrants may be noted as early as late February. By late May non-breeders throughout the state have departed for their northern breeding grounds.

Gadwall. *Anas strepera.*

Common summer resident east of the Cascade Mts. Common to rare transient and winterer throughout the state.

The Gadwall is a common summer resident east of the Cascades, where the greatest numbers utilize the large marshes of Harney, Lake and Klamath Cos. As an example, 3,300 breeding pairs were at Malheur N.W.R. in 1980. In recent years it has been found to nest in small numbers in western Oregon, especially Clatsop Co.

This duck occurs throughout the state as a migrant. It is generally uncommon as a migrant west of the Cascades and common east of the Cascades. The Gadwall is a fairly common transient in the Rogue Valley and in Coos Co. Migrants west of the Cascades are rarely reported as early as mid-July, but the species is not of widespread occurrence until late September. Numbers peak from mid-October to the end of November. East of the Cascades it is one of the more common migrant ducks.

51

In winter the Gadwall is uncommon to locally common west of the Cascades. Small numbers winter along the coast, more near Coos Bay. Typically about 500 winter annually there, and as many as 2,000 have been reported some winters. It is uncommon in winter in the inland valleys of western Oregon. Two hundred fifty to 300 typically winter in Multnomah Co. East of the Cascades the Gadwall is generally uncommon in winter, but is rare in many areas, and common in the Klamath Basin and at Summer L. Its presence and numbers are determined by the severity of the winter.

The Gadwall nests in marshes. Transients and winterers utilize lakes, marshes, wet fields, and coastal estuaries. This species often utilizes deeper ponds than do other dabbling ducks, as it is adept at diving for submerged plant life.

Eurasian Wigeon. *Anas penelope.*

Uncommon winter visitant west of the Cascade Mts. Locally uncommon to rare transient and winter visitant east of the Cascades.

The Eurasian Wigeon is an uncommon transient and winter visitant west of the Cascades. It is most numerous near Portland, in the lower Columbia R. lowlands, and along the coast. East of the Cascades the Eurasian Wigeon is generally a rare transient and a very rare winter visitant. In the Klamath Basin and northern Lake Co. it is an uncommon transient and a rare winterer.

Migrants appear in mid-October and depart by late April or early May. This species is typically found among flocks of American Wigeon. Wigeon flocks in Oregon utilize shallow estuaries, lakes, and flooded fields. Much feeding is done in short grass fields or on lawns, such as those in city parks or golf courses. Hybrids of the two species have been noted in the state.

American Wigeon. *Anas americana.*

East of the Cascade Mts. an uncommon summer resident and winterer, and a common transient. West of the Cascades a common transient and winter visitant, and a rare non-breeding summer visitant.

The American Wigeon is an uncommon summer resident east of the Cascades, where the greatest numbers of breeders occur in the marshes of Harney, Lake, and Klamath Cos. Smaller numbers breed at widely scattered locations elsewhere. It is a common transient and an uncommon winterer east of the Cascades, except in the Klamath Basin where it is fairly common in winter. Banding data indicates that a large percentage of birds migrating through eastern Oregon spend the winter in the central valley of California, with lesser numbers traveling as far as the Salton Sea.

West of the Cascades the American Wigeon is a common transient and winter visitant. In western Oregon in winter it is most common near Portland, on Sauvie I., along the lower Columbia R., and on the coast. This species is a rare non-breeding summer visitant in western Oregon.

The spring migration is from mid-February through early May. A few migrants are occasionally noted into late May. Fall migrants appear in western Oregon in late July, usually first on the larger coastal estuaries. Peak numbers occur from mid-October to early December west of the Cascades, and from early October to mid-November east of the Cascades.

Canvasback. *Aythya valisineria.*

Locally uncommon to fairly common resident, common transient, and generally uncommon but locally common winter resident east of the Cascade Mts. Uncommon transient and winter visitant in the inland valleys of western Oregon. Fairly common transient and winter visitant along the coast. Very rare summer visitant in western Oregon.

The Canvasback is a locally uncommon to fairly common summer resident in the large marshes of Harney, Lake, and Klamath Cos. Numbers fluctuate widely from year to year, probably due to varied water levels; in optimum years 500 pairs may breed at Malheur N.W.R. Canvasbacks have declined in Oregon in the past several decades. East of the Cascades smaller numbers breed on available marshes, ponds, and sloughs. There are a few records for western Oregon in summer, none of which have involved nesting.

This species is a common transient east of the Cascade Mts. Fall migrants appear from interior northern breeding areas by early October, and exceptionally in late August. Peak numbers are reached by early November. The majority of migrants east of the Cascades winter south of Oregon.

The species is generally an uncommon winter resident east of the Cascade Mts., but may be locally common at favored localities such as the Columbia R. and Upper Klamath L. The severity of the winter is an important factor in its winter abundance.

The Canvasback is an uncommon transient and winter visitant in the interior valleys of western Oregon. It is a fairly common transient and winter visitant along the coast, where winter rafts form on Tillamook, Alsea, and Coos Bays, and on the Columbia R. estuary. The species typically appears in early October and exceptionally in late August. Peak numbers of fall migrants occur in November.

Spring migrants occur from March through April, with occasional birds lingering away from breeding areas into early May.

Redhead. *Aythya americana.*

Locally common summer resident and fairly common transient east of the Cascade Mts. Uncommon to rare winter visitant throughout the state.

The Redhead is a locally common summer resident east of the Cascade Mts. in the large marshes of Harney, Lake, and Klamath Cos. Malheur N.W.R. supports up to 7,000 breeding pairs in some years. It is often absent from the Columbia R. basin in summer, but Umatilla N.W.R. has supported a few pairs in recent years (U.S.F.W.S. Peak Monthly Reports). Elsewhere east of the Cascades it breeds in smaller numbers where suitable deep marsh habitat exists.

East of the Cascades the fall migration is early, with peak numbers usually moving through the state in August and September. Numbers decline sharply until November, after which few transients are observed. Migration is much heavier east of the Cascades than west. Typical August peaks at Malheur N.W.R. number

5,000 birds, while Upper Klamath N.W.R. reports August peaks averaging 800-1,000 migrants (U.S. F.W.S. Peak Monthly Reports). In western Oregon it is a very uncommon migrant, except in the Coos Bay area, where it is fairly common. The majority of migrants west of the Cascades continue south.

The Redhead is a generally uncommon winter resident east of the Cascade Mts., but remains common during milder winters. Five hundred to 1,000 commonly winter on the Columbia R., and as many as 600 may winter on Upper Klamath L., with generally lesser numbers elsewhere. It is a very uncommon winter visitant west of the Cascade Mts., and is rare or absent over much of this area. This species is fairly common in winter on and near Coos Bay. A flock of up to several dozen birds usually winters on Yaquina Bay. Flocks of as many 25 Redheads are exceptional elsewhere west of the Cascades. It is more typically noted in numbers from one to several birds, and often is associated with other species of diving ducks.

Spring migrants move into Oregon from southern winter areas by February, and numbers rise until peaking in April. Numbers away from breeding locations decline steadily until May.

Ring-necked Duck. *Aythya collaris.*

Very local summer resident in the Cascade Mts. Local and very uncommon summer resident, fairly common transient, and rare to uncommon winter visitant east of the Cascades. Fairly common to locally common transient and winter visitant west of the Cascades.

Ring-necked Ducks in Oregon utilize lakes and ponds (often wooded), sewage lagoons, and much less frequently rivers and coastal estuaries. It breeds locally at scattered, typically forested, lakes in the Cascade Mts. and eastward. A few pairs breed annually at Trillium L., Clackamas Co.

There are also breeding records from northeastern Oregon, Upper Klamath L., and Malheur N.W.R. There are additional records of summering birds east of the Cascades, some of which may pertain to breeding birds. Non-breeders are very rarely noted west of the Cascades in summer.

It is a fairly common to common spring and fall transient on both sides of the Cascade Mts. The main fall migration is in October and November, and migrants appear exceptionally as early as late August. East of the Cascades peak numbers are recorded by early November, while peak numbers pass through western Oregon two to three weeks later.

The Ring-necked Duck is a rare to uncommon winter resident east of the Cascade Mts., with the availability of open water the main criterion. It is probably most numerous east of the Cascades in winter in Klamath Co. West of the Cascades it is a locally common transient and winter visitant. More than 1,000 have been recorded in early December at Henry Hagg L., Washington Co., but the species is more frequently noted in flocks of a few to several dozen birds.

Tufted Duck. *Aythya fuligula.*

Vagrant.

The Tufted Duck is nearing annual occurrence on the sewage ponds and lakes of western Oregon, with about 18 total records. Individual birds typically spend most of the season in a small area and are readily re-located. Most are found in mid-winter but there are records as early as October 15 and as late as May 4.

A hybrid Tufted Duck/scaup returned to the Monmouth sewage ponds, Polk Co., for several years in the late 1980s. Hybrids of various types should be considered when reporting rare diving ducks in Oregon.

Greater Scaup. *Aythya marila.*

Common coastal transient and winter visitant, and very uncommon summer visitant. Rare to uncommon transient and winter visitant in inland western Oregon. Rare transient and winter visitant east of the Cascade Mts., except along the Columbia R. where it is locally common.

The Greater Scaup in Oregon is primarily a coastal species. It occurs more typically on larger bodies of water and is much more likely to be found on salt water than is the Lesser Scaup. It is a common transient and winter visitant on estuaries, sewage lagoons, and to a lesser extent freshwater lakes. This species is much more numerous as a transient than a winterer.

Fall migrants appear in late September, and peak in number in mid-November. The majority of winter visitants concentrate on the larger estuaries such as the Columbia R. estuary, Tillamook Bay, Yaquina Bay, the Umpqua R., and Coos Bay. Spring transients appear in early March and peak near the end of that month or in early April. Transients are often noted into early May. Small numbers often remain through the summer on coastal estuaries and occasionally elsewhere.

The Greater Scaup is a rare to uncommon transient inland in western Oregon. It is of most regular occurrence on large lakes and sewage lagoons. One summered at Portland in 1969, and another at Baskett Slough N.W.R. in 1984.

East of the Cascade Mts. it is generally a rare transient, and also winters rarely on large lakes and reservoirs. In recent years the Greater Scaup has been found along the Columbia R. from Hood River to Umatilla Cos. both in the winter and during the periods of migration. Rafts there sometimes number in the hundreds.

Lesser Scaup. *Aythya affinis.*

East of the Cascade Mts., locally common but generally uncommon summer resident. Common transient and winter visitant throughout the state. Rare summer visitant in western Oregon.

The Lesser Scaup breeds at the margins of marshes and in nearby uplands at scattered localities east of the Cascade Mts. As many as 1,000 pairs breed on Upper Klamath L., while Klamath Marsh N.W.R. supports 200-300 pairs. It is an uncommon summer resident at the large marshes of Lake and Harney Cos., and in lesser numbers elsewhere over a wide range east of the Cascades. It is a rare summer visitant west of the Cascades where it is found regularly at a few lakes and sewage treatment ponds.

The Lesser Scaup is a common transient and winter visitant throughout Oregon. Fall migrants begin moving throughout the state in late September, with peak numbers observed east of the Cascades in late October, and in western Oregon in late November. Although far greater numbers occur during migration, the species remains common during winter throughout the state where open water remains.

The spring migration is protracted. Small numbers of transients move into the state in mid-February. In western Oregon numbers decline after early March, while in some areas east of the Cascades the peak migration period is delayed until mid-April. Spring transients are uncommonly noted into May.

Steller's Eider. *Polysticta stelleri.*

Vagrant.

A male was at the north jetty of Coos Bay from Feb. 10-17, 1992, for the only Oregon record. Photographs were taken.

King Eider. *Somateria spectabilis.*

Vagrant.

This duck is a very rare visitant, with most records found in scoter flocks off coastal headlands. A female was at Garibaldi, Tillamook Co., on March 10-17, 1976; a female was found dead on the beach at Cape Arago, Coos Co., on Nov. 18, 1980; two subadult males were at Seaside, Clatsop Co., from Feb. 16 into March 1981; an immature male was at Cape Arago Dec. 19-26, 1985; one female stayed at Bandon, Coos Co., from November 1991 to Feb. 29, 1992; and an immature male was at Florence, Lane Co., Oct. 22, 1993. Two additional females, most likely of this species, were seen around the mouth of Coos Bay on Nov. 6, 1992.

Harlequin Duck. *Histrionicus histrionicus.*

Rare summer resident in the northern and central Cascade Mts. Formerly nested in the Wallowa Mts. but no recent records. Fairly common transient and winter visitant, and a very uncommon summer visitant along the coast. Very rare elsewhere in the state.

The Harlequin Duck is a fairly common transient and winter visitant along the coast where small flocks of several to a dozen birds are typical, but exceptional groups as large as 70 birds have been noted. Small numbers of non-breeders summer at coastal locations.

The Harlequin Duck is a rare summer resident on swift mountain streams in the Cascade Mts. Fewer than 10 sightings have been reported from the Wallowa Mts. since 1970, and the last verified nesting record for that area was from 1935. A female with four ducklings on the Nestucca river on July 1, 1994 is the only known Coast Range breeding record.

In 1993, O.D.F.W., the Forest Service, and the B.L.M. surveyed 420 miles of known or suspected breeding habitat in the Oregon Cascades, and compiled reports from other sources. Eighty-nine pairs and 26 broods were observed, with a total of 354 individuals, though some may have been duplicate sightings. Three new nests were found to bring the total number of historical records to eight.

Breeding was confirmed in the Hood, Deschutes, Sandy, Clackamas, Molalla, North Santiam, McKenzie, and upper Willamette R. drainages. Individuals were also observed on the Middle Santiam, South Santiam, and Umpqua Rivers. Birds were noted on only one stream east of the Cascade crest, the White R. of Hood River and Wasco Cos., where a brood was observed. An old record on June 14, 1958, in Klamath Co. was also on the east slope but out of breeding habitat. A migrant was below the John Day Dam, Sherman Co., on Sept. 6, 1989.

The Harlequin Duck's habitat along the coast is the ocean and lower parts of estuaries where the shore and ocean floor are rocky. They are often seen resting on rocks at high tide and feeding about exposed rocks at low tide. This species is sometimes attracted to the mouths of small coastal streams.

Harlequin Duck

Oldsquaw. *Clangula hyemalis.*

Very uncommon transient and winter visitant along the coast. Rare transient and winter visitant inland.

The Oldsquaw is a very uncommon transient and winter visitant along the coast. Numbers vary considerably from year to year. The great majority of Oregon birds are either immatures or females. Normally only one or two individuals are present at a single locality. However, in 1976-77 up to 10 wintered at Yaquina Bay. The largest number counted at a single estuary was 12 on March 21, 1976, at Yaquina Bay. Nine, five of which were adult males, were on the Nehalem sewage lagoons on Oct. 18, 1981.

Transients and winterers are typically noted from late October to mid-April, and rarely to mid-May. A male in Tillamook Co. in July, 1977, and one during the summer of 1982 represent rare summering birds, while a female at Yaquina Bay on June 3, 1990 could have been either a late migrant or summering. A male was at Yaquina Head on June 12, 1993, and was also reported several times to early August.

Inland, the Oldsquaw is rare as a transient and winter visitant, usually to large bodies of water. Most Columbia R. counties have records, as well as those in southeastern and central Oregon. There is a record from the high Cascades, one at Big L., Linn Co., on Oct. 24, 1987.

Along the coast Oldsquaws utilize estuaries, the ocean near shore, and occasionally sewage lagoons or freshwater ponds. They are often found with scoters.

Black Scoter. *Melanitta nigra.*

Uncommon transient and winter visitant, and very rare summer visitant on the coast.

The Black Scoter is an uncommon transient and winter visitant in coastal estuaries and on the ocean near shore. The first fall migrants may appear as early as late August, although the bulk of the migrants arrive after late September. In winter, individuals or small flocks numbering less than 30 are typically noted, although flocks of up to 100 are sometimes noted in good habitat. An exceptional group of 700 was noted north of Yaquina Head, Lincoln Co., on Feb. 12, 1989.

Northern migrants are evident from March into early May. Browning (1973) reported 573 Black Scoters in 27 flocks passing Goat I., Curry Co., on March 23-26, 1966. Flights of lesser numbers have been noted as late as the second week of May. Occasional migrants may linger into late May. There are five July records, all from Yaquina Bay, and an August 9 record from Bandon, Coos Co.

Inland records include one shot at Sauvie I., Dec. 26, 1967; one found shot at Summer L., Lake Co., Nov. 15, 1955; one at the Monmouth sewage ponds, Polk Co., Oct. 16, 1984; one at Cascade Locks, Hood River Co., on Dec. 11, 1984; one at Salem, Marion Co., on Nov. 4, 1987; one at Haystack Res., Jefferson Co., on Oct. 15, 1989; and one at Willow Creek Res., Morrow Co., Oct. 20, 1990.

Surf Scoter. *Melanitta perspicillata.*

Common transient and winter visitant, and an uncommon summer visitant along the coast. Rare transient and winter visitant inland.

The Surf Scoter is a common transient and winter visitant along the coast. Fall migrants arrive in early September, reaching peak numbers in October and November. In winter numbers diminish but the species remains common. The spring migration begins in March, and most have departed by early June. On April 15, 1979, 3,000 per hour were reported to pass the S. Jetty of the Columbia R. That number subsided to about 225 per hour by May 6. The Surf Scoter remains an uncommon non-breeder along the coast throughout the summer.

The species utilizes coastal estuaries, the ocean near shore, and occasionally freshwater habitats near the ocean. The lower part of estuaries are preferred to the more brackish upper areas.

Inland the Surf Scoter is a rare but regular transient and winter visitant on both sides of the Cascade crest. The more than 40 records for east of the Cascades are from Malheur N.W.R., Summer L., Upper Klamath L. and a variety of other large lakes and rivers. It is also occasionally found in fall on lakes in the high Cascades and during fall and winter in the Rogue, Umpqua, and Willamette Valleys.

White-winged Scoter. *Melanitta fusca.*

Common transient and winter visitant, and an uncommon summer visitant along the coast. Rare transient inland.

The White-winged Scoter is a common transient and winter visitant along the coast, and remains as an uncommon non-breeder throughout the summer. Some early fall migrants arrive in late July, but peak numbers are reached in October and November when the species is very common. Numbers are reduced in mid-winter. It has been estimated that approximately 30 percent of the state's wintering scoters are this species, while Surf Scoters and Black Scoters comprise about 60 percent and 10 percent respectively. The spring migration takes place from March through late May.

The White-winged Scoter is a rare transient inland. Most inland records are from October and November, but there are a few spring records as well. The species is nearly annual in Deschutes Co., and has also been recorded away from the coast at a variety of locations east and west of the Cascade crest.

Although this species primarily uses the lower parts of coastal estuaries and the ocean near shore, small numbers also occur on upper bays, sloughs, and freshwater lakes.

Common Goldeneye. *Bucephala clangula.*

Common to very uncommon transient and winter visitant statewide.

The Common Goldeneye is a locally common transient and winter visitant along the coast. It is an uncommon to very uncommon transient and winter visitant in the inland valleys of western Oregon, and a common transient and winter visitant east of the Cascade Mts.

Fall migrants arrive by mid- or late October, and peak in number in late November and early December. The spring migration is relatively early, with some movement noted in late February and peak numbers reached in March.

Numbers decline rapidly in April and the species is usually absent from Oregon by May. The latest spring record at Malheur N.W.R. is May 29, 1980. There are several summer records of individuals from the coast. It is also reportedly a rare summer visitant to northeastern Oregon.

In Oregon the Common Goldeneye utilizes coastal estuaries, slow and rapid moving rivers and streams, small ponds and large lakes, and even flooded fields.

Barrow's Goldeneye. *Bucephala islandica.*

Very uncommon local summer resident on subalpine lakes of the Cascade Mts. Uncommon transient and winter visitant in northeastern Oregon and Klamath Co. and uncommon to rare transient and winter visitant elsewhere east of the Cascades and on reservoirs along the western slope of the Cascades. Very rare winter visitant west of the Cascades.

The Barrow's Goldeneye breeds in small numbers on the subalpine lakes of the Cascade Mts., utilizing tree cavities or nest boxes for nest sites. Breeding records are available for a number of lakes in the central Cascades of Clackamas, Linn, Deschutes, Douglas, and Klamath Cos.

This species is an uncommon transient and winter visitant in northeastern Oregon and in Klamath Co. It is an uncommon transient and winter visitant elsewhere east of the Cascades and on lakes and reservoirs on the western slope of the Cascades, though substantial numbers can congregate at favored locations like Diamond L., Douglas Co., Hatfield L., Deschutes Co., and along the Columbia R.

The Barrow's Goldeneye is a very rare winter visitant and transient in inland western Oregon and along the coast.

Bufflehead. *Bucephala albeola.*

Locally uncommon summer resident in the Cascade Mts. Common transient and winter visitant throughout the state.

The Bufflehead is an uncommon local breeder in the central and southern Cascade Mts. Nesting normally occurs near lakes in holes made by Northern Flickers. It has been found nesting at a number of lakes at the higher elevations of Linn, Deschutes, Klamath, and Douglas Cos.

The Bufflehead is a common transient and winter visitant throughout the state. The first fall migrants normally appear in late September, and peak in late October or early November. Although it is common throughout the state in winter, it is especially numerous at coastal locations in sheltered freshwater lakes, ponds, sewage lagoons, rivers, and estuaries. In large bays the Bufflehead prefers to feed in shallow water over tidal mudflats. Maximum coastal counts in December range from 3,075 at Coos Bay to 707 at Tillamook Bay. Inland it is particularly common near Klamath Falls, where 2,204 were counted on a Christmas Bird Count in 1987. Smaller numbers winter on unfrozen lakes, ponds, or larger rivers elsewhere in the state. The peak of the spring migration is from mid-March through late April. A few migrants linger into late May.

The Bufflehead is very rare in summer away from Cascade Mts. breeding locations. Non-breeders have summered in Multnomah, Clatsop, Lincoln and Tillamook Cos.

Smew. *Mergellus albellus.*

Vagrant.

An adult male Smew was seen and photographed on both the Oregon and Washington sides of the Columbia R. in the vicinity of Government Cove, Hood River Co., from Jan. 27 to April 1, 1991. Presumably the same bird returned the next winter to the same area. It was seen from Feb. 1-16 on the Oregon side; on the latter date it appeared injured and apparently did not survive.

Hooded Merganser. *Lophodytes cucullatus.*

Locally uncommon summer resident and an uncommon transient and winter resident west of the Cascade Mts. Rare to locally uncommon winter resident east of the Cascades.

The Hooded Merganser is a locally uncommon summer resident west of the Cascade Mts. and in the Cascades to middle elevations. Wooded habitat adjacent to a pond, lake, or river is a requirement, as the species nests in tree cavities or nest boxes. It is an uncommon to locally fairly common transient and winter visitant west of the Cascades. Concentrations of up to 110 birds have been found, but the species is more typically seen in small flocks of up to 10 birds.

East of the Cascades the Hooded Merganser has been recorded in summer in Wallowa, Union, Grant, Deschutes, and Klamath Cos. Although breeding may be widespread, the only reported nest was found in a large quaking aspen near Sisters, Deschutes Co., in early May, 1954 (Griffee 1954). Nesting is very probable at Upper Klamath L. It is an uncommon transient, and generally a rare winter visitant, east of the Cascades except in the Klamath Basin where it remains uncommon through the winter.

Hooded Mergansers in Oregon utilize ponds, lakes, reservoirs, some sewage lagoons, streams, rivers, and sometimes coastal estuaries. They more frequently use small bodies of water than does the Common Merganser, especially ponds surrounded by trees.

Common Merganser. *Mergus merganser.*

Fairly common summer resident and a common transient and winter visitant throughout the state.

The Common Merganser is a fairly common to common summer resident throughout the state. It nests from tidewater to high in the Cascade Mts. (for example, Crater Lake). This species is also a common transient and winter visitant throughout the state where water remains open. It utilizes lakes, ponds, rivers, and the brackish upper ends of coastal estuaries.

Winter numbers vary significantly from year to year at particular areas with changes in food supply and weather. Fern Ridge Res. supports up to a thousand birds, and Upper Klamath L. also hosts significant numbers.

Fall migrants generally peak in number in November or early December. In spring Common Mergansers disperse to breeding areas through March and April.

Red-breasted Merganser. *Mergus serrator.*

Common transient and winter visitant along the coast. Very rare transient and winter visitant inland. Rare in summer along the coast.

The Red-breasted Merganser is a common winter visitant and transient along the coast, where it utilizes estuaries and to a lesser extent the ocean near shore. It generally shuns fresh water. In some winters as many as 300 may be present on such favored estuaries as Coos Bay and Tillamook Bay. This species is a rare non-breeder along the coast in summer. Some reports of Red-breasted Merganser in summer may pertain to young Common Mergansers that often visit the brackish parts of estuaries in July and August.

Fall migrants appear in late August, although the peak occurs after late November. The major spring movement is from late March through late April with small numbers into mid-May. Possible migrants have been noted as late as May 23.

The Red-breasted Merganser is a very rare transient and winter visitant inland on both sides of the Cascade crest. Most records from the Willamette Valley are in November or December. In 1965-66 a male and female wintered in a pond at Medford, Jackson Co., until mid-March. It has been recorded at scattered locations east of the Cascades. There is also one summer record from Klamath Co.

Ruddy Duck. *Oxyura jamaicensis.*

Locally common summer resident east of the Cascade Mts., and common transient and winter resident. West of the Cascades, a common transient and winter visitant, and a rare summer resident.

67

The Ruddy Duck is a common summer resident east of the Cascades, particularly in the great marsh regions of Harney, Lake, and Klamath Cos. The Harney Basin typically supports about 6,000 nesting Ruddy Ducks, with similar numbers in the lake basins in Lake and Klamath Cos. Smaller numbers breed on widely scattered marshes elsewhere. West of the Cascades one to several pairs have bred at Delta Park in Portland, and a few have bred near Eugene, Lane Co., in recent years. Summering non-breeders have been noted in several Willamette Valley counties, and along the coast in Tillamook and Clatsop Cos.

Ruddy Ducks move into western Oregon in September, with their numbers increasing into November inland and into December at coastal locations. Upper Klamath L. and Malheur N.W.R. are important for migrants. Fall migrants normally peak in October east of the Cascades. The spring migration west of the Cascades is from February through early April, with occasional individuals lingering into early May along the coast.

Order FALCONIFORMES
Family Cathartidae

Turkey Vulture. *Cathartes aura.*

Common summer resident and transient throughout most of Oregon. Very rare in winter in western Oregon.

This conspicuous raptor is a common summer resident through most of the state, breeding to about 5,000 ft. It is generally uncommon over large tracts of dense forest, but is a familiar sight over farmland, mixed forest, desert, and grasslands.

It is much less common in parts of northeastern Oregon, with very few records for Morrow Co. It is also very scarce in Umatilla and Wallowa Cos., and only somewhat more regularly noted in the Grande Ronde Valley.

Turkey Vultures return to the southwestern part of the state in mid-February, and to the Willamette Valley by March. Numbers increase through mid-April. The southward migration starts in late August, peaks in September, and is typically over by the latter half of October. There have been occasional winter records in the last few years, mostly from the southwestern part of the state.

East of the Cascades, most migrants return from mid-March through April. February 18 is the earliest arrival date for Malheur N.W.R. The autumn migration begins in August, peaks in September, and few remain by early October. The latest records are from the last week of October.

Turkey Vultures often roost in groups of as many as a hundred in open-canopied trees, on snags, towers, and cliffs.

California Condor. *Gymnogyps californianus.*

Extinct in Oregon. Last seen in 1904.

California Condor bones at least 9,000 years old have been unearthed by archaeologists in Oregon Indian middens. Gabrielson and Jewett (1940) detail the condor sightings made in Oregon during the 1800s and early 1900s: from 1805 (Lewis and Clark) to 1854 condors were noted in spring and fall by several naturalists along the Columbia R., where they were said to feed on dead salmon. At least one Oregon specimen is still extant. After 1854 the next and final reliable sightings were at Drain, Douglas Co., in July 1903, three birds, and in March 1904, four birds. At about this same time one was reported killed on the southern Oregon coast, and a few were observed by woodsmen in southwestern Oregon. Wilbur (1973) suggested that the Oregon population may have been exterminated by egg and skin collectors, as were similar isolated populations in California.

Family Accipitridae

Osprey. *Pandion haliaetus.*

Uncommon to common local summer resident near water from the Cascade Mts. to the coast. Uncommon summer resident east of the Cascades. Migrates near water throughout Oregon. In winter very rare west of the Cascades, and three records from eastern Oregon.

The Osprey is a local, uncommon to fairly common summer resident around lakes, streams and rivers from the forested east slope of the Cascades west to the Pacific. The species is more numerous along the south coast than the north. It inhabits lakes up to timberline, and is locally common on the many lakes of northwest Klamath Co. and southwest Deschutes Co., where Crane Prairie Res., Deschutes Co., hosts about 200 birds. Large numbers bred near Lower Klamath L. early in the century, but almost all are gone due to changes in water levels and loss of nesting trees.

Further east of the Cascades, Ospreys are an uncommon summer resident along lakes and rivers in the Blue and Wallowa Mts., and occasionally nest near water in open country, provided there are suitable nesting trees. Ospreys increased in Oregon during the 1970s, after having reached a low in the 1950s and 1960s due to pesticide poisoning.

The southward migration begins in August, peaks in September, and few are noted by mid-October. During migration Ospreys increase throughout the state and are often noted over waters where breeding does not occur. In winter Ospreys are very rarely noted (annually in recent years) at lower elevations west of the Cascades. Most winter records are from the Rogue Valley, Jackson Co., and the south coast. There are three winter records from eastern Oregon: one in January in the 1970s along the Deschutes R., near Warm Springs, Jefferson Co.; and one on Dec. 20, 1987 and one on Dec. 20, 1992, both in Wallowa Co.

White-tailed Kite. *Elanus leucurus.*

On the coast and in the interior valleys of western Oregon, rare to locally fairly common fall and winter visitant from late August through April, and very rare summer resident. East of the Cascade Mts., very rare in winter in the Klamath Basin and fewer than 10 records elsewhere.

The first Oregon records of the White-tailed Kite were a single bird near Portland in the mid-1920s and one at Scappoose, Columbia Co., Feb. 23, 1933. There were several scattered sightings west of the Cascades in the 1960s. This increase in observations during the 1960s accelerated in the early 1970s and apparently leveled from the late 1970s to about 1990. The rise in the Oregon population corresponded with a population increase and range expansion in California. Since 1990 there has been a noticeable decrease in numbers in Oregon, which has coincided with a reported population decrease in California. As of 1993, the species may be increasing again.

70

Today the White-tailed Kite is a local, very uncommon to fairly common winter visitor (late August through April) to agricultural land, fields, marshes, and grassy dunes of the coast. In open habitats in the Rogue and Umpqua Valleys, and the southern Willamette Valley, especially in Lane Co., they are locally uncommon. The area around Fern Ridge Res. is especially favored. Numbers in Oregon fluctuate widely from year to year. Local concentrations of more than ten have occurred some years in coastal pasturelands, the Rogue R. Valley and Lane Co. In the northern Willamette Valley it is a very rare August to April visitant. In the Klamath Basin and elsewhere east of the Cascades there are fewer than 10 records scattered from March through December.

White-tailed Kites begin arriving in Oregon during late August (early August on the south coast) and increase through September and October. They usually depart in late March and April.

In summer (before August) they are very rare on the coast and in the interior valleys of western Oregon, with most records in July. There are very few nesting records from Oregon: near Medford, Jackson Co., in 1976 and Finley N.W.R., Benton Co., in 1977 (probably 1976 also), and near Tillamook. More recently, a pair fledged four young near Fern Ridge Res. in the summer of 1992. Nesting was also suspected in the Rogue R. Valley in 1983 and 1984.

Bald Eagle. *Haliaeetus leucocephalus.*

Fairly common summer resident around Upper Klamath L., and common winter visitant throughout the Klamath Basin. Elsewhere in Oregon, uncommon local summer resident on the coast, along the Columbia R. and in the southern Cascade Mts. Rare local summer resident in the north Cascades and very rare summer resident in northeastern Oregon mountains. In winter, uncommon to locally fairly common on the coast, along the Columbia R., and in the Willamette Valley, and rare on lower-elevation rivers and lakes throughout the state.

Approximately 205 Bald Eagle pairs nested in Oregon in 1992, and numbers are increasing. A substantial number use the Klamath Basin, where most nest in forest around Upper Klamath L. In this area Bald Eagles are fairly common in summer. Elsewhere in Oregon the greatest number of nests occur on the coast, along the Columbia R. (especially near the mouth) and around lakes in the Cascades from Deschutes Co. south. Further north in the Cascades Bald Eagles are rare and very local summer residents near large lakes and rivers. Only two nests are currently known in the mountains of northeast Oregon.

Migrants from north of Oregon begin arriving in late October and November. Local breeders generally remain near their nesting areas in winter, but some move to lower elevations. About 600 Bald Eagles currently winter in the Klamath Basin, where they feed primarily on waterfowl. This is the largest wintering concentration in the lower 48 states. Five communal roosts in the Basin are used by the wintering eagles, the most important of which is in Bear Valley. This protected, timbered roost was added to the Klamath Basin N.W.R. system in 1979. Bald Eagles winter widely outside of the Klamath Basin, primarily along the coast and the Columbia R., where they are uncommon. About 30 now winter annually on Sauvie I., near Portland. Increasing numbers are also using the southern half of the Willamette Valley, where they reportedly scavenge for dead sheep. Wintering Bald Eagles usually depart for northern breeding areas in late March and early April.

Northern Harrier. *Circus cyaneus.*

East of the Cascade Mts., common to locally uncommon summer resident and migrant, and common to rare in winter. West of the Cascades, locally common to uncommon in the interior valleys, and in open country along the coast in winter. Breeds locally along the northern coast and in the Willamette Valley.

East of the Cascades in summer, the Northern Harrier is common in large wetlands, fairly common in agricultural lands and grasslands, and locally uncommon in sagebrush. From late July into September dispersing and migrating Northern Harriers occur more frequently over rangelands and above timberline. In winter it is common in the Klamath Basin, generally fairly common over lower-elevation marshes and agricultural lands, and uncommon in lower-elevation sagebrush country. At Malheur N.W.R. it is fairly common in winter.

West of the Cascades, it is a local summer resident in the Willamette Valley (e.g. Sauvie I., Fern Ridge Res.) and along the coast from northern Lincoln Co. northward (e.g. Salmon R. marshes, Bayocean sandspit, Wilson River marsh lands, and near the Columbia R. mouth). It is common as a transient and winterer in the valleys and coastal lowlands of western Oregon. Transients are occasionally noted over forested areas.

Sharp-shinned Hawk. *Accipiter striatus.*

Uncommon permanent resident.

The Sharp-shinned Hawk is an uncommon summer resident throughout Oregon from sea level to timberline in deciduous and coniferous forests, occasionally including juniper stands. During the southward migration, which begins in mid-August and peaks in mid-September, many birds move through Oregon to winter further south. Transients move through open country where they are attracted to brush and trees, along the coast, and along ridge tops.

In winter, Sharp-shinned Hawks are uncommon at lower elevations in woodlands and semi-open country throughout the state, including urban areas. Spring migration occurs from mid-March through April.

Cooper's Hawk. *Accipiter cooperii.*

Uncommon summer resident in forests statewide, and in winter uncommon to fairly common at lower elevations. Migrates through open and forested country.

In Oregon the Cooper's Hawk is an uncommon summer resident from sea level to timberline, inhabiting coniferous and deciduous forest, and rarely juniper woodlands. During fall migration, which begins in mid-August and peaks in September and October, many transients pass through Oregon. Migrating Cooper's Hawks are less common than Sharp-shinned Hawks. Like Sharp-shinned Hawks, they often migrate over open country, along ridges and above timberline.

During winter Cooper's Hawks are uncommon to fairly common throughout Oregon in forests and semi-open country at lower elevations. Generally they are slightly less common than Sharp-shinned Hawks in winter, but this varies regionally. Spring migration occurs primarily in March and April, with a few noted in open country into early May.

Northern Goshawk. *Accipiter gentilis.*

Uncommon permanent resident of forests in the Cascade Mts., Siskiyou Mts., and the mountain ranges of eastern Oregon. Rare to uncommon transient and winterer at lower elevations east of the Cascades. Rare to very rare in winter and migration west of the Cascades.

The Goshawk is an uncommon summer resident in dense forests up to timberline in the Siskiyous, Cascades, and all major mountains eastward. It even occasionally nests in isolated stands of trees on such desert mountains as Steens and Hart Mts. Nesting has not been proven from the coast range, but it may breed there in small numbers at high elevations, as birds are occasionally reported in summer.

From September through early May, migrants from the north or birds from higher elevation within the state are rare to uncommon at lower elevations east of the Cascades. Many local breeders remain in the mountains throughout the winter.

West of the Cascades, the Goshawk is rare to very rare as a winter visitant and transient. Some reports of this species may pertain to the Cooper's Hawk.

Red-shouldered Hawk. *Buteo lineatus.*

Uncommon fall, winter, and spring visitant to the coastal lowlands of Curry and Coos Cos.; very rare to the coastal lowlands north and to the interior valleys of western Oregon. Very rare visitant to south-central and southeastern Oregon.

Bendire found two nests and collected eggs and an adult at Archie's Creek, Harney Co. in 1878, but there were no further Oregon records until one was observed Oct. 3, 1971 near the Winchuck R. mouth, Curry Co. Since then it has been recorded annually in the lowlands of that county, and it is now an uncommon visitant from early August through March. Birds have been noted on several occasions engaging in courtship or carrying nesting material, so the species may nest in very small numbers. The Coquille Valley of Coos Co. has also consistently supported a few in recent years.

North of Coos Co., the Red-shouldered Hawk is a very rare visitant from late August through March. There are about eleven records from the coastal lowlands of Lane, Lincoln and Tillamook Cos.

The first Willamette Valley record was an immature on Sauvie I., Jan. 3, 1973, and the second, an adult at Fern Ridge Res. on Jan. 11, 1977. Since the second observation, Red-shouldered Hawks have been noted almost every winter in the Willamette Valley, usually in Lane Co., but there are also recent records from Linn, Benton, Washington and Multnomah Cos. There are also a few summer records from around Fern Ridge Res.

In the Rogue Valley of southwestern Oregon, an adult was observed during the springs of 1976, 1977, and 1978; and in the summer of 1978 adults were seen repeatedly on and near an island behind Gold Ray Dam on the Rogue R., where nesting may have occurred. Since 1978 the species has been noted almost annually in the Rogue Valley during fall, winter, and spring, but there have been no additional summer sightings. It has also been found to be a very rare visitant to the Umpqua Valley.

East of the Cascade Mts., the Red-shouldered Hawk is very rare in south-central and southeastern Oregon. There are records from Klamath, Lake, Harney, Deschutes, and Wheeler Cos. Since 1986 it has been of almost annual occurrence (one to three birds) on or near Malheur N.W.R. in September. East of the Cascades birds have occurred mostly in fall and winter, but there is one recent summer record: one at Lower Klamath N.W.R., Klamath Co., July 9, 1983.

Red-shouldered Hawks prefer wooded river bottoms, especially when associated with open meadows or shallow marshes.

Broad-winged Hawk. *Buteo platypterus.*

Vagrant.

Single immature Broad-winged Hawks were observed at Malheur N.W.R., May 29 and Oct. 2, 1983 and in September 1987; near Timber, Washington Co., Aug. 6, 1983; at Cascade Head, Tillamook Co., Sept. 29, 1985; and at Roaring Springs Ranch, Harney Co., on May 23, 1992.

Swainson's Hawk. *Buteo swainsoni.*

Rare to locally fairly common summer resident in open country east of the Cascade Mts. Arrives in April and departs in September. Vagrant spring and fall in the interior valleys of western Oregon and along the coast.

The Swainson's Hawk breeds east of the Cascades in open country with scattered trees. Gabrielson and Jewett (1940) considered it a common summer resident, although they reported a noticeable decrease in the years just prior to publication. It has continued to decline and today is rare to locally common in rangelands of sage, bunchgrass, and juniper, ascending the foothills to the forest borders. Occasionally large meadows and prairies in forested country are inhabited. It is locally fairly common in agricultural areas planted with alfalfa and hay.

Most migrants return to Oregon during April. The earliest record is for February 24, and a few migrants are noted into mid-May. The fall migration peaks during late August and early September, and a few are occasionally noted into late September. Early October records are exceptional. There are several winter reports, none well enough documented to be acceptable.

There are several spring and fall reports from the interior valleys of western Oregon, where most observations have been made in April and September. The only coastal record was of one photographed near Tillamook on May 1, 1993.

The cause of the Swainson's Hawk's decline is unclear. Hunting through the first half of this century and displacement by unfavorable agricultural practices are probably major factors. The spread of junipers caused by fire control and the erection of utility poles has made many areas more favorable for Red-tailed Hawks, which compete directly with the Swainson's Hawk for prey and territories (Janes 1987). Pesticide levels in local populations are low and apparently have little or no deleterious effect (Henny and Kaiser 1977).

Osprey

Red-tailed Hawk. *Buteo jamaicensis.*

Common summer resident throughout Oregon. In winter, common at lower elevations west of the Cascade Mts., and uncommon to locally common east of the Cascades.

The Red-tailed Hawk is a common summer resident throughout Oregon and inhabits a wide variety of habitats, from agricultural lands and arid sagebrush country to open forests on the highest mountains, where it often hunts above timberline. In summer, it is the only *Buteo* regularly seen in western Oregon and the most common *Buteo* east of the Cascades.

Migrating Red-tailed Hawks pass through Oregon in spring and fall. Many local birds probably depart and are replaced in winter by northern birds. Large numbers of migrants are occasionally seen, usually along ridges or on mountain tops. For example, on Oct. 4, 1967, 250 were seen over the Rogue Valley, Jackson Co.

During winter, Red-tailed Hawks are common at lower elevations west of the Cascades. Throughout Oregon, higher elevation forests are abandoned in winter. In the Willamette, Umpqua, and Rogue Valleys, they may be locally very common in winter. East of the Cascades in winter, Red-tailed Hawks are locally common in central and northeastern Oregon agricultural lands at lower elevations. In the Klamath Basin they are locally abundant, and elsewhere east of the Cascades in winter, they are fairly common to uncommon in open and semi-open country.

Ferruginous Hawk. *Buteo regalis.*

Generally rare to uncommon summer resident in open country east of the Cascade Mts., but in northeastern and north-central Oregon, locally fairly common. Very rare during winter east of the Cascades. Vagrant to western Oregon.

The Ferruginous Hawk breeds east of the Cascades in grasslands and sagebrush country with few trees, where it nests on cliffs, rocky outcrops, and in trees. It is the least abundant of the three *Buteos* that nest east of the Cascades, but the population appears to have remained fairly stable since 1940. In central Oregon from

Wasco and Sherman Cos. south to Klamath and Lake Cos., it is a rare to uncommon summer resident, and in southeastern Oregon it is very uncommon and local. In northeastern Oregon and in the Columbia R. Basin from Gilliam Co. east it is generally a very uncommon summer resident, but is locally fairly common. At Zumwalt Prairie, Wallowa Co., it is common.

The fall migration is protracted, beginning in August, peaking in September, with birds noted regularly into November. In August and September, birds are occasionally noted above timberline in the Cascades and mountains of northeast Oregon. A few winter in open country at lower elevations east of the Cascades. Spring migrants return in early March.

Ferruginous Hawks are vagrants to the interior valleys of western Oregon, where they are not recorded most years. One photographed on Sauvie Island, Columbia Co., on May 20, 1972, and one near Sheridan, Yamhill Co., in April of 1978 are the only spring records from western Oregon. One was near Eugene, Lane Co., Sept. 28-29, 1992. Most records from western Oregon are from the Rogue Valley. Several recent records from that area are one Aug. 29, 1989, one Sept. 28, 1989, and one on Jan. 12-18, 1992. There are no proven records from the coast.

Rough-legged Hawk. *Buteo lagopus.*

Uncommon to common during winter in open country throughout Oregon. Arrives in October and November and departs in March and April.

During winter the Rough-legged Hawk is uncommon to common east of the Cascade Mts. in open country. Numbers vary greatly from year to year. The greatest concentrations occur in agricultural lands and meadows. In open country of the western interior valleys and along the coast, Rough-legged Hawks are generally uncommon, and less common further south. Some years they may be locally common. That status has changed since 1940, when Gabrielson and Jewett considered them rare stragglers west of the Cascades.

The first Rough-legged Hawks usually arrive in mid-October (earliest September 15), but the peak of migration occurs in November. Some pass through Oregon and winter farther south. In spring most depart in late March and early April, and

79

by May few remain. Exceptionally late individuals have been recorded into the fourth week of May.

Golden Eagle. *Aquila chrysaetos.*

Uncommon to fairly common permanent resident in open country east of the Cascade Mts. Very uncommon summer resident high in the Cascades, and a rare breeder in southwestern Oregon and in foothills adjacent to the southern Willamette Valley. Rare to very rare west of the Cascades in winter.

The Golden Eagle is an uncommon to fairly common summer resident east of the Cascades in sagebrush country, grasslands, agricultural land, and open forests. It is rare in forests of the Cascade, Blue, and Wallowa Mts. Nests are located on cliffs and in large trees. East of the Cascades in winter, Golden Eagles remain uncommon to fairly common, but retreat from higher elevations.

West of the Cascades, Golden Eagles are very rare summer residents inhabiting open country and open forests in the Siskiyou Mts., and in the foothills of the Rogue, Umpqua, and southern Willamette Valleys. A few migrate into the Rogue and Umpqua Valleys in fall and winter, when they are rare. In the Willamette Valley and along the coast in winter, Golden Eagles are very rare. Some coastal reports may involve misidentified immature Bald Eagles.

Family Falconidae

American Kestrel. *Falco sparverius.*

Common permanent resident in the interior valleys of western Oregon. On the coast, uncommon permanent resident. East of the Cascade Mts., common in spring, summer and fall and fairly common in winter.

The American Kestrel is a common permanent resident of the interior valleys and foothills of western Oregon, where it inhabits open country of all types. In fall there in an influx of birds from outside the valleys, so that during migration and winter they are more common. In open country along the coast kestrels are uncommon throughout the year. On the west slope of the Cascades, the species takes advantage of clear-cuts to colonize forested areas. Throughout mountainous areas of Oregon, beginning in August, there is a post-breeding movement to higher elevations, where small concentrations often occur above timberline.

East of the Cascades, American Kestrels are common summer residents in open country where trees or cliffs provide nesting habitat. From late August through mid-September and again in late March and April many migrate through the region and may be locally very common. In winter they are common in the Klamath Basin, Klamath Co., and fairly common in agricultural areas at lower elevations in central Oregon. Elsewhere east of the Cascades they are generally uncommon in winter, except in the Wallowa Valley where they are rare or absent most winters.

Merlin. *Falco columbarius.*

Uncommon winter visitant and transient.

The Merlin formerly nested east of the Cascade Mts. where Gabrielson and Jewett (1940) considered it to be a very rare breeding bird. There are no breeding records from recent decades; despite several summer sight records of birds in the 1970s and 1980s.

The Merlin is currently an uncommon winter visitant and transient in lowland areas along the coast and in inland western Oregon. East of the Cascades it is uncommon to rare as a transient, and generally rare at lower elevations in winter. Transients are occasionally noted in the Coast Range and Cascades.

Migrants occur in more diverse habitats, but wintering birds most often are seen near coastal beaches and estuaries, in agricultural lands, and in towns.

The first fall migrants appear in early September, or exceptionally in the last days of August. Spring migrants are typically gone by the end of April, but are occasionally noted to mid-May.

The "Black" Merlin (*F. c. suckleyi*) is the subspecies that occurs most frequently on the coast, but also occurs inland. The "Taiga" Merlin (*F. c. columbarius*) occurs throughout Oregon, most frequently east of the Cascades.

American Kestrel

Peregrine Falcon. *Falco peregrinus.*

Very rare breeder. Uncommon transient and winter visitant along the coast. Uncommon to rare transient and winter visitant elsewhere.

The Peregrine Falcon once occurred as a widespread summer resident and winterer in many parts of Oregon. In the 1930s, about 40 nest sites were known; the greatest numbers along the coast, the Columbia Gorge, and near the large marshes of southeastern and south-central Oregon. Rapid decline both of nesters and visitants from outside the state began in the 1940s as a result of use of the pesticide DDT.

Of the three subspecies that occur in Oregon, the nesting "American" Peregrine Falcon (*F. p. anatum*) was hit the hardest. By the early 1970s, very few pairs were known to still breed in the state. "Peale's" Peregrine Falcon (*F. p. pealei*), primarily a transient and winter visitant along the coast, was less affected because its prey (seabirds and estuarine birds) had much less DDT residue in its tissues. The third subspecies, the "Tundra" Peregrine Falcon (*F. p. tundrius*) is a very rare spring and fall transient throughout the state, and may have been so even before the species' general decline.

In 1980, the eggs of the last known Oregon pair failed to hatch at their Crater Lake eyrie. Throughout the early 1980s, introductions were attempted at several Oregon sites with varying success. By the mid-1980s it was evident that the 1972 ban on DDT in North America was showing positive results. By the 1990s the species had recovered sufficiently to be a fairly frequent sight again in favored habitats. At present, the species is a very rare breeder (more than 20 pairs) in several parts of the state, including coastal and inland locations.

Along the coast, the species is an uncommon transient and winter visitant, the great majority in winter being of the *pealei* form. Waterfowl and shorebirds are hunted along the rocky coast, in pasturelands, and especially around the larger estuaries.

Inland, the species is an uncommon transient and winterer, most likely to be found where waterfowl or Rock Doves are numerous. One or two Peregrine Falcons have wintered in the center of Portland in recent years, using the ledges of tall buildings much as they would natural cliffs, and feeding on the Rock Doves that are numerous in that urban setting. More typically Peregrines are found at locales such at Sauvie I. and the Klamath Basin.

Gyrfalcon. *Falco rusticolus.*

Vagrant.

The Gyrfalcon is a vagrant to Oregon that is not recorded every year. Most records are from the northern counties, but there are several records from Deschutes Co., and some of the counties in the central and southern Willamette Valley. The species has also occurred in Curry Co. and in the Klamath Basin. Records extend from mid-October to late April.

Gyrfalcons usually occur in open country near concentrations of waterbirds, and at larger sandspits along the coast. Dark forms are seen in Oregon.

Prairie Falcon. *Falco mexicanus.*

Uncommon to locally fairly common permanent resident in open country east of the Cascade Mts. Rare fall and winter visitant west of the Cascades.

The Prairie Falcon is an uncommon to locally fairly common summer resident in open country east of the Cascades, including sage- and grass-covered mountains like Steens Mt., Harney Co., and Hart Mt., Lake Co. Nests are placed on cliff ledges. Where extensive cliffs exist, such as along portions of the Snake R. canyon, Prairie Falcons may be fairly common. Many leave areas east of the Cascades in fall, so that by winter they are uncommon and restricted to lower elevations.

West of the Cascades, Prairie Falcons have nested very locally in the Rogue Valley, and are rare but annual fall and winter visitants there. In the Umpqua and Willamette Valleys and along the coast they are rare winter and fall visitants. The species is most regular in the southern and central Willamette Valley, where it occurs annually in winter in very small numbers.

Order GALLIFORMES
Family Phasianidae

Gray Partridge. *Perdix perdix.*

Introduced permanent resident.

The species was introduced east of the Cascade Mts. in 1900, and is now established in many areas. The greatest concentrations are in north-central Oregon and in the valleys of the north-eastern part of the state. Introductions west of the Cascades were not successful. It is usually found near areas of wheat production or other farming areas. It is also established in some desert areas and areas of grassland, far from cultivation.

Chukar. *Alectoris chukar.*

Introduced permanent resident.

This palearctic species was successfully introduced east of the Cascade Mts. in the 1950s. It is now widespread, and fairly common. Its preferred habitat is steep, rocky areas with brush or grass. It avoids heavily forested areas.

Ring-necked Pheasant. *Phasianus colchicus.*

Introduced permanent resident.

This Asian species is an introduced permanent resident in many parts of the state. Its is most common in the grain growing areas of north-central Oregon and the agricultural areas of Malheur Co., but it is also fairly common in many other areas. It also occurs in some larger urban parks, and in suburbs. Numbers have declined greatly in the Willamette Valley in recent decades due to changes in agricultural practices. It is generally absent as a self-sustaining species along the coast. It is not found in heavily forested areas, in higher mountains, and in most of the vast deserts of southeastern and south-central Oregon.

Blue Grouse. *Dendragapus obscurus.*

Permanent resident.

The Blue Grouse is a common to uncommon permanent resident of coniferous forests throughout the state, and can at times be found from sea level along the coast, to above timberline on the state's highest mountains in late summer and early autumn. It is readily heard in the correct habitat during the breeding season, though its ventriloquial territorial calls are difficult to follow to their source.

Spruce Grouse. *Dendragapus canadensis.*

Permanent resident of the Wallowa Mts.

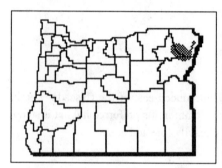

The Spruce Grouse is an uncommon permanent resident from moderate to high elevations in the Wallowa Mts. of Union, Wallowa, and Baker Cos. Its numbers have probably declined due to logging. It is most often found in dense, undisturbed coniferous forests, though most birds move into subalpine areas in late summer and fall.

White-tailed Ptarmigan. *Lagopus leucurus.*

Introduced, possibly extirpated.

This alpine species was introduced to the Wallowas from the Rocky Mts. in the 1960s. Its current status is uncertain, but it may be extirpated. No certain records have been received in the past several years. The species has been removed from the official state list by the Oregon Birds Records Committee.

Ruffed Grouse. *Bonasa umbellus.*

Permanent resident in forested areas.

The Ruffed Grouse is a common permanent resident throughout the state where significant forested areas remain. It prefers habitats with both deciduous and coniferous trees. It is typically absent from the higher elevations in the Wallowa, Blue and Cascade Mts. The species does fairly well even to the edges of some cities so long as suitable forested areas remain.

Sage Grouse. *Centrocercus urophasianus.*

Permanent resident east of the Cascade Mts.

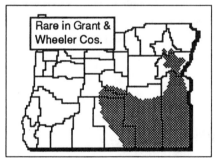

This large grouse is an uncommon permanent resident of the sage country east of the Cascades. Its range formerly included all of the counties east of the Cascades except Wallowa Co. Due to various ranching practices, and probably over hunting, it is now restricted to the area from southeastern Klamath Co., north to eastern Deschutes Co., north-east to Wheeler and Grant Cos., east and north into Baker Co., and east and south of these described limits.

This spectacular bird is still declining within its present range, probably because of grazing practices that have in many areas damaged its habitat.

Sharp-tailed Grouse. *Tympanuchus phasianellus.*

Extirpated, and recently reintroduced.

The Sharp-tailed Grouse was once a common permanent resident over most of the state east of the Cascade Mts., where it inhabited sagebrush and bunch grass habitats. It had declined greatly by the early part of this century, and by the 1950s was restricted to a small part of Baker Co. A few credible reports continued from that county into the early 1980s, but the native population is now very likely extirpated.

It has recently been introduced to an area in Wallowa Co., but it is too early to know whether a self-sustaining population can be established.

Wild Turkey. *Meleagris gallopavo.*

Uncommon introduced resident.

The Turkey has been introduced as a game bird to several areas of the state. The most successful introductions have been along the eastern slope of the Cascade Mts. in Wasco Co. and adjacent areas. The other stronghold is the oak-covered foothills of the Rogue and Umpqua Valleys, with smaller populations extending into Klamath Co. In northeastern Oregon, there are discontinuous populations in Morrow Co., Umatilla Co., and Wallowa and Union Cos. that may prove to be self-sustaining.

Northern Bobwhite. *Colinus virginianus.*

Introduced permanent resident.

This familiar species of the eastern states was widely introduced to agricultural areas of the state during the first six decades of this century. It has been largely extirpated from most areas where it once seemed to have been successfully introduced, such as most of the Willamette Valley. Small self-sustaining populations are believed to persist in the farming areas of Malheur Co., and until recently they were still present in northern Umatilla Co. Record snowfall in 1993 apparently eliminated the latter population. Sightings from other areas may be attributed to escaped birds from sportsmen who use them in dog training, private introductions, or perhaps in some cases, populations that have persisted for several decades without reintroduction.

California Quail. *Callipepla californica.*

Permanent resident, native in some areas and introduced elsewhere.

This familiar quail is native to Jackson, Josephine and Curry Cos., to southern Lake and Klamath Cos., and possibly the interior valleys of Douglas Co. In all of these areas it is a common permanent resident. It has also been widely introduced around the state, and has established itself as a common resident in many areas. It prefers brushy and semi-wooded habitats, with grassy areas. It finds suitable habitat in many agricultural areas, and does fairly well in some suburbs and on the edges of smaller towns. It is generally not established along the coast north of Coos Bay, in any heavily forested areas, or at higher elevations.

Mountain Quail. *Oreortyx pictus.*

Permanent resident in many areas of the state.

This quail is a permanent resident in the mountainous and hilly areas throughout the state. In western Oregon it prefers brushy foothills, emergent clear cuts, clearing edges, and younger forested areas with grassy and brushy openings. It is especially common in the dry, brushy habitats typical of the foothills that surround the Rogue and Umpqua Rivers. Most Oregon birders would be surprised by how common it is in many areas of the Cascades and Coast Range to the northern border of the state. It also occurred in fairly good numbers in brushy habitats at lower and middle elevations in the Blue and Wallowa Mts., and at scattered other locations east of the Cascade summit, but has declined greatly in recent years. According to local residents, a population on Steens Mt. declined severely following the introduction of Chukar to that massif, though it was still at least locally present as of 1977.

The Mountain Quail is much less tolerant of human presence than is the California Quail, though clear-cutting has expanded its habitat in many areas. It typically avoids agricultural areas. It is generally absent in the first few miles inland from the ocean, but may be found occasionally near the ocean in winter.

Order GRUIFORMES
Family Rallidae

Yellow Rail. *Coturnicops noveboracensis.*

Very local summer resident of the Klamath Basin. Vagrant elsewhere.

A Yellow Rail was flushed off a nest and eggs were collected at Aspen L., Klamath Co., on May 23, 1926. Other occurrences in the early 1900s were reported from that county without details (Griffee 1944).

A single bird was heard calling and its voice was recorded near Ft. Klamath, Klamath Co., on June 19-20, 1982. Since its rediscovery in the state, it has been found to be a very local summer resident in short vegetation marshes and wet meadows north of Upper Klamath L., and at the Klamath Marsh N.W.R. Nesting has also been reported during at Sycan Marsh and Camas Prarie, both Lake Co. (Stern *et. al.* 1993). The wet mountain meadows of southern Grant Co. should be checked for possible breeding birds.

The only other confirmed record for the state is of a bird collected near Scio, Linn Co., on Feb. 1, 1900. There have been sight records elsewhere in the state.

Virginia Rail. *Rallus limicola.*

Fairly common summer resident throughout the state. In winter uncommon west of the Cascade Mts. and very rare east of the Cascades.

The Virginia Rail is a fairly common summer resident throughout Oregon, inhabiting primarily freshwater marshes, but also occurring at the marshy borders of watercourses, lakes and ponds, and sparingly in brackish marshes along the coast. It has been found in mountain marshes and bogs at over 5,000 ft. Summer residents are fairly common both east and west of the Cascades, although the vast marshes of Klamath, Lake, and Harney Cos. provide the most extensive habitat.

Fall migrants are observed from mid-August through October and frequently occur in vegetation bordering brackish and salt water, in flooded fields, and exceptionally even on barren lake shores. Virginia Rails are uncommon winter residents in lowland marshes west of the Cascades (most common on the coast), and are rare in winter east of the Cascades. Spring migrants apparently return in late March.

Sora. *Porzana carolina.*

Locally common summer resident throughout the state. Very rare in winter west of the Cascade Mts.

The Sora breeds throughout Oregon in freshwater marshes from sea level to at least 5,000 ft. It is abundant in the large marshes of Klamath, Lake, and Harney Cos., and fairly common in many smaller marshes east of the Cascade Mts. West of the Cascades it is locally common where habitat exists.

The fall migration occurs from late August through October. There are very few winter records for east of the Cascade Mts. West of the Cascades they are not recorded every year in winter, though they are probably present each winter in the Rogue Valley and in Curry Co. Winter records are widespread west of the Cascades. Spring migrants have been observed in early April, but the height of the migration occurs in late April and early May.

Common Moorhen. *Gallinula chloropus.*

Vagrant.

Single adult Common Moorhens have been observed in Oregon on about 10 occasions. There are at least five records from Malheur N.W.R.: single individuals were seen from Cole Island Dike on May 20, 1972; from May 22 through June 5, 1981; on May 16, 1982, in early May, 1992 at Dredger Pond; and one at an unspecified location on the refuge in August 1993. The remaining records are one at Garrison L., Curry Co., on May 5, 1976 (photo); one near Tillamook Bay, May 6, 1983; one at Ken Denman Wildlife Management Area, Jackson Co., May 30, 1982; and one seen in May in the early 1970s on Sauvie I. Outside of the May and early June pattern of occurrence was a male collected Feb. 13, 1983 on Winema Creek, near Neskowin, Tillamook Co.

American Coot. *Fulica americana.*

East of the Cascades Mts., common summer resident and uncommon to common in winter. West of the Cascades locally uncommon to common summer resident and common in winter.

The American Coot breeds in marshes and along the marshy edges of bodies of water throughout Oregon. It is common in the tule marshes of Klamath, Lake, and Harney Cos. and common at many marshes elsewhere east of the Cascades. On the east slope of the Cascades, coots are locally common summer residents up to at least 4,500 ft. In the lowlands west of the Cascades they are widespread summer residents, but are only common on the comparatively few large marshes, such as at Fern Ridge Res.

From late August through December local birds and migrants from the north congregate on large bodies of water both east and west of the Cascades. The greatest numbers occur in November and December, when concentrations of 10,000 have been observed in Klamath and Harney Cos. Late fall aggregations on Diamond L., Douglas Co., also are substantial.

Coots are locally common during winter in western Oregon, congregating in flocks that locally number in the thousands. At that season they occur on estuaries, lakes, rivers, and sewage ponds. East of the Cascades they are usually fairly common on lakes and reservoirs at lower elevations, but during especially cold winters when waters freeze, they may be very uncommon. In March and April the wintering flocks disband and birds return to the breeding areas.

Family Gruidae

Sandhill Crane. *Grus canadensis.*

Local summer resident in south-central and eastern Oregon. Uncommon spring and fall transient in western Oregon valleys and east of the Cascades. Common on Sauvie I. in spring and fall, and present in small numbers in winter.

Two subspecies of Sandhill Crane occur in Oregon. The Central Valley population of Greater Sandhill Cranes (*G. c. tabida*) breeds in eastern and south-central Oregon and northeastern California, and winters in the Central Valley of California. Approximately 2,500 birds in the population summer in Oregon, and about 2,000 of these actually breed. The Harney Basin supports the greatest number of breeders, with 250 pairs in recent years (Stern *et. al.* 1987). Smaller numbers breed elsewhere in Harney Co., and in Lake, Klamath, Grant, Baker, Union, and Deschutes Cos. Individual pairs have nested just west of the Cascade summit at various locations. A pair far from nesting habitat along the upper Elk R. drainage, Curry Co., on July 11, 1993, defies categorization.

Greater Sandhills return to their meadow and marsh territories in late February and March. At higher elevations birds arrive in late March. February 7 is the earliest arrival date at Malheur N.W.R. In September and October 2,300 to 3,000 Greaters congregate at Malheur N.W.R., peaking there in mid-October. Numbers staging here are swelled by migrants from the British Columbia population. By November most have left but some linger into mid-November and one wintered in 1980-81.

The Lesser Sandhill Crane (*G. c. canadensis*) is a transient and occasional winter visitant in Oregon. Lessers, migrating north in spring from wintering areas in the Central Valley of California, and south in fall from southwestern Alaska breeding grounds, primarily follow two migration routes through Oregon. Birds from the southern Central Valley, numbering over 20,000, cross the Sierra Nevada and enter Oregon in Lake and Klamath Cos. during late February and March. Their major spring stopover is in Harney Co. on the meadows south and east of Burns, where 6,000 are often present in late March and April and up to 14,000 have congregated during inclement weather. Migrants of this race also congregate in the Klamath Basin. By early May nearly all of the Lesser Sandhill Cranes have departed regions east of the Cascades.

Southbound Lessers appear east of the Cascades in late September and October, and follow the same migration corridors as in spring. Autumn migrants at Malheur N.W.R. do not attain the large numbers found in spring, and the occurrence in fall of thousands of Greater Sandhills makes estimating the population of Lessers difficult. Most have departed by early November. Single Lessers have wintered near Baker City, in 1972-73 and at Malheur N.W.R. in 1980-81.

Lessers from the northern Central Valley population, numbering only 1,400, migrate from early March to early May, passing through Jackson and Douglas Cos. and the Willamette Valley. Although small numbers stop at many places, especially in the Willamette Valley, Sauvie I. is the primary stopover site. Spring numbers on the Island seldom exceed 400 during the peak in late March and early April and all have usually departed by mid-May.

In autumn Lessers usually first return to the Willamette Valley in early September, but occasionally small numbers are noted in late August. The peak on Sauvie I. is usually in the latter half of October, when 2,000-2,500 are present. Hundreds often persist into early November, and in recent years over 100 have typically wintered. There are also a few winter records for elsewhere in the Willamette Valley. There are about six coastal records, and only one for winter. A bird wintered near Florence, Lane Co., in 1972-73. There are two summer records of non-breeding individuals from Sauvie I.

Order CHARADRIIFORMES
Family Charadriidae

Black-bellied Plover. *Pluvialis squatarola.*

Common spring and fall transient, and locally common in winter along the coast. Uncommon transient inland. In winter, rare to locally uncommon in inland valleys west of the Cascade Mts.

In Oregon the Black-bellied Plover utilizes ocean beaches, coastal estuaries, wet and short grassy fields, and the margins of lakes. The vanguard of the southward migration typically arrives on the coast in early July. It becomes common by August and remains so into November. It is fairly common at favored estuaries throughout the winter, especially those with nearby pasture lands such as Nehalem Bay, Tillamook Bay, Coos Bay, and the Coquille R. estuary.

Spring transients are present from late March through early May, with a few occasionally reported until the end of May. Small numbers are rarely seen through June, a situation that makes its migratory movements more difficult to understand.

It is an uncommon fall transient throughout the interior. The latest fall record at Malheur N.W.R. is October 18. Birds thought to be transients are noted through

November west of the Cascade Mts. It is less numerous inland in the spring, with most observed between early April and mid-May.

This plover is generally a rare winter visitant in the inland valleys of western Oregon, but is locally uncommon at Fern Ridge Res., Sauvie I. and in the lower Columbia R. bottoms from Sauvie I. to the ocean.

American Golden-Plover. *Pluvialis dominica.*

Uncommon to rare fall transient, and a very rare transient in spring statewide.

The American Golden-Plover and its near relative the Pacific Golden-Plover were recognized as distinct species by the A.O.U. only in 1993. Most published records until recent years have referred to Lesser Golden-Plovers, the species that included both the American and Pacific Golden-Plovers. In addition, little was known until recent years regarding reliable identification the two forms. The status of both therefore remains to be fully established.

There are records of some type of Golden-Plover for every month, but there are none safely ascribable to American Golden-Plover from mid-November through March. The species has been occasionally reported from the coast from mid-April through mid-May. One was photographed on June 18, 1986 at Tillamook Bay, which could represent either a late spring migrant or an early fall transient. One at Malheur N.W.R. on May 8 and 23, 1967, seems more likely to pertain to this form than the Pacific Golden-Plover, but this is entirely speculative. Adults in breeding or partial breeding plumage have been reported in small numbers along the coast from early July through early November. An adult near Klamath Falls on July 29, 1978 was probably of this species. Juvenile American Golden-Plovers occur along the coast and to a lesser extent inland from late August to at least the end of October. Although always uncommon in Oregon, the greatest numbers of juveniles have been noted from about the first week of September to the first week of October.

Pacific Golden-Plover. *Pluvialis fulva.*

Uncommon fall transient along the coast; rare spring transient along the coast. Vagrant inland.

95

Refer to the preceding species for words of caution about our present knowledge of the status of these two closely related species, only recently recognized as being distinct.

The Pacific Golden-Plover is a rare spring transient along the coast. It is usually found as single birds, but small flocks have also been noted. This species has been reported from early April through early June.

It occurs as an uncommon transient in the fall along the coast, from early August through early November. Juveniles have been reported from late August through early November. The species has also been found at least three times in late September and October in northern Morrow and Umatilla Cos.

There are a few December, January, and February records from coastal locations, and one record from the Willamette Valley, that have been described as being of this species. These birds probably wintered or attempted to do so.

Mongolian Plover. *Charadrius mongolus.*

Vagrant.

This Asian species has been recorded in Oregon three times: a juvenile at Tillamook Bay, Tillamook Co., Sept. 11 to 17, 1977; a juvenile at the South Jetty of the Columbia R., Clatsop Co., Oct. 16 to 21, 1979; and an adult in breeding plumage from July 11 through Aug. 14, 1986, near Bandon, Coos Co. The birds fed on estuarine flats and used open sandy beaches during high tide. The Tillamook bird constituted the first record for the Pacific coast south of Alaska. All three records were confirmed by photographs.

Snowy Plover. *Charadrius alexandrinus.*

Locally uncommon permanent resident along the coast. Locally fairly common summer resident inland in Harney Co., Lake Co., and periodically and very locally in Klamath Co.

The Snowy Plover is an uncommon and local permanent resident along the coast, where it utilizes the less-disturbed flat, sandy beaches both as nesting habitat and for wintering. Some flocking and migratory movement occurs after the nesting season.

Until recent years the species was found in small numbers in Clatsop, Tillamook, and Lincoln Cos. As many as 19 adults had been seen in a day from Gearhart, Clatsop Co., north to the Columbia R. mouth as late as 1983. Six or seven pairs were still using the Bayocean Sandspit, Tillamook Co. in the early 1980s. These breeding populations have since been extirpated. The small population on the southern Washington coast may account for the occasional individual that has been reported after the breeding season on the northern Oregon coast in recent years.

Small numbers (fewer than 200 birds) still breed on the coasts of Douglas, Coos, and Curry Cos. Favored locations include the North Spit of Coos Bay, Ten Mile Creek Spit, the beaches south of Bandon, and the beaches near Floras L., Curry Co. The coastal population has recently been listed as Threatened by the United States Department of Interior.

The Snowy Plover is a fairly common summer resident in Harney and Lake Cos., where it inhabits the margins of alkaline playas, lakes, and ponds with little or no vegetation. An extensive population survey conducted in 1980 in Harney and Lake Cos. counted 1,047 adults at 11 sites. Harney L. had about 400, and smaller numbers were located elsewhere in the Harney Basin. The Alvord Basin, Harney Co., had 67. In Lake Co., the Summer L. basin had 193 and Lake Abert 345. The observers noted that water levels were too high on some alkaline playas where Snowy Plovers doubtlessly occur when conditions are suitable. In 1987 a total of 651 adults were censused in Lake Co. Small numbers are found some years at White L. in southern Klamath Co. Numbers, or even the species' presence, at inland locations varies greatly with water levels.

The only confirmed record for inland western Oregon was of a bird found injured along the Willamette R., between Portland and Salem, and brought to the Portland Audubon Society Bird Rehabilitation Center on Sept. 22, 1992. One reported from near White City, Jackson County, on May 6, 1984 also seems credible.

Semipalmated Plover. *Charadrius semipalmatus.*

Common transient, rare winter visitant along the coast. Uncommon transient inland.

The Semipalmated Plover is a common transient along the coast in spring and fall. Northward transients are evident in early April, and are typically common

97

from mid-April through mid-May, with small numbers reported through early June. Occasional reports throughout June may pertain to transients or non-breeding summer visitants. Southward transients begin arriving in the last week of June, and are typically common by early July. Concentrations of over 100 have been noted at Tillamook Bay as early as July 8. Over 350 at Tillamook Bay on Aug. 3, 1979 is the largest concentration reported from the state.

This species remains common through September, after which numbers decline rapidly. Small numbers remain through early November. A few typically winter at favored estuaries, such as Tillamook Bay and Coos Bay

Small numbers of spring and fall transients occur inland on both sides of the Cascade Mts., where they are usually found in small flocks or as individuals.

In Oregon Semipalmated Plovers favor coastal estuaries, open sandy beaches, lake shores, and wet fields with little or no vegetation.

Remarkably, a pair was found to produce young at Malheur N.W.R. during the summers of 1987, 1988 and 1989. This constitutes the southernmost breeding record of the species anywhere.

Piping Plover. *Charadrius melodus.*

Vagrant.

The only record of this species for Oregon was a single bird seen on the open sandy beach near Manzanita, Tillamook Co., on Sept. 6 and 8, 1986. The record has been accepted by the Oregon Bird Records Committee, but some commentators believe the description is of a leucistic Semipalmated Plover.

Killdeer. *Charadrius vociferus.*

Common summer resident and transient statewide. Uncommon to abundant in winter west of the Cascades. Rare to uncommon in winter east of the Cascades.

The Killdeer is a common summer resident throughout the state in short grass, agricultural and sparsely vegetated habitats. It avoids high mountain areas. This species has probably increased as a result of the abundant habitat provided by the conversion of large parts of the state to agricultural uses.

The Killdeer is an uncommon to abundant winter resident of western Oregon, with numbers variable depending on the severity of the weather. It is especially numerous in winter in the southern Willamette Valley, where concentrations numbering in the thousands occur. Large numbers have been noted on agricultural land along the coast when snow or ice covers inland habitats. East of the Cascade Mts., Killdeer are locally uncommon in valleys in winter or rare to absent during severe winters.

Mountain Plover. *Charadrius montanus.*

Vagrant.

There are five Oregon records of this species: two with a flock of Killdeer near Corvallis, Benton Co., on Jan. 2 1967, and one was still there to March 10, 1967 (one had been collected); one at the Bayocean Spit, Tillamook Co., on Nov. 19-26, 1977; one at and near Siletz Bay, Feb. 3-26, 1983; one at Tahkenitch Beach, Douglas Co., Jan. 23, 1988; and two on the beach at Bandon State Park, Coos Co., Dec. 6, 1989.

Family Haematopodidae

American Black Oystercatcher. *Haematopus bachmani.*

Fairly common permanent resident along the coast.

The Black Oystercatcher is found throughout the year on rocky shores, offshore rocks, and rocky estuary mouths the length of the coast. It is occasionally seen on sandy beaches, especially where fresh water enters the ocean.

A survey of the Oregon breeding population conducted in 1988 estimated 350 birds (Lowe pers. com.). Despite this small number, the species apparently fills its available habitat. Small flocks of up to 30 birds occur in the winter.

Family Recurvirostridae

Black-necked Stilt. *Himantopus mexicanus.*

Locally common summer resident in Klamath, Lake, Harney, and Malheur Cos., and sporadically elsewhere east of the Cascades Mts. Vagrant or rare to western Oregon.

The Black-necked Stilt nests in the counties of Oregon's Great Basin. In that area the species is a summer resident that is highly variable in abundance from one year to the next. It is generally a fairly common to uncommon summer resident, but may be common some years, and very scarce at particular areas in other years. In Oregon it is a bird of shallow lakes, open marshes, and flooded or irrigated fields. Fresh water and strongly alkaline habitats are used. These habitats are variable within its normal nesting range, due primarily to the vagaries of precipitation. Its centers of abundance are the Malheur N.W.R., the lakes of southern Lake Co, and the southern half of Klamath Co.

Nesting has occurred sporadically and in small numbers north to Baker, Union, Umatilla, and Morrow Cos. The stilt is also a rare to very rare spring and summer visitant elsewhere east of the Cascades in spring, summer, and early fall.

East of the Cascades the species generally occurs from mid-April to early September. The vanguard in spring sometimes arrives in the latter part of March. There are a few fall records extending into mid-October.

The Black-necked Stilt is a vagrant to western Oregon. It is unrecorded some years and occasionally stages small-scale spring invasions. Records are for April and May, and include almost the length of the coast as well as the major inland valleys. West of the Cascades it is most regular in the Rogue Valley, where the few sites of suitable habitat have produced a disproportionate percentage of the western Oregon records. There are also a few records in fall from early August through early September, but the species is much more likely to stray to western Oregon in spring. West of the Cascades it has utilized flooded fields, the edges of ponds and lakes, sewage treatment ponds, and estuaries.

American Avocet. *Recurvirostra americana.*

Locally abundant to uncommon summer resident of Klamath, Lake, Harney, and Malheur Cos. Smaller numbers locally elsewhere east of the Cascades. Vagrant to western Oregon.

The American Avocet is a common summer resident of the great alkaline lakes, shallow open marshes, flooded grazing lands, and other shallow wetlands without dense or tall vegetation in southeastern Oregon. Numbers vary at any given locale depending on whether relative drought or wet conditions exist. It is also a locally uncommon to rare summer resident in the limited suitable habitat north into Baker, Union, Umatilla, and Morrow Cos. Spring and fall transients, and summer visitants are rare to uncommon elsewhere east of the Cascades.

East of the Cascades the spring migration usually begins in mid-March, but the earliest returning birds have been noted in late February. The main movement takes place in the first weeks of April. The fall migration begins in early July, and peaks in August. Although numbers begin to decline in September, there are many birds still present at the favored locales through October. The last depart in early November. The latest fall record for Malheur N.W.R. is November 18 (Littlefield, 1990). Post-breeding concentrations are sometimes spectacular in numbers. As an example, over 15,000 have been recorded at Stinking L. on the Malheur N.W.R. in mid-August (Littlefield, 1990). Up to 50,000 have been at Summer L., Lake Co., also in August. A count of 2,350 at Summer L. on Nov. 10, 1984, was late for such a large concentration (Paulson, 1993).

The avocet is a spring and fall vagrant both to the coast and the inland valleys west of the Cascade Mts. A few birds are noted most years. Most records are from mid-April to mid-May, and from mid-August to mid-September. Flooded fields, lake margins, sewage treatment ponds, and estuaries are the major habitats that have been used.

Two were at a frozen marsh in Klamath Co. on Dec. 7-16, 1978, and two were seen for a day at Coos Bay on Dec. 12, 1980 (Paulson, 1993).

Family Scolopacidae

Greater Yellowlegs. *Tringa melanoleuca.*

Common transient throughout the state. Uncommon winter visitant to western Oregon, and very rare east of the Cascades in winter. Has bred.

The Greater Yellowlegs is primarily a transient through Oregon, although there are records for every week of the year. The first spring migrants are sometimes noted in late February in western Oregon, but the latter half of March is more typical for the species' arrival. The peak of migration is from the last days of March through the first two weeks, or some years, the first three weeks of April. Some transients are occasionally noted into late May. Typically this species is seen individually or in flocks of fewer than 20 birds, but some spring concentrations have been noted that approach 200 birds. The occasional record from late May through mid-June may pertain to summering non-breeders or transients going in either direction. By the last week of June the first adults are noted returning from the north, and the species becomes common by about the middle of July. Numbers noticeably decline by mid-October. Birds that are obviously transients continue to be seen into November, and sometimes well into December. From December through February it is rare west of the Cascades, both along the coast and in the interior valleys, except at Coos Bay where small numbers winter. At that season it is very rare east of the Cascades, with most records corning from the Klamath Basin, but there are records from many areas.

To further complicate any description of the species' status, a few have bred at Downy L., Wallowa Co., in at least four seasons since 1980 (Evanich 1992).

In Oregon the Greater Yellowlegs utilizes lake margins, ponds, wet meadows and flooded grazing lands, mud flats, open marshes, and coastal estuaries, in which it prefers the more brackish upper reaches, and the mouths of small fresh water streams.

Lesser Yellowlegs. *Tringa flavipes.*

Common fall transient and an uncommon to rare spring transient statewide. Very rare in winter.

The Lesser Yellowlegs is almost exclusively a transient in Oregon. In spring it is typically uncommon to rare. Spring transients occur from early April to about mid-May. The first returning migrants from the north are sometimes noted in the latter third of June, and from early July to near the end of that month the species is uncommon throughout the state. The adults of the species move through in July, and as is the case with several other species of shorebirds, there is something of a gap before the juvenile birds make their appearance. The juveniles begin appearing after about August 10, and peak in numbers in the last third of August and the first third of September. Concentrations of over a hundred have been noted occasionally at favored locations during that time period, both along the coast and inland. Few birds remain by early October. It is a rare transient from late October through November.

The Lesser Yellowlegs is very rare in winter. Most records are from coastal locations and the interior valleys of western Oregon, but there are a few records for east of the Cascades as well. Some of the winter records have been substantiated by photographs, and many have been of birds that accompanied Greater Yellowlegs. Extreme caution is recommended when reporting this species in winter due to its similarity with the Greater Yellowlegs.

Its habitat choices are very similar to those of the Greater Yellowlegs. Both utilize lake and pond edges, shallow open marshes, flooded fields and wet meadows, mud flats, and coastal estuaries, where they favor the brackish upper reaches and the mouths of streams.

Spotted Redshank. *Tringa erythropus.*

Vagrant.

The only record for Oregon of this palearctic species was a bird at the S. Jetty of the Columbia R., Clatsop Co., Feb. 21 through March 15, 1981. The record was substantiated by photographs.

Solitary Sandpiper. *Tringa solitaria.*

Uncommon to rare transient statewide. Has bred.

The Solitary Sandpiper is generally an uncommon to rare transient through Oregon in spring and fall. Numbers are never large, and as its name implies, concentrations of more than two or three birds are infrequent. In spring it occurs from about April 10 to about May 15. By far the greatest numbers of birds are recorded from the last ten days of April and the first ten days of May, and the species is difficult to find outside this narrow window of time. There are a few records from as early as the first week of April, and one from Fields, Harney Co., as late as May 30. Fall records extend from early July to early October. Most are seen in the latter half of August and the first half of September.

In the 1980s, Gold Lake Bog in the central Cascades of Lane Co. in some years supported a pair or two that appeared to have successfully bred. Territorial displays were seen, as well as very young juveniles. No nests have actually been seen in Oregon.

The Solitary Sandpiper uses small ponds (including stock ponds, farm ponds, and wooded lakes and ponds), irrigation ditches, sloughs, sheltered corners and edges of larger lakes and open marshes, and flooded fields. The species generally avoids salt water habitats.

Willet. *Catoptrophorus semipalmatus.*

Common summer resident in Malheur, Harney, Lake, and Klamath Cos. Rare visitant spring through early fall elsewhere east of the Cascades. Very rare spring and early fall visitant in inland western Oregon. Rare transient and winter visitant along the coast.

The Willet is a common summer resident in Malheur, Harney, Lake, and Klamath Cos., where it inhabits wet meadows and the edges of marshes and lakes. The first of the species arrive at the nesting areas in early to mid-April. The earliest records are from late March. Birds begin departing from the nesting areas in the latter half of June. The species is present through July and much of August, but is very scarce by early September. Numbers at Stinking Lake on the Malheur N.W.R. have exceeded 3,000 in mid-July (Littlefield, 1990). East of the Cascades away from its nesting areas it is a rare to very rare spring and early fall transient, within the same time frames mentioned above.

West of the Cascades it is a very rare transient in both spring and fall at inland sites, again within the time frames of occurrence on its breeding range. The Willet is very rare to rare along the coast as a spring transient from mid-April to early June, and rare from mid-July to October. One to several often winter at Yaquina Bay and Coos Bay, and in some winters at the Coquille R. estuary. Winter records elsewhere along the coast are very rare. Along the coast it utilizes estuaries, and occasionally open ocean beaches.

Wandering Tattler. *Heteroscelus incanus.*

Fairly common spring and fall transient along the coast. Very rare in winter. Vagrant inland.

The Wandering Tattler is a fairly common transient along the Oregon coast in both spring and fall. The spring migration begins in the last days of April, and rarely as early as about April 10. Transients are regular through May, and a few records extend into the second week of June. The fall migration begins about the end of the first week of July, with a few records earlier than that. Juvenile birds begin to arrive in mid-August. By the end of August almost all of the adults have gone to the south. After the third week of September the juveniles become uncommon, and only a few are present through October.

There are several records for winter, but the species is typically only reliably reported a few times per decade at that season. The winter of 1977-78 was remarkable in that about a dozen birds were reported along the Oregon coast (Paulson, 1993).

There are five autumn records from inland locations, all east of the Cascades in Klamath, Lake, and Grant Cos.

Gray-tailed Tattler. *Heteroscelus brevipes.*

Vagrant.

There is one sight record of this species in Oregon, a calling adult at the mouth of the Coquille R., Coos Co., on Aug. 18, 1990.

Spotted Sandpiper. *Actitis macularia.*

Common to rare summer resident and transient throughout the state. Rare in winter, primarily along the coast.

The Spotted Sandpiper is a common to rare summer resident throughout the state from sea level to over 6,000 ft. It breeds on the margins of lakes, rivers, streams, and mountain ponds.

Migrants appear from the south in the last days of April, and peak in numbers in the first ten days of May. Some birds that are still obviously in migration are found through the first two-thirds of May. The southward migration occurs from July through early October, with the main migration in August and early September. Migrants prefer freshwater habitats, but a few also occur along the edges of coastal estuaries and even on ocean jetties.

The species is rare in winter, at which time it is most regularly found on coastal estuaries or along coastal rivers near their mouths. At such places it prefers sheltered coves with driftwood and other debris. It is rarer inland in winter west of the Cascade Mts., where it is found along rivers, ponds, lakes, and reservoirs. It is very rare in winter east of the Cascade Mts. in similar habitats.

Upland Sandpiper. *Bartramia longicauda.*

Very local summer resident east of the Cascade Mts.

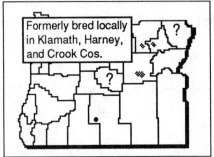

Formerly bred locally
in Klamath, Harney,
and Crook Cos.

The Upland Sandpiper is a summer resident in a few small areas east of the Cascades. The Bear and Logan Valleys of southern Grant Co. have several dozen breeding pairs. One to several pairs have also been found in recent years near Ukiah, Umatilla Co.; at Sycan Marsh, Lake Co.; at Summit Prairie in the Ochoco Mts., Crook Co.; near LaGrande, Union Co.; and near Enterprise, Wallowa Co. The species is present at its breeding sites from early May into the latter half of July. Transients have also been noted at Malheur N.W.R. in both spring and fall (May 2, 1987 and Aug. 12, 1987) (Littlefield, 1990). One was at Lost Valley, Gilliam Co., on May 30, 1994.

In Oregon the Upland Sandpiper nests in ungrazed or lightly grazed grasslands, usually with scattered forbs.

The only record for western Oregon is of a bird that was at the Hatfield Marine Science Center near Newport, Lincoln Co., July 23 to 28, 1987.

Whimbrel. *Numenius phaeopus.*

Fairly common spring and fall transient. Uncommon non-breeding summer visitant and rare winter visitant along the coast. Very rare transient inland.

The Whimbrel is a fairly common transient in spring and fall along the coast. Numbers at favored estuaries such as Tillamook Bay, Siletz Bay, Yaquina Bay, and Coos Bay sometimes exceed 100 birds.

Northward transients usually first appear in early April. The greatest number passes through in late April and May, with small numbers seen into June, which may be late transients. A few non-breeders occasionally remain throughout June, especially at Yaquina Bay.

Southward transients begin arriving in early July. The greatest numbers are present from late July through mid-September with some obvious transients noted into early November. Small numbers are occasionally present throughout the winter, especially at Yaquina Bay and Coos Bay.

Inland the Whimbrel is a very rare transient throughout the state, with spring records predominating. There are inland records on both sides of the Cascade Mts. Flocks of up to 15 have been noted, but most reports are of individuals.

On the coast the Whimbrel utilizes muddy and sandy estuaries, sandy and occasionally rocky beaches, and pasture lands, especially when freshly cut. Inland birds have been found on mud flats and in fields.

There is a single record of the Asian race *variegatus*, from Clatsop Beach, Clatsop Co., on Sept. 25, 1985.

Bristle-thighed Curlew. *Numenius tahitiensis.*

Vagrant.

The only record was that of two birds at Bandon Sept. 16, 1981. Supportive photographs were obtained. The sighting followed a storm front from the Pacific.

Long-billed Curlew. *Numenius americans.*

Locally common summer resident and transient east of the Cascades. Rare transient west of the Cascades, primarily along the coast.

The Long-billed Curlew is locally a common summer resident in Harney, Lake, Klamath, Umatilla, Morrow, Union, and Baker Cos. Smaller numbers are found in other counties east of the Cascade Mts. Migrants arrive on their breeding grounds beginning in the last week of March. Some depart the breeding grounds as early as June, but most adults are still present into the middle or latter part of July. Juveniles are sometime noted near the breeding areas into the middle of August. The are a few records east of the Cascades as late as October and even into November.

West of the Cascades this large curlew is rare as a transient along the coast in spring and in fall. Spring birds are usually noted in April and early May. Fall transients sometimes occur in very small numbers from the middle of June to October. Individuals have summered along the coast a few times. There are several records of birds that wintered at the larger estuaries along the coast or in coastal pasture lands. In the inland valleys of western Oregon the species is a very rare transient, more frequently noted in spring than fall.

Hudsonian Godwit. *Limosa haemastica.*

Vagrant.

There are 12 records of this species for Oregon, all but one are from the autumn migration. All involve one or two birds, except for the flock of 16 found at Tillamook Bay during a wet weather front on Aug. 17, 1980. The spring record was one at the S. Jetty of the Columbia R., Clatsop Co., on May 31, 1983. The remaining records are from Bandon, Coos Co., Sept. 18-20, 1978; S. Jetty of the Columbia R., Aug. 23, 1979; near Malheur N.W.R., Sept. 21, 1984; S. Jetty of the Columbia R., Aug. 23-Sept. 4, 1985; Bandon, Oct. 6-27, 1985; Summer L., Lake Co., Aug. 22-Sept. 17, 1987; S. Jetty of the Columbia R., Aug. 31, 1988; Nehalem sewage ponds, Tillamook Co., Aug. 10, 1989; at the mouth of the Siuslaw R., Lane Co, on Sept. 18, 1990; and two at the S. Jetty of the Columbia R. on Sep. 1, 1991.

Bar-tailed Godwit. *Limosa lapponica.*

Vagrant.

The Asian race (*L.1. baueri*) has been recorded on the Oregon coast on 13 occasions. The spring records are: one at Newport, Lincoln Co., April 25, 1980; four at Bandon, Coos Co., May 14, 1988; one near Mohler, Tillamook Co., on May 28, 1978; and one at the S. Jetty of the Columbia R., June 1, 1980. The autumn records are one at Yaquina Bay, Lincoln Co., July 8, 1993; one at Coos Bay, Aug. 25-29, 1980; one at Bandon, Aug. 27-30, 1987; one at Tillamook Bay, Sep. 7, 1990; one at Bandon, Sep. 8 -Oct. 2, 1990; two at Bandon, Sept. 11-12, 1977; one at Newport, Sept. 14+, 1979; one at Bandon Sept. 23, 1976; and two at Bandon, Oct. 4-5, 1980.

Marbled Godwit. *Limosa fedoa.*

Uncommon transient and a very rare winter visitant along the coast. Rare to very rare transient inland.

Along the coast the Marbled Godwit is an uncommon transient, seen more frequently in the fall migration than in spring. It is usually found at the larger estuaries such as Coos Bay and Yaquina Bay, but the rich feeding habitat at the Coquille R. estuary is perhaps the most reliable place in Oregon to see this species. Open sandy beaches and smaller estuaries and river mouths are also sometimes utilized. The migration in spring typically extends from April through early May. Some birds thought to be spring migrants have been noted into the first week of June. Birds presumed to be fall migrants are occasionally seen in the latter part of June. The main migration is from mid-July through early October. It is most common from the last week of August through the first two weeks of September, when juvenile birds reach the state.

Flocks of more than 30 birds are rare along the coast, although exceptional flocks have had over a hundred birds. The 250 at the Coquille R. estuary on April 27, 1981 was the largest flock ever reported for the state. Small flocks of six to 15 are more typical.

There are a few winter records from large coastal estuaries, particularly those with nearby meadows that provide feeding habitat during high winter tides.

Inland, the species is a rare to uncommon transient through Malheur, Harney, Lake, and Klamath Cos., and the counties of northeastern Oregon, within the same time frames as are noted for coastal locations. The species is rare to very rare elsewhere east of the Cascades.

Inland west of the Cascades it is a very rare transient in fall in the Willamette Valley. It is rare in spring and fall in the Rogue Valley, but on several occasions spring flocks of over a hundred birds have been recorded, usually associated with inclement spring weather. Individuals are also more frequent in the Rogue Valley than further north.

Ruddy Turnstone. *Arenaria interores.*

Fairly common transient along the coast; rare in winter. Vagrant during migration inland.

The Ruddy Turnstone is a fairly common transient along the coast in spring and fall. The fall migration begins during the second week of July, and the number of adult birds peaks from about July 15 through the end of the month. At the Bandon Marsh N.W.R., in the Coquille R. estuary, the July peak often exceeds a hundred birds, and has exceeded 400 birds in some years. Smaller numbers are typically found elsewhere, but the species is well scattered along the coast. Numbers decrease in early August, and begin increasing again in mid-August when the juvenile birds begin to arrive. It remains fairly common to uncommon well into September. By October it is decidedly uncommon, and rare through the winter. The spring migration begins in the latter half of April, peaks in the first half of May, with only a few birds present as late as the third week of May. A flock of 86 at Tillamook Bay on May 9, 1990 is an example of a large flock for the spring.

Along the coast the Ruddy Turnstone is found on rocky shores (particularly those with small stones, shells, and other debris), jetties, sand flats, and mud flats. On occasion it can be found at sewage treatment ponds, wet meadows, and lake margins. It often associates with Black Turnstones and Surfbirds, but is much less dependent upon rocky shorelines than either of those species.

It is a vagrant inland. There are two records for west of the Cascade Mts. in September (Washington Co., and Jackson Co.), and four in May, all from Jackson Co. There are more records east of the Cascades, where it is recorded in spring or fall on nearly an annual basis, with fall records predominating. While most records east of the Cascades pertain to individual birds, as many as four have been found together. Spring records east of the Cascades range from May 8 to June 4. Fall records east of the Cascades range from August 3 to September 10.

Black Turnstone. *Arenaria melanocephala.*

Common winter visitant and spring and fall transient. Vagrant inland.

The Black Turnstone is a common winter visitant and transient along the coast, where it is found along rocky shores and jetties. To a lesser extent it also feeds on sandy beaches and estuarine mud flats. It often associates with Surfbirds, but is less restricted to rocky habitats. During high winter tides and storms it can sometimes be found feeding in wet meadows, or even on the lawns of coastal homes.

The Black Turnstone is present in varying numbers along the Oregon coast almost the entire year. Migrants arrive from the north during the first week of

July, and the species is quite common by the middle of the second week of July. It remains common throughout the fall migration, and as a common winter visitant the length of the coast. Numbers peak during the spring migration during the second half of April, and it becomes uncommon after mid-May. Records are few after mid-May, with the latest record being June 6, 1980.

Inland it is a vagrant, rarer than the Ruddy Turnstone. There are five inland records for western Oregon: two from fall or early winter, and three from late April to mid-May. Most surprising is the record of two birds east of the Cascades Mts. at Ochoco Res., Crook Co., on Sept. 8, 1985.

Surfbird. *Aphriza virgata.*

Common transient and fairly common winter visitant along the coast.

The Surfbird is a bird of the rocky shores and jetties of the coast. At times it is found on sandy beaches near rocky areas. It usually associates with Black Turnstones. These mixed flocks sometimes also contain Rock Sandpipers and Ruddy Turnstones. It occasionally feeds on the mud flats near the mouth of the Coquille R. estuary, but in recent years has seemed to do so less frequently.

It is most common as a transient in both spring and fall, but is also a fairly common winter visitant. It is found along our coast throughout most of the year, from early July into May. Fall migrants arrive in small numbers during the first week of July. Spring transients are mostly gone by the first of May, but a few can sometimes be found into mid-May.

Great Knot. *Calidris tenuirostris.*

Vagrant.

There are two records of this Asian species for Oregon: an adult at Yaquina Bay on Sept. 28, 1978; and a juvenile at the Coquille R. estuary near Bandon from Sept. 1-19, 1990. The latter bird was well photographed. Photographs supporting the Yaquina Bay sighting were also taken, although some commentators believe that the photographs do not eliminate Red Knot.

Red Knot. *Calidris canutus.*

Along the coast, a fairly common to uncommon spring transient, and a rare to very uncommon fall transient. Very rare along the coast in winter. Rare to very rare transient spring and fall inland.

The Red Knot is a fairly common to uncommon transient along the coast in spring. The main migration is during the first two weeks of May, but the it may extend from mid-April through the end of the third week of May. Flocks are usually small, but groups of over a hundred have been noted. In fall the species is much less common, and is rare during most years. At that season it is more typical to see individuals or very small flocks of fewer that a dozen birds at favored locales such as the Coquille R. estuary or at Coos Bay. There are a few records of wintering birds from various coastal locations.

Inland it is very rare in spring and fall in the interior valleys of western Oregon. East of the Cascades it is a rare spring and fall transient and has been recorded from numerous locations, but is most frequently reported from Malheur N.W.R. and from the large lakes of Lake and Klamath Cos.

Sanderling. *Calidris alba.*

Abundant transient and fairly common to common winter visitant along the coast. Uncommon to rare transient inland. Rare winter visitant in the Willamette Valley.

The Sanderling is present along the coast in varying numbers almost the entire year. Fall migrants appear in early July and are typically common by August. It becomes abundant from August through October. Numbers are greatly reduced by mid-winter, but it remains common at favored localities such as the Clatsop Co. beach from Gearhart to the S. Jetty of the Columbia R.

The spring migration is during April and May, with significant numbers present in at least some years into early June. A total of 30,000 were estimated along a three-mile stretch of beach in Clatsop Co. on May 25, 1978. Occasional individuals have been recorded throughout June, which may represent transients or non-breeding summer visitants.

The Sanderling is an uncommon fall and rare spring transient inland. The largest concentration reported from east of the Cascade Mts. is a flock of 28 at

Harney L., Sept. 25, 1981. Inland transients are typically individuals or small flocks.

It is a rare winter visitant in the Willamette Valley, and a rare winter visitant in the Columbia R. bottoms from Portland to the ocean. Winter flocks of as many as 62 birds have occurred on Sauvie I., but have not done so in recent years.

The Sanderling is primarily a bird of sandy ocean beaches. To a lesser extent coastal birds utilize muddy and sandy estuaries and flooded fields during winter high tides. It occurs inland on mud flats, alkaline flats, and in flooded fields.

Semipalmated Sandpiper. *Calidris pusilla.*

Rare to uncommon transient in fall, very rare transient in spring.

The Semipalmated Sandpiper has in the past fifteen years proven to be a rare to uncommon fall transient throughout the state. The earliest arrival date is June 29 at Tillamook Bay. Adults have been recorded throughout July and into early August. Juveniles begin to arrive in the second or third week of July, and peak between August 10 and September 10. After mid-September there are very few records, with the latest documented record September 25 (Tillamook Co.). The highest count for the state is the 15 at Tillamook Bay on August 18, 1985.

It is very rare in spring. As far as we know, only the one at Tillamook Bay on May 12, 1979 has been proven by photograph. At least some other reports must be correct, but the comparative difficulty of its identification in spring might lead to some misidentification.

Western Sandpiper. *Calidris mauri.*

Uncommon to abundant fall and spring transient. Rare to uncommon along the coast in winter. Very rare inland in winter.

Spring migrants begin to arrive in the middle of April, peak during the last week of April, and decline in number rapidly after the first week of May. A few transients can sometimes be found into the third week of May, and there are several records into the first week of June, both inland and along the coast. In spring its greatest numbers are along the coast, where it is often abundant. Counts at the Bandon Marsh N.W.R. have reached 15,000. Other coastal estuaries also provide habitat to concentrations of up to several thousand. Inland in spring it is generally less numerous, but still common, both in the inland valleys of western Oregon and east of the Cascades. The largest concentrations occur when water levels are right at the large lakes in Lake and Harney Cos. Spring concentrations in those areas sometimes exceed 10,000 in late April and early May.

The fall migration begins as early as mid-June when very small flocks or individuals are occasionally noted. Large flocks of adult birds begin arriving in the first week of July, especially along the coast. The earliest juvenile birds arrive in the latter part of July. Numbers decline noticeably near the end of July and through about the first third of August, as adults depart to the south, and before the main movement of juvenile birds arrive. The juvenile birds arrive in large numbers beginning after the first third of August, and continue in large numbers into early September, after which they begin to decline rapidly. It remains common throughout September, and becomes uncommon in October. Numbers decline rapidly after October 1 east of the Cascades, and in inland western Oregon. By November almost all have departed from inland areas.

There are few authenticated records inland after the end of October. The flock of seven at Malheur N.W.R. on Feb. 14, 1990 is inexplicable. The species is often reported on Christmas counts in the Willamette Valley, and occasionally elsewhere at inland locations. None of these reports have been verified by photograph as far as we are aware. We suspect that many if not all such inland winter records are inaccurate. There is potential for an occasional inland winter record, but we await photographic evidence.

Along the coast it is an uncommon winter visitor, found almost exclusively on the larger estuaries. At that season it is vastly outnumbered by Dunlin, with which it often associates. Numbers vary considerably from year to year. The species may be somewhat over-counted on some coastal Christmas counts.

Rufous-necked Stint. *Calidris ruficollis.*

Vagrant.

There are four certain records of this Asian breeder for Oregon. Three are from the Bayocean Spit, Tillamook Co.: June 20, 1982; July 3, 1982; and Aug. 21-26, 1982. The other was at the Coquille R. estuary, Coos Co., on June 25, 1984. July 3, 1982. All of the records are of single birds in full or partial breeding plumage.

Little Stint. *Calidris minuta.*

Vagrant.

This palearctic species has been recorded twice in Oregon: Sept. 7, 1985, at Bayocean Spit, Tillamook Co. (diagnostic photographs), and at Bandon, Coos Co., on Sept. 12, 1986 (supportive photographs).

Long-toed Stint. *Calidris subminuta.*

Vagrant.

There are two records of this Asian species for Oregon. A juvenile was photographed and its calls recorded at the S. Jetty of the Columbia R., Clatsop Co., on Sept. 2-6, 1981. An adult was there July 17, 1983. These records were the first for North America away from various Alaskan islands. This species is very similar to the Least Sandpiper, and several other reports of it occurring in Oregon are not considered to have eliminated that species.

Least Sandpiper. *Calidris minutilla.*

Common transient. In winter, uncommon along the coast, uncommon to rare inland west of the Cascades, and very rare east of the Cascades.

The Least Sandpiper is a common transient throughout the state in both spring and fall. Spring migration begins in March west of the Cascades, and typically in mid-April east of the Cascades. The peak of the migration is in late April and early May. An estimate of 5,000 at Abert L., Lake Co., on April 28, 1994 is the largest from the state of which we are aware. By the third week in May numbers are in rapid decline. There are a few records of late migrants into early June. The earliest fall migrants sometimes are noted in the last third of June. The first juvenile birds begin to appear during early August. This species is common by about July 10, and remains so into early October. Numbers decline rapidly after early October east of the Cascades, and do so much more gradually west of the Cascades.

The Least Sandpiper is uncommon along the coast in winter. It is uncommon to rare in the Willamette Valley in winter (depending on the particular year and location); and has been recorded at that season in the Umpqua and Rogue Valleys. It is very rare into December east of the Cascades, and only a few records exist for January through March.

It generally prefers drier areas on the edges of wetlands than do Western Sandpipers. The Least Sandpiper utilizes both mud flats and vegetated areas, including very low vegetation, and taller marshes where there are openings in the vegetation. Even small rain puddles or wet fields often attract Least Sandpipers. Gravel covered estuaries are also used. It is rarely found on the margins of alkali lakes or sandy ocean beaches.

Baird's Sandpiper. *Calidris bairdii.*

Uncommon transient in fall. Rare transient in spring.

Oregon is not in the species' main migratory path at any season. It occurs in Oregon mostly during the fall migration, when it is generally an uncommon transient. Greater numbers may occur east of the Cascades than west. Although gatherings of several dozen have been noted, the species is most typically seen as individuals or in flocks of up to ten birds. Adults are rare in the fall migration. The earliest fall record is July 5. A few adults are typically noted through July. Juveniles have been recorded by early August, but are more regular by the middle of August. The peak of the migration is from mid-July to the end of the third week of September. A few birds are typically reported into early October. East of the Cascades there are a few records into mid-October. Along the coast there are several records into November, the latest being Nov. 23, 1988 at Nehalem, Tillamook Co., and Nov. 28, 1976 from Yaquina Bay.

In spring Baird's Sandpiper is a rare transient anywhere in the state. Most records are from western Oregon, where most of the observers are, but the species may occur more regularly east of the Cascades at that season. Spring records range from April 8 (Harney Co.) to June 6 (Lincoln Co.). Most records are from the latter third of April and the first third of May. Flocks of as many as twenty birds have been recorded in spring, but such occurrences are very rare. The more typical spring occurrences involve single birds.

In Oregon, the Baird's Sandpiper utilizes a wide variety of habitats. Along the coast it is found most frequently along the drier edges of estuaries and along the open ocean beaches above the wet sand. In the mountains in the fall migration it uses the area above timberline, where it can be found along the sides of snow patches and in low vegetation, or in barren areas. East of the Cascades it uses the margins of alkali lakes and ponds. Anywhere in the state, it can be found in

116

short grass habitats (sometimes far from water), and along the margins of lakes, ponds and rivers. It prefers the drier parts of the shores of these bodies of water.

Pectoral Sandpiper. *Calidris melanotos.*

Uncommon to common fall transient. Very rare to rare spring transient.

During the fall migration, adults of this species occur as transients throughout the state from mid-July through early September, with some records as early as the first week of July. A bird near the S. Jetty of the Columbia R. on June 20, 1970 was probably a southward migrant. The vast majority of Pectoral Sandpipers that occur in the state are juveniles in the fall migration. The first juveniles appear during the last ten days of August, and are often common through September and October. Numbers decline quickly at the end of October, and the species is rare after the first week of November. There are a few coastal records into the last week of November. Numbers vary greatly from year to year. During exceptional years several hundred have been found at favored coastal and inland locations.

In spring the Pectoral Sandpiper is only a rare to very rare transient statewide. Records extend from early April to the first days of June. Records of individuals are most frequent, but small flocks of up to six have been noted.

In Oregon the Pectoral Sandpiper utilizes short vegetation marshes, mud flats, both dry and wet grassy fields, plowed fields, and the margins of small ponds and lakes. It uses both fresh and salt water habitats.

Sharp-tailed Sandpiper. *Calidris acuminata.*

Very rare fall transient in western Oregon. Vagrant in fall east of the Cascades.

The Sharp-tailed Sandpiper is a very rare fall visitant to the coast and Willamette Valley from its Siberian breeding grounds. It has proven to be of annual occurrence in the last fifteen years or so. Numbers vary considerably from year to year. All Oregon records are of juvenile birds. The species tends to occur in larger numbers in years when juvenile Pectoral Sandpipers also occur in relatively large numbers. It is usually encountered in Oregon as a single bird associated with dowitchers, Dunlin, smaller calidrids, or Pectoral Sandpipers. Up to four have been noted together.

117

Oregon records range from September 2 to November 12. Most records are for the latter half of September and the first three weeks of October.

There are four records for east of the Cascade Mts., all of individual birds: Wamic, Wasco Co., Sept. 8, 1990; Lower Klamath N.W.R., Klamath Co., Sept. 24, 1991; Malheur L., Harney Co., Sept. 28, 1991; and Hatfield L., Deschutes Co., Oct. 17, 1987.

In Oregon the Sharp-tailed Sandpiper has been found using the mud flats of coastal estuaries, short vegetation coastal marshes, the bare margins of small ponds and large lakes, wet grassy fields, and plowed fields.

Rock Sandpiper. *Calidris ptilocnemis.*

Uncommon to rare winter visitant along the coast.

The Rock Sandpiper is an uncommon to rare winter visitant and transient along the coast, being more numerous in the northern counties. It is found on jetties, the rocky outer shore, rocky estuaries, and very rarely on estuarine mud flats. Rock Sandpipers usually arrive in early November (earliest August 21, Coos Co.) and depart in April (latest May 14, Clatsop Co.).

Numbers are never very large, groups of up to 30 being exceptional. It often associates with Black Turnstones and Surfbirds.

Dunlin. *Calidris alpina.*

Common transient and winter resident along the coast and in the Willamette Valley. Uncommon transient and winter visitant in the Rogue and Umpqua Valleys. Uncommon to locally common spring and fall transient east of the Cascade Mts.

The Dunlin is a common transient in both spring and fall along the coast and in the Willamette Valley. Fall birds have been noted as early as the first week of July, but these individuals are rare. It is not until the last days of August that the first birds are typically noted along the coast. The species occurs in small numbers until about the latter third of September when a significant increase begins. Transient numbers peak in October and November. It remains common at some locations throughout the winter. Thousands winter along the lower Columbia R. in Clatsop Co. Significant numbers also are found at the larger coastal estuaries. Tillamook Bay and Coos Bay, not surprisingly, host the largest concentrations away from the Columbia R. Thousands also winter in the Willamette Valley unless they are driven out by unusually cold or snowy conditions. The birds wintering in the Willamette Valley mostly utilize the large expanses of wet agricultural fields, but do not need the presence of standing water. The spring migration takes place from early February to about mid-May. The most obvious transients are from late March through early May. Only small numbers persist through the end of May. Apparent northward transients have been noted into the first third of June.

In the inland valleys of western Oregon south of the Willamette Valley, the Dunlin is an uncommon transient in spring and fall, and winter visitant depending on the availability of suitable habitat during the particular season in any given year.

East of the Cascade Mts. it is generally only an uncommon transient in both spring and fall. The spring migration is from the last days of March to about the beginning of the last third of May. Most transients are noted in the latter half of April and early May. The large lakes of Klamath Co., Harney Co., and especially Lake Co. sometimes have concentrations of over 300 birds. Lake Co. flocks have exceeded a thousand individuals. Three thousand were estimated at Abert L., Lake Co., on April 28, 1994. The status of the species in fall east of the Cascades is presently mired in some controversy. Based on the best evidence currently available to us the species is a very rare transient in July, August, and until the last days of September; and an uncommon transient from the last days of September or early October to the latter part of November. Most east of the Cascade reports are from October. There are a few December records into the latter half of that month.

Stilt Sandpiper. *Calidris himantopus.*

Rare to very rare fall transient.

In the last 20 years the Stilt Sandpiper has proven to be of annual occurrence during fall migration in Oregon. The normal migratory path of this species is east of the Rocky Mountains, but small numbers are encountered every fall in Oregon. It has occurred in almost every part of the state.

Numbers vary considerably depending on the year, with only a few birds noted some years. In the best years as many as several dozen have been found. Adults are occasionally noted from early July (July 5, Clatsop Co.), and have been seen as late as September 18 (Tillamook Co.). Most records from Oregon are of juvenile birds. The earliest record is August 2 (Clatsop Co.), the latest October 22 (Coos Co.). Most birds are seen from late August through the first days of October.

Curlew Sandpiper. *Calidris ferruginea.*

Vagrant.

This vagrant from Eurasia has been recorded at least five times in Oregon, all but one of the birds were adults in at least partial breeding plumage: July 21, 1976, Yaquina Bay; Aug. 16, 1976, Seven Devils Wayside, Coos Co.; July 25-30, 1985, Bandon, Coos Co.; Aug. 17-18, 1985, Tillamook Bay; and Aug. 20-25, 1985, Tillamook Bay.

Buff-breasted Sandpiper. *Tryngites subruficollis.*

Vagrant.

The Buff-breasted Sandpiper occurs in very small numbers almost annually during the fall migration. Most records are from along the coast, where it has been found along open beaches, on the drier edges of estuaries, in short grass and plowed fields, at airports, and at sparsely vegetated sand flats behind coastal fore dunes.

Numbers vary considerably in number from year to year. In some years over a dozen have been reported. In others only one or two are found. Small concentrations of six or seven have been reported on several occasions. All of the fall birds reported from Oregon appear to have been in juvenile plumage. The earliest record is for August 15. The latest is for October 17. There is one spring record, a bird in a field near Tillamook on April 12, 1981.

The species is even more rare inland in western Oregon. There are several records from Sauvie I., the Willamette Valley, and the Rogue Valley. All of these are within the same time frames as the coastal occurrences. The only record from east of the Cascades is of a bird near Prineville, Crook Co., from Sept. 23 through Oct. 5, 1990.

Ruff. *Philomachus pugnax*

Vagrant.

This primarily Old World species is a fall vagrant, but has also occurred in spring, and there is one winter record. Numbers vary considerably from year to year. In a good year there may be five to eight reported. In some years there are only one or two reported. Most Oregon records have been of juvenile birds. Although most Oregon records are of individuals, as many as four birds have been seen together. Most records are from the coast. Inland records are from Sauvie I., where one to several have occurred almost annually in recent years; and from Summer L., Lake Co.

Fall adults have occurred from July 26 to August 11. Juveniles in fall have occurred from August 11 to October 11. Most records of juveniles have been noted in the last week of August to the end of the third week of September.

There are two spring records: April 12, 1991, Summer L., Lake Co., and June 2, 1984, Tillamook Co. The winter record is from the Coquille Valley, Coos Co., on Jan. 18, 1980.

Short-billed Dowitcher. *Limnodromus griseus.*

Common transient along the coast in spring and fall. Uncommon to rare spring and an uncommon to fairly common fall transient through the interior valleys of western Oregon. Rare spring and fall transient east of the Cascade Mts.

The Short-billed Dowitcher is a common transient along the coast in spring and fall. Numbers in Oregon do not approach the concentrations in the large bays of Washington, but the species visits almost all of the Oregon estuaries, and also to a lesser extent uses wet and plowed fields, and fresh water habitats. Spring migrants are sometimes noted in the last days of March, and are common from mid-April through about the first week of May. A few transients are sometimes noted as late as the mid-May. A few fall migrants may appear in the last week of June, but it is more typical for the vanguard to be noted during the first week of July. Most adults move through Oregon by the third week of July, and a few are sometimes still present in mid-August when the juvenile birds begin to appear. The peak of the migration of juveniles is in the last two weeks of August and the first week of September. Numbers decline rather rapidly after early September. By October few are left. There are very few November records. None of the few reported in winter have been verified, although some reports may be correct.

In the interior valleys of western Oregon the Short-billed Dowitcher is an uncommon to rare spring transient and an uncommon to fairly common fall transient within a similar migratory time table to that along the coast. Fall adults are rare inland. Only the occasional adult individual or small flock has been noted inland in fall. The species is not usually noted until the latter third of August when juvenile birds arrive from the north.

East of the Cascade Mts. the Short-billed Dowitcher is a rare transient in both spring and fall, with spring records from the last week of April to the latter third of May, and fall records from the first week of July to the third week of September.

Long-billed Dowitcher. *Limnodromus scolopaceus.*

Common transient in spring and fall statewide. Uncommon in winter along the coast and in the interior valleys of western Oregon. Rare in winter east of the Cascade Mts.

The Long-billed Dowitcher is a common transient throughout Oregon in both spring and fall. Transients begin arriving from the south as early as late February or early March along the coast. The peak of the spring migration inland west of the Cascades is from mid-April through mid-May. Only an occasional straggler is sometimes located into the last week of May or the first week of June. East of the Cascades the peak of the migration is in the first half of May.

In fall, the earliest migrants are sometimes noted in the last days of June, but more typically are found in early July. August numbers at Malheur N.W.R. sometimes have exceeded 30,000. Large flocks also use the lakes of Lake and Klamath Cos., and Sauvie I. The species is common through October, but drops off rapidly after that month east of the Cascade Mts. West of the Cascades it remains common through November. It is generally uncommon, but rare in many areas, in the lowlands of western Oregon in winter. East of the Cascades there are a few records into December and January. A Feb. 22, 1975 record from Malheur N.W.R. was probably an early spring arrival.

The Long-billed Dowitcher is primarily a bird of fresh water habitats, but it will also use brackish and even salt water habitats as well. It feeds in shallow ponds, mud flats, flooded fields, estuaries, and similar habitats where it can probe in soft mud for its prey.

Common Snipe. *Gallinago gallinago.*

Common summer resident east of the Cascade Mts. and in the Cascade Mts. Uncommon and local summer resident west of the Cascades. Common transient spring and fall statewide. Common to uncommon winter resident at lower elevations west of the Cascade Mts. Generally uncommon east of the Cascade Mts. in winter.

The Common Snipe is a common summer resident east of the Cascades. West of the Cascades it is a local and uncommon summer resident in the Willamette Valley and in suitable habitat in the Cascade Mts. Nesting takes place in wet meadows and marshes of sedge or grass; and to a lesser extent where cattail marshes provide openings or edges.

As a transient in spring or fall it can be found almost anywhere in the state. Presumed fall migrants are sometimes noted away from breeding sites in mid-July. Breeding birds in the great wetlands of Klamath, Lake, and Harney Cos. typically arrive between the first week of March to the last third of March depending on the elevation and weather.

In winter the Common Snipe is generally uncommon to locally common at lower elevations along the coast and in the inland valleys. There has been a significant decrease in the species in the last two decades. East of the Cascade Mts. in winter it is generally uncommon, but can be more scarce or absent over vast areas during very cold weather. In winter, wet or damp fields, and marshes are used. Although the species has a decided preference to fresh water habitats, brackish habitats are also utilized.

Wilson's Phalarope. *Phalaropus tricolor.*

Common summer resident and transient east of the Cascade Mts.; very rare summer resident west of the Cascade Mts. Rare transient along the coast and in the inland valleys of western Oregon.

The Wilson's Phalarope is a common nesting bird of the marshes east of the Cascades, especially in the great marshes of Klamath, Lake and Harney Cos. Small marshes and wet meadows also provide suitable nesting situations. Smaller nesting populations occur elsewhere in many areas east of the Cascades. Transients occur widely at areas where breeding does not take place.

Significant breeding populations occur in the marshy lakes up to at least 5,000 ft. in the central Cascades, especially in Deschutes and Klamath Cos., but also in Douglas Co. It has probably nested at various marshes in the interior valleys of western Oregon in very small numbers some years.

Wilson's Phalarope typically arrives on the nesting areas during the last week of April, or the first two weeks of May. Migrants from the south have on rare occasions been noted as early as the first week of April. The arrival times are similar west of the Cascades, where the species is typically only a rare spring transient. The small numbers seen west of the Cascades are probably lost birds. More are seen west of the Cascades in the latter half of May and the first half of June, than during the time that is typical for migration east of the Cascades, a fact that also supports the conclusion that the birds west of the Cascades are vagrants rather than birds within the species normal migratory path.

The fall migration east of the Cascades begins very early. Obvious transients on the way south become evident by the latter half of June. Thousands congregate on some of the lakes of Harney and Lake Cos. from late June through mid-August. Few adults are in the state by the middle of July. Flocks of juveniles in late July to about mid-August have been estimated to be as high as 50,000 at Lake Abert, Lake Co., and to over 10,000 at Summer Lake, Lake Co. Large numbers also stage on the playas in the Harney Basin (Harney L., Boca L.). After mid-August numbers drop rapidly. By the end of the first week of September almost all are gone. A few stragglers are sometimes noted into the last week of September. The individual noted at Summer L. on Dec. 19, 1989 was an injured bird that had survived to that date during a mild early winter.

West of the Cascades the species is even more rare in fall than spring. Since non-breeders or transients have been noted at times in every week of June, it is hard to say exactly which birds are moving through to the south. There are records for every week from the first of July through September 18. Very few fall birds west of the Cascades are adults. In fall west of the Cascades it is usually seen individually, or exceptionally in small groups up to five.

Wilson's Phalarope nests in marshy and wet meadow habitats. Migrants use a variety of fresh water habitats. The alkaline lakes are heavily used in migration. The species forages much more readily on mud flats than do the other two phalaropes. Only rarely is an occasional bird seen on salt water habitats along the coast.

Red-necked Phalarope. *Phalaropus lobatus.*

Common transient spring and fall.

The Red-necked Phalarope is a common, sometimes abundant transient along the coast. Most transients pass off shore, up to several miles out. During stormy weather or when influenced by other conditions, very large numbers are seen on shore and from land. In addition to the open ocean they utilize the coastal estuaries, fresh water ponds, and sewage treatment ponds.

Most of the spring movement occurs in May, while fall migration is more extended, with records from late August through late November. Although there are a number of winter reports, the species is not proven to occur after early December.

Red Phalarope. *Phalaropus fulicaria.*

Common offshore transient in spring and fall. Status uncertain, but probably rare offshore most winters; but has been found to be common offshore during at least one winter. Irregular transient along the coast on shore and within the sight of land. Rare to very rare transient in fall, and very rare transient in spring inland.

Great numbers of this most pelagic of all shorebirds migrate off the coast in both spring and fall. Their migrations typically keep them far beyond the sight of land-based birders. Birding pelagic trips often locate the transients, but at times they are further at sea than the boats are able to navigate. On occasion, especially in the fall, large numbers flying over and swimming on the ocean are visible from land. This happens when strong storms move onshore, and less frequently when their food supply is disrupted by changes in water temperatures or perhaps other factors. Small numbers are sometimes found along the coast even during normal conditions.

The species is a rather late migrant in spring. Obvious migrants have been noted as early as the middle of April, but the normal migration is from early May through about the first week of June. Some transients have been noted even into the third week of June. Since an occasional bird has been noted in every week of June and July, there are sometimes questions as to whether an individual bird is summering, or if a transient, which way it is going. Small numbers of southbound adults have been noted as early as the middle third of July, and concentrations of up to several thousand have been noted by the latter third of July. Juvenile birds begin arriving in the last week of August, and in some years what are believed to still be transients have been recorded into the first half of January. Large numbers, sometimes in the thousands, have been recorded from the latter part of September through the middle of December.

There are a few scattered records for coastal areas for the latter half of January, February and March. A strong storm on Jan. 18, 1986 brought many to the coast, so at least that year the species was apparently wintering off the coast in considerable numbers. Its normal status offshore in winter is unknown, but it is probably absent most winters.

Inland the Red Phalarope is a very rare transient in spring both in the valleys of western Oregon and east of the Cascade Mts. Records east of the Cascades extend from the first week of May to the last week of June. All have been of individual birds, that have typically associated with other species of phalaropes. The 10 at the Kirtland Sewage Ponds, Jackson Co., on May 22, 1990 represents a very unusual spring record inland since it involved a flock of birds. The species is also rare to very rare inland on both sides of the Cascades in fall, with extreme dates from July 24 to at December 22. The powerful Pacific storms that sometimes cause large number to appear along the coast also on occasion bring birds inland, particularly to locations west of the Cascades. Such storms usually occur from late October to early December, but have also brought birds inland in spring as well.

Although while in Oregon the Red Phalarope is primarily a bird of the open ocean, during other occasions it is found in almost any wetland habitat. Like other phalaropes, when away from the ocean it is particularly attracted to nutrient-rich sewage treatment ponds.

Family Laridae

Pomarine Jaeger. *Stercorarius pomarinus.*

Fairly common fall and rare spring transient offshore. Occasionally observed from shore. Vagrant inland.

The Pomarine Jaeger is most frequently observed more than five miles offshore, but occasionally birds occur in estuaries and along beaches, particularly after storms. At sea it is usually more abundant than the Parasitic Jaeger. Many can be found around large fishing vessels where they pirate food from congregating gulls. Fall transients have been recorded from July 14 to November 17, but the greatest number are observed in late August and September.

Inland records include two birds at Fern Ridge Res. on Nov. 10, 1975, following a storm with fierce westerly winds, and one at McNary Dam, Umatilla Co., on Sept. 2, 1985. The late date of the Fern Ridge record suggests that a few transients may regularly be offshore into November.

During the winter it is a rare visitor, and records include Dec. 10, 1987, Jan. 3, 1987 and Jan. 19, 1986 at Yaquina Bay, Lincoln Co.; Dec. 30, 1983 at Florence, Lane Co.; and Dec. 15, 1990 at Tillamook Bay. In spring it is a rare transient off the coast from late April to the end of May, only very rarely seen from shore.

Parasitic Jaeger. *Stercorarius parasiticus.*

Uncommon spring and fairly common fall offshore transient. Regularly observed along the coast. Rare inland.

The Parasitic Jaeger is the jaeger most frequently observed on the Oregon coast. A few are sighted each year from headlands, along beaches, and in estuaries. It generally migrates closer to shore than other jaegers, and during pelagic trips is seen most often within 10 miles of land. There are a few records for June and July, indicating that some may spend the summer off Oregon.

Parasitic Jaegers are seen most often from late August through early October, with the migration peaking in September. There are numerous fall records for lakes and reservoirs in the Willamette Valley, those often occurring following storms with strong westerly winds. The latest inland record was six individuals observed on three Lane Co. reservoirs on Nov. 10, 1975, after a violent storm. The latest coastal record was one observed Dec. 3, 1977, on Tillamook Bay.

Little research has been conducted off the Oregon coast in winter, but such late sightings of Parasitic Jaegers indicates that a few may regularly occur into the winter. There are about 40 records for east of the Cascade Mts. falling between July 5 and October 18. Most of these records are from Malheur N.W.R. where as many as 20 individuals were present in September 1985.

Parasitic Jaegers are far less frequently observed in spring than in fall. Birds have been noted along the coast and offshore from April 9 to May 31, and dead birds have been found on beaches March 3 and March 30. The infrequency of spring ornithological ventures offshore has limited our understanding of the migrations of many species, but information from California and Washington corroborates that Parasitic Jaegers are less abundant in spring than in fall. Many pelagic transients follow this pattern, and it is possible that in spring these species migrate farther offshore, resulting in their infrequent detection by birdwatching cruises which seldom go more than 20 miles from shore.

Long-tailed Jaeger. *Stercorarius longicaudus.*

Uncommon fall and rare spring offshore transient. Very rarely observed from shore. Vagrant inland.

The Long-tailed Jaeger is usually observed beyond 10 miles from land, preferring the relatively warm waters that occur farther offshore. Fall transients have been observed between July 13 and October 15, but most sightings occur in late August and September.

Long-tailed Jaegers are very rare inland in fall, and there are no inland spring records. Following a storm with strong westerly winds two were observed at Fern Ridge Res., Lane Co., on Aug. 30, 1977. Two were noted Sept. 19, 1978, over the

Columbia R. near Umatilla, Umatilla Co.; one was at Fern Ridge Res. on July 21, 1987; one was at Haystack Res., Jefferson Co., on Aug. 30, 1987; and an immature was collected Aug. 14, 1976, in sagebrush desert in Harney Co. east of Steens Mt.

The only spring records are of a bird found dead on the coast near Boiler Bay, Lincoln Co., on May 8, 1976, and two seen May 31, 1976, at the Columbia R. mouth. Long-tailed Jaegers are undoubtedly regular spring transients far offshore.

South Polar Skua. *Catharacta maccormicki.*

Rare to very uncommon fall pelagic migrant. Very rarely observed from shore.

The South Polar Skua nests in the Southern Hemisphere and migrates north during our summer and fall to the west coast of North America. No specimens have been collected in Oregon, but several have been photographed.

This skua was first recorded in Oregon in the fall of 1972, and has been observed nearly every fall since. Skuas have been seen in Oregon between June 27 and October 7, though most are sighted after mid-August. The greatest number observed in a day was seven west of Newport, on Sept. 30, 1978. A late record is a bird found on the beach north of Florence, Lane Co., on Dec. 23, 1988. Skuas are usually observed more than 10 miles from shore, but there are also records nearer to shore and a few from headlands.

Laughing Gull. *Larus atricilla.*

Vagrant.

An adult in breeding plumage was photographed at Lower Klamath N.W.R., Klamath Co., on April 24, 1983.

Franklin's Gull. *Larus pipixcan.*

Breeds at Malheur N.W.R. and is common during summer in the Harney Basin. Locally very uncommon elsewhere in Harney and Malheur Cos. Rare in spring, summer, and fall in other counties east of the Cascades. Rare to very rare all seasons in western Oregon.

The Franklin's Gull was first recorded in Oregon in 1943 at Malheur N.W.R. The first pair was found nesting at Malheur L., in 1948. This colony has gradually increased, and in 1981, a record 1,330 pairs nested (Littlefield, 1990). The number varies considerably from one year to the next.

Franklin's Gulls arrive at Malheur N.W.R. in late April and early May, with the earliest date March 16. During the summer small flocks and individuals are widespread and fairly common in the Harney Basin, and occasionally are seen in the Alvord Basin and the Catlow Valley. Foraging flocks have been noted as far north as southern Grant Co. Small flocks, possibly of non-breeders, have also been observed during late June on agricultural lands in the Snake and Owyhee R. Valleys. Birds usually depart the Malheur L. colony during the first week of August, and most apparently leave the state at this time, though there is a January 13 record from Chickahominy Res. In recent years it has visited Lake and Klamath Cos. in increasing numbers during the same time periods in which it occurs in Harney Co. Franklin's Gulls frequent marshes, lake shores, and agricultural lands, especially when wet or recently plowed.

Outside the previously mentioned counties there are perhaps 30 scattered records for east of the Cascades. Most are recorded in late May and June, but birds have been observed as late as September 29.

Fall migrants are found nearly every year on the coast and in the interior valleys of western Oregon. There are records, usually of immatures, extending from early July to November 22. Adults are much less frequently encountered.

There are several winter records, generally immatures: Feb. 15, 1975, Dec. 20, 1977, and Dec. 20, 1988 at Yaquina Bay, Lincoln Co; one at the Monmouth sewage ponds during December of 1988; and one at Sauvie I., Multnomah Co., Feb. 14-16, 1985. There are about 15 spring records for west of the Cascades, ranging from early April to late May. These records are nearly evenly divided between the coast and interior valleys. Immatures have summered near Medford, Jackson Co., and Portland.

Little Gull. *Larus minutus.*

Vagrant.

There are five records of this primarily Eurasian species for Oregon. All except the Sherman Co. bird were adults: one at Yaquina Bay, Lincoln Co., Aug. 11 to at least early October, 1979; one at Tillamook Bay on Oct. 10, 1981; one at Yaquina Bay and the Nye Beach area Oct. 13 and 25, and on Dec. 15, 1981 (presumably the same bird); one at Tillamook Bay on Nov. 4, 1975; and one at the John Day Dam, Sherman Co., Nov. 21-28, 1989.

Common Black-headed Gull. *Larus ridibundus.*

Vagrant.

There are two records of this Palearctic species for Oregon, both adults: one near Astoria, Clatsop Co., on Dec. 20, 1981; and one at the Bay City sewage ponds, Tillamook Co., Dec. 3-19, 1992.

Bonaparte's Gull. *Larus philadelphia.*

Common spring and fall transient on the coast. Very uncommon to locally common transient inland on large bodies of water. Uncommon in summer and very uncommon in winter on the coast. Rare inland in summer and winter.

The Bonaparte's Gull is a common fall transient on the Oregon coast and an uncommon transient inland, though it is locally common near large bodies of water such as Upper Klamath L., and Fern Ridge Res. An influx of fall migrants is first noted in late July, and numbers increase gradually into October. The peak of migration is from late September through November but varies somewhat

131

from one year to another. Hundreds often occur on estuaries at this time. Inland, over 1,000 at one time have been recorded in late October and November in the Klamath Basin and at Fern Ridge Res.

On the coast, migrating Bonaparte's Gulls usually fly over the ocean within sight of land, but flocks, generally of fewer than 20 birds, have been observed as far as 40 miles from shore. Resting and feeding birds frequent estuaries, sewage ponds, flooded fields, and the near shore ocean. Inland birds are usually associated with large bodies of water.

By December nearly all birds have left the state, but a few occur on the coast during the winter and very rarely small numbers are found inland in western Oregon. The spring migration is often spectacular along the coast, but in some years numbers are much reduced, many birds apparently migrating over the ocean. Transients first appear in early April, peak during the first two weeks of May, and flocks continue to be seen into mid-June. In late April and early May over 500 per hour have often been observed flying north just offshore. Inland, Bonaparte's Gulls are very uncommon spring transients throughout most of the state, however in the Klamath Basin they are fairly common in some years.

Bonaparte's Gulls are rare inland during the summer, but may appear anywhere. Congregations of over 100 are occasionally noted in June at favored localities such as Upper Klamath L. Small flocks have been noted inland into early July. These flocks typically are comprised of immature birds, and may represent late spring transients or birds that ultimately summer south of the breeding grounds. They are uncommon along the coast in summer but a few are usually to be found at favored estuaries. Over 250 were at the mouth of the Columbia R. during the summer of 1978.

Heermann's Gull. *Larus heermanni.*

Common late summer and fall visitant along the coast. Vagrant inland.

Heermann's Gulls breed in early spring on islands off the Mexican coast and migrate north along the western North American coast in summer. They are common along the Oregon coast from mid-July through early November. Heermann's

Gulls are occasionally observed in Oregon in May, but more typically are first detected in late June. In recent years they have been noted earlier with more frequency. The northward migration usually peaks in the latter half of July when over 100 birds per hour are sometimes observed passing coastal promontories. An extremely heavy movement of over 500 birds per hour was noted passing Newport on July 28, 1979. Migrating Heermann's Gulls fly individually and in small flocks over beaches and just offshore. In Oregon they are almost always observed within a mile of shore.

In summer and fall they occur most frequently over the surf and beaches and at the mouths of estuaries. They are also seen regularly inside estuaries. Large numbers often rest on beaches with other gulls, especially California Gulls. Feeding birds are often found in association with cormorants and Brown Pelicans. Heermann's Gulls frequently congregate at the mouths of the larger rivers, and from mid-July to November there are often more than 200 at the Columbia R. mouth. Most of the birds found in Oregon are adults.

The southward migration begins in late September with few remaining by late November. The largest concentration recorded during the southward migration was an estimated 1,200 with other gulls on Sunset Beach, Clatsop Co., on Oct. 28, 1980. In some years a few are observed through late December.

There are about 12 inland records from the valleys of western Oregon. The record from Portland on Dec. 20, 1949 was also a late individual.

There are at least three records from east of the Cascades. One was on the Columbia R. at Mosier, Wasco Co., on Nov. 14, 1977; one was at Thompson Res., Lake Co., on Oct. 16, 1990; and one was at the mouth of the Deschutes R., Wasco and Sherman Cos., on Oct. 31, 1993.

Mew Gull. *Larus canus.*

Abundant winter visitant to the coast and common along the lower Columbia and Willamette Rivers; uncommon in the rest of the Willamette Valley. Very rare winter visitant to the Klamath Basin and to inland southwestern Oregon. Immatures are rare on coastal estuaries in summer.

Migrant Mew Gulls are first observed on the coast during late July, and increase gradually through September. The height of migration occurs from mid-October through early December, and during this period concentrations of 10,000 or more are occasionally noted, particularly in Tillamook Co. Mew Gulls also appear along the Columbia and Willamette Rivers at this time. They frequent estuaries, large rivers and pastures, and are rarely observed at sea more than a mile from shore.

Mew Gulls are abundant along the coast during winter and especially large concentrations occur on and around Tillamook Bay. They are common winter visitants along the lower Columbia and Willamette Rivers, often congregating on nearby agricultural fields and attending the spring smelt runs. In the Willamette Valley south of Oregon City, individuals and small groups are uncommon among flocks of other gulls. They are rare winter visitants to the Umpqua and Rogue Valleys.

East of the Cascades, the species follows the Columbia R. inland as far as Umatilla Co. There are also a few scattered records from elsewhere in eastern Oregon.

In March Mew Gulls begin migrating north and small numbers of migrants are noted through May. In recent years very small numbers of immatures have spent the summer at estuaries along the northern coast of Oregon.

Ring-billed Gull. *Larus delawarensis.*

Locally common near nesting colonies and fairly common elsewhere east of the Cascade Mts. during summer. Uncommon non-breeding summer visitant, and fairly common transient and winter visitant west of the Cascades. Very uncommon in winter east of the Cascades, except in the Klamath Basin and along the Columbia R. where fairly common.

Ring-billed Gulls share long-established as well as temporary breeding colonies with California Gulls in Lake, Klamath, and Harney Cos. Few of these colonies approach 500 pairs in size, and Ring-billed Gulls usually comprise less than 40 percent of nesters. Probably fewer than 1,500 pairs nest in the southeastern Oregon colonies. Along the Columbia R. 960 pairs nested on Miller Rocks, near the Deschutes R. mouth in Sherman Co., and 4,380 pairs nested at Three Mile Canyon I., near Boardman, Morrow Co., in 1977. These colonies have supported similar numbers in recent years. A small colony has been active near Baker City, Baker Co., since 1973. Ring-billed Gulls are increasing in population and expanding their breeding range in the Pacific Northwest.

Non-breeding adults and immatures are uncommon in western Oregon valleys and on coastal estuaries throughout the summer. East of the Cascades non-breeders are fairly common during summer at lakes, reservoirs, and rivers. In August and September, migrants from the Oregon colonies and from colonies east and north of the state are common at large bodies of water east of the Cascades. During this period most birds move west. From August through October they are common on the coast and in the inland valleys of western Oregon.

Ring-billed Gulls remain fairly common through winter in the Willamette Valley, where flocks of over 500 are occasionally observed on agricultural lands. In other interior western Oregon valleys they are generally uncommon. They are fairly common, though less abundant than in the Willamette Valley, in estuaries and on coastal pastures. Winter coastal flocks rarely exceed 100 birds, often mixed with Mew Gulls, and feed on flooded fields.

East of the Cascades they are very uncommon during winter except in the Klamath Basin and along the Columbia R., where their status varies with winter severity from fairly common to uncommon. Summer residents return to the Harney Co. colonies in late February and early March.

California Gull. *Larus californicus.*

Uncommon to locally common summer resident east of the Cascade Mts. Common near nesting colonies. Uncommon non-breeding summer visitant and rare to locally common winter visitant in western Oregon. Locally uncommon in winter east of the Cascades. Uncommon to locally common spring and fall transient throughout the state.

The California Gull breeds locally east of the Cascades in Lake, Klamath, and Harney Cos., and along the Columbia R. Colonies are located on islands in lakes and rivers, and usually also include Ring-billed Gulls. The Oregon breeding population is poorly understood due to the inaccessibility of colony sites, the widely fluctuating size of colonies, and the constant shifting of colonies from one location to another. In recent years over 2,000 pairs have nested in the Klamath Basin, Klamath Co., and over 500 pairs have nested in the Harney Basin. There are several islands in the Columbia R. east of the Cascades that support colonies. The Columbia R. population is currently estimated at over 5,000 pairs. There is also a small colony near Baker City, Baker Co. Non-breeding summer visitants are locally uncommon to common on estuaries and large bodies of water throughout the state.

California Gulls begin leaving the nesting colonies in late June, and in July and August are locally common throughout Oregon as birds move toward the coast. Many of these migrants breed in central Canada and in the north-central United States, and apparently use the Columbia R. as a major migration route. From August to October this is the most common gull offshore; large numbers occur to at least 70 miles from land. Concentrations of thousands are occasionally observed on the coast from July to October. A heavy southward migration is observed along the coast from July through October and occasionally later.

In winter California Gulls are found throughout the state. East of the Cascades they are locally uncommon near large bodies of water, though in severe winters when waters freeze they may be rare in all areas except the Klamath Basin. They are uncommon to locally common in winter on the Columbia R. and in the Willamette Valley, where flocks of 100 or more occasionally gather on agricultural land, golf courses, and even lawns. They are uncommon in winter along the coast, and are absent from many areas along the coast in winter.

Migrating adults are abundant on the coast and along the Columbia R. in March and April, often flying in small flocks. In March thousands congregate on the Columbia R. during the smelt runs. Spring migrants are locally common inland and often follow rivers north. A moderate northward movement of birds that are probably non-breeders occurs along the coast during late May and June.

Herring Gull. *Larus argentatus.*

Uncommon to common spring and fall transient on the coast. Uncommon to fairly common winter visitor on the coast, offshore, in the Willamette Valley, and along the lower Columbia R. Rare elsewhere in fall, winter, and spring.

Migrant Herring Gulls are first observed on the Oregon coast in late August, and very rarely by early August. Numbers increase gradually into October and November, when they are fairly common. Very heavy migrations are noted in some years between mid-October and mid-November, when great streams of this and other species pass along beaches and past promontories. An increase in numbers is infrequently observed following strong fall and winter gales. The number along the coast is reduced by December, and they are uncommon in winter. Occasionally they are fairly common at garbage dumps and on estuaries, though the large numbers recorded on some coastal Christmas Bird Counts should probably be viewed with suspicion.

At sea Herring Gulls are fairly common in fall and spring. They are common offshore in winter and sometimes are the most abundant gull. They occur regularly to at least 700 miles from shore.

Herring Gulls are locally fairly common in winter along the lower Columbia R. and in the northern Willamette Valley. They have been observed in these areas as early as late August, but large numbers do not arrive until October. Many congregate at refuse dumps, and flocks of over 500 have been observed gathered on fields in the Portland area and on Sauvie I. They are uncommon in the southern Willamette Valley, except near Eugene, where they are fairly common.

Elsewhere inland during winter, they are uncommon along the Columbia R. east of The Dalles Dam and uncommon in the Klamath Basin. It is a rare to very rare transient and winter visitant to larger bodies of water elsewhere east of the Cascades, away from the Columbia R. The species is apparently only a rare visitant to the Rogue and Umpqua Valleys.

During the March smelt runs birds may be fairly common along the Columbia R. but numbers are much reduced after mid-April, the latest departing by mid-May. Northbound migrants are common along the coast during April and May in some

137

years, while uncommon in others. Several worn-plumaged immatures have been noted in July in Tillamook Co., and it is possible that very small numbers occasionally summer on the coast.

Thayer's Gull. *Larus thayeri.*

Fairly common fall and spring transient on the coast. Uncommon winter visitant to the coast, and fairly common winter visitant to the lower Columbia R. and the Willamette Valley. Rare elsewhere.

The Thayer's Gull was considered a subspecies of the Herring Gull until 1973, when it was designated a full species. Prior to 1973 little information had been gathered on its distribution and abundance in Oregon. The taxonomic status of this and several other large *Larus* gulls is still being debated.

Migrating Thayer's Gulls are first noted on the coast in late September, but it is mid-October before they are observed regularly. There is an exceptional early record of August 22 in Tillamook Co. In the Willamette Valley they are rarely noted before mid-November. Most coastal transients are gone by December.

Thayer's Gulls are uncommon in winter on the coast, but inland they are fairly common on Sauvie I. and in the Portland area, where they occur primarily on lawns, agricultural lands, and at refuse dumps. Concentrations of several hundred have been recorded. Lesser numbers regularly winter in the Salem and Eugene areas of the Willamette Valley. It is rare in winter in the Klamath Basin, and other eastern Oregon records include one from Haystack Res., Jefferson Co., on Feb. 16, 1991, and one at Umatilla, Umatilla Co., on Nov. 11, 1992. This species has been found well offshore in California and probably also occurs in small numbers off the Oregon coast.

The height of spring migration on the coast occurs in March and early April, with some noted into May. Few remain in the Willamette Valley by April, and hundreds are attracted to the smelt runs on the Columbia R. in late February and March.

Slaty-backed Gull. *Larus schistisagus.*

Vagrant.

A large gull flock on Sauvie I., Multnomah Co., contained several Slaty-backed Gulls in the winter of 1992-93. One adult was first located December 27 and sightings continued to March 20. At least two adults were present, and as many as four adults and two subadults of distinct plumage patterns were reported. Photographs of some of these birds were obtained.

Western Gull. *Larus occidentalis.*

Common permanent resident along the coast. Rare to uncommon winter visitant on the lower Columbia R. and in the Willamette Valley. Very rare elsewhere.

During the breeding season the Western Gull is the most abundant gull on the Oregon coast. Nearly all steep headlands and offshore rocks are utilized for nesting. A small number of nests are located on pilings, channel markers, and bridge supports. A comprehensive survey of the Oregon population conducted in 1979 counted 4,950 breeding pairs (Varoujean and Pitman 1979). Seven colony sites supported nearly half the population, each of these with between 250 and 550 pairs: Haystack Rock, Clatsop Co.; Three Arch Rocks and Haystack Rock, Tillamook Co.; Table Rock, Coos Co.; and Island Rock, Hunter's I. and Goat I., Curry Co.

Throughout the year Western Gulls are fairly common at sea within 50 miles of shore, but are rarely noted beyond 70 miles. Young birds disperse widely. Birds banded in Oregon have been recovered both north and south of the state. Western Gulls banded in California have been found in Oregon.

During August and September, Western Gulls are far outnumbered by California Gulls, and from November through winter the Glaucous-winged Gull is more common. In October and November many adults and immatures migrate south along the coast. In winter Western Gulls are less abundant than in summer, though still common. Small numbers of adults and immatures occur along the lower Columbia R. and in the Portland area during fall and winter. A few are noted nearly every year in the Eugene area, but are very rare elsewhere in western Oregon interior valleys.

East of the Cascades, the Western Gull occurs rarely up the Columbia R. to at least John Day Dam, and there are several records from Umatilla Co. A specimen was taken near Klamath Falls (date unknown) that had been banded on the Farallon Is., California, and there are at least two other records from the Klamath Basin. Another was seen at Summer Lake, Lake Co., on Nov. 11, 1989.

The breeding subspecies for the Oregon coast is *L. o. occidentalis*. Individuals of the more southerly race (*L. o. wymani*) are very rarely found along the coast. Hybrids between the Western Gull and the Glaucous-winged Gull are common in Oregon, especially in winter, and are much more common inland than pure Western Gulls.

Glaucous-winged Gull. *Larus glaucescens.*

Local breeder. In winter abundant on the coast and lower Columbia R., fairly common in the Willamette Valley, and uncommon in the interior valleys of southwestern Oregon.

The Glaucous-winged Gull is at the southern extreme of its breeding range in Oregon. The largest breeding colony in Oregon is at the mouth of the Columbia R. on Sand Island, where over 360 pairs were estimated in 1975. From the mouth of the Columbia R. south to Yaquina Bay, there are probably fewer than 100 pairs scattered among colonies of Western Gulls; a coastal survey in 1988 found at total of 376 breeding birds.

Remarkably, breeding has occurred inland along the Columbia R. east of the Cascade Mts. In 1974, three pairs were observed among the California and Ring-billed Gulls at the Little Memaloose Island gull colony and four pairs were noted at the California and Ring-billed Gull colony on Miller Rocks, Sherman Co., which lie upstream from the mouth of the Deschutes R. in the Columbia. A few pairs were observed at the Miller Rocks colony each year through at least 1987, and have been seen locally through 1994. A pair of presumed Western X Glaucous-winged Gull hybrids nested on a piling at Willamette Falls, Clackamas Co. in 1993.

140

Non-breeders are uncommon along the entire coast and offshore in summer and are regularly observed on the Columbia R. as far east as the John Day Dam, Sherman Co., and occasionally farther. Non-breeders are also found sparingly in the Portland area during summer.

In September migrants from the north begin arriving in Oregon. The greatest numbers of migrants are observed in October and November. Many are transients that winter south of Oregon. In winter Glaucous-winged Gulls are abundant on the coast, on the Columbia R. as far east as Bonneville Dam, Multnomah Co., and in the Portland area. They are common on the Columbia R. east of Bonneville Dam to at least the John Day Dam. They are fairly common in the Willamette Valley south of Portland. In the interior valleys of southwestern Oregon they are uncommon. One was observed at Malheur N.W.R. on Dec. 19, 1988, one was at Farewell Bend, Malheur Co., on Nov. 16, 1987, and small numbers are regularly observed in the Klamath Basin.

Concentrations of several thousand are sometimes observed in the winter on the coast and along the lower Columbia R. during the early spring smelt run. Glaucous-winged Gulls are the most common bird on the open ocean in winter and are occasionally common 100 miles offshore. Wintering birds migrate in March, April, and early May. Northward migrants are often observed passing by coastal headlands in large numbers.

Glaucous-winged Gulls frequently interbreed with Western and Herring Gulls in areas where their ranges overlap. Hybrids with intermediate characteristics are regularly observed in Oregon. In addition, an occasional apparent hybrid with the Glaucous Gull is noted.

Glaucous Gull. *Larus hyperboreus.*

Rare winter visitant to the coast and the Willamette Valley. Very rare east of the Cascade Mts.

Glaucous Gulls are rare during winter on the Oregon coast, offshore, and in the Willamette Valley. Numbers vary greatly from year to year. During the winter of

1992-1993 there were several dozen on Sauvie I. alone. Most observations involve the nearly white second-winter immatures, but the pale brown first-winter birds are being seen with greater frequency. Fully adult birds are very scarce. Occasional reports from June and July may pertain to worn-plumaged immature Glaucous-winged Gulls. Glaucous Gulls are typically found at large bodies of water, open ocean beaches, on agricultural lands, and at garbage dumps.

Glaucous Gulls typically occur in Oregon from December through March. The species has been recorded as early as mid-October, and there are a number of May records. One was photographed at Tillamook Bay on June 20, 1982.

There are about six winter records of individuals east of the Cascades.

Black-legged Kittiwake. *Rissa tridactyla.*

Fairly common transient and uncommon winter visitant offshore. Uncommon and irregular transient and winter visitant along the coast. Uncommon and irregular summer visitant along the coast and offshore. Vagrant inland.

The Black-legged Kittiwake occurs primarily far offshore in Oregon but exceptional concentrations have been observed in May and June at the mouth of the Columbia R. The largest concentration recorded in the state was 1,000 observed June 20, 1965, at the Columbia R. mouth.

Away from the Columbia R., Black-legged Kittiwakes are occasionally seen within the larger estuaries but are typically very uncommon on the coast and offshore during summer. Small numbers of subadults, and to a far lesser extent adults, are non-breeding summer visitants along the coast.

The fall migration is seldom obvious, but increased numbers are observed from September through November. Occasionally birds are observed migrating with other gulls along the coastline.

The number wintering in Oregon fluctuates widely from year to year, but typically small numbers are observed on beaches and from coastal promontories. Small numbers also occur offshore in winter, and during some winters many dead kittiwakes are washed onto Northwest beaches, usually following storms. From late January through March, 1976, as many as 35 dead birds per mile were found on Oregon beaches. The largest concentration of Black-legged Kittiwakes observed during winter in Oregon was 200 recorded at the Columbia R. mouth on Feb. 24, 1977. Another large number was 165 on the Yaquina Bay CBC in 1986.

The spring migration is conspicuous in some years, while unobserved during others. Heavy northward migrations have been noted from early April through early June. As many as 200 birds per hour have been observed passing the Columbia R. mouth in late May and early June.

Black-legged Kittiwakes are very rarely found in the Willamette Valley following fall and winter storms. In addition, a bird was observed east of the Cascade Mts. at Heppner, Morrow Co., on Nov. 12, 1967, and one was observed on Sauvie I., on Aug. 25, 1977.

Red-legged Kittiwake. *Rissa brevirostris.*

Vagrant.

There are seven records of the Red-legged Kittiwake for Oregon, all but one have been of individual birds dead found dead or injured on ocean beaches. All have been adults: Cannon Beach, Clatsop Co., on Dec. 30, 1981; Rockaway, Tillamook Co. on Jan. 16, 1989; at Lincoln City, Lincoln Co.; on Jan. 24, 1982 at Sunset Beach, Clatsop Co.; on Jan. 28, 1933; near Nehalem, Tillamook Co. on March 12, 1955; near Waldport, Lincoln Co. on March 25, 1951; and a live bird photographed on the railing of a fishing boat 15 nautical miles west of Tillamook Head, Clatsop Co. on Aug. 7, 1983. The number of specimens involved hints that the species may be somewhat more frequent off the Oregon coast in winter than current evidence indicates. Too few bird observers get offshore in the winter to have an accurate indication of the birdlife at that season.

Ross' Gull. *Rhodostethia rosea.*

Vagrant.

There is a single record of this species for Oregon, a winter-plumage bird that frequented Yaquina Bay, Lincoln Co., from Feb. 18 to March 1, 1987. Many photographs were obtained.

Sabine's Gull. *Xema sabini.*

Uncommon to fairly common spring and fall transient offshore, rarely observed from land. Very rare transient inland.

The Sabine's Gull is an uncommon to fairly common transient offshore during both spring and fall. Only rarely have as many as 50 been noted in a day on pelagic birding trips, although several hundred have been seen in a day when observers are fortunate enough to hit the height of migration. Rarely birds are seen from coastal promontories, beaches, or jetties, or on ponds, estuaries, or ocean beaches.

Autumn records fall between July 21 and Nov. 20, with the height of the migration in late August and September. Exceptionally late individuals, probably transients, were off Cape Arago, Coos Co. on Dec. 17, 1978, and Dec. 20, 1981, and at the S. Jetty of the Columbia R. on Dec. 15, 1979. There is also a late winter record, one in breeding plumage at Yaquina Bay, Lincoln Co., on Feb. 22, 1992. The northward migration occurs in May and early June.

Sabine's Gull is a very rare transient inland on both sides of the Cascades, with at least 20 inland records. Most occurrences fall between early September and late November, with one record near Medford, Jackson Co., May 3, 1993.

Caspian Tern. *Sterna caspia.*

East of the Cascade Mts. locally fairly common summer resident near nesting colonies and locally fairly common to rare transient and summer visitant elsewhere. On the coast, common transient and fairly common in summer at the Columbia R. mouth. Uncommon but increasing transient through inland western Oregon.

144

The Caspian Tern nests very locally east of the Cascades, usually on barren islands in association with gull colonies. The largest Oregon colony is on Three Mile I., in the Columbia R. of Morrow Co., where in recent years 210-220 pairs have nested. Historically, it was a regular summer resident on the large lakes of Klamath, Lake, and Harney Cos. but since 1960 only small colonies have been recorded. There is also a small colony on an island in the Snake R. north of Ontario, Malheur Co. Non-breeders are rare to locally uncommon in summer around large bodies of water east of the Cascades.

Non-breeders summer at the mouth of the Columbia R. annually, and in some years as many as 300 may be present. Small numbers of non-breeders have also been observed summering at other estuaries on the coast. A few nest on Sand I. in the mouth of the Columbia R. At Howard Prairie Res., Jackson Co., as many as six birds have been observed during recent summers but there is no evidence of nesting. In recent years small numbers of non-breeders have been noted at various locations along the coast.

Oregon birds depart breeding colonies in late June and July. Transients are observed throughout the state migrating individually and in small flocks from late June through October. Adults in fall are often followed by begging juveniles.

East of the Cascades transients are locally fairly common to rare near large bodies of water, and are especially common along the Columbia R. The fall migration peaks in late July and August. One at Sunriver, Deschutes Co., on Nov. 18, 1974 is a late record for east of the Cascade Mts.

Fall transients are common along the coast, where they occur in estuaries and over the ocean near shore. The coastal migration begins in late June, and peaks from mid-July through early September. Very small numbers sometimes persist into November. The origin of most coastal migrants is probably the large colonies on the Washington coast, which were first established in the late 1950s. Before this time transients were rarely recorded on the Oregon coast. In inland western Oregon fall transients were rare until about fifteen years ago. Since then the species has become regular, and while still generally uncommon, numbers at Sauvie I. sometimes exceed a hundred birds. It is now of regular occurrence in fall at almost any of the large lakes and reservoirs of western Oregon. Transients also follow the Columbia R. from inland nesting sites to the ocean.

Spring transients are common on the coast, first appearing in late March and peaking in April, during which as many as 35 birds per hour have been noted passing coastal points. The species is generally very scarce along the coast, away from the Columbia R. mouth, by the end of May. East of the Cascades spring transients are locally common and the migration occurs slightly later than on the coast. The average arrival date at Malheur N.W.R. is May 8, and the earliest record is March 30. In inland western Oregon where spring transients are rare, late migrants have been observed in early June.

Elegant Tern. *Sterna elegans.*

Irregular post-breeding visitant along the coast.

The Elegant Tern was first recorded in Oregon during the El Niño warming of the Pacific during the summer of 1983. The first record was at Coos Bay when 29 were found on Aug. 7, 1983. Hundreds were later found the length of the coast, with peak numbers in the second week of September. As many as 225 were at the mouth of the Rogue R., Curry Co., at that time. Some stayed until mid-October.

Including 1983, invasions have occurred in seven out of the last 11 years, with varying numbers apparently keyed to water temperature. Timing has generally followed the pattern of the original occurrence. Warm water in 1990 and 1992 brought large numbers to the state.

Common Tern. *Sterna hirundo.*

Fairly common spring and fall transient along the coast. Very uncommon fall transient inland. Very rare spring transient inland.

The Common Tern is a fairly common transient on the coast, where it occurs on beaches, in estuaries, and over the ocean near shore. The spring migration some-times extends from late April to early June, but the greatest numbers are observed during the first three weeks of May. The latest spring record is June 17, 1976,

146

when 25 were noted at the Columbia R. mouth. During some springs few Common Terns are noted, but during other years as many as 500 per hour have been observed steadily flying north along the coast in early and mid-May. There are fewer than ten inland records during the spring.

The fall migration occurs from late July through October. The greatest numbers are observed in September and early October, when flocks of up to 400 have been noted in the large estuaries. Inland, fall transients are very uncommon to rare, occurring both east and west of the Cascades. In the interior they frequent lakes, reservoirs, and larger rivers. The latest Oregon fall record was one in Lincoln Co. on Nov. 24, 1986.

Difficulty in the identification of the three *Sterna* terns, Common, Arctic, and Forster's, has made the reliability of many records suspect and confuses our understanding of the distribution and abundance of these species.

Arctic Tern. *Sterna paradisaea.*

Fairly common pelagic transient, rare transient along coast. Vagrant inland.

The Arctic Tern is primarily an offshore transient, occurring in small flocks or as individuals. Only rarely have more than 50 birds been noted in a day. Small numbers are rarely found along the coast, usually with Common Terns on beaches and in estuaries.

The heaviest fall movement is in late August and September, but birds have been reported from mid-July to mid-October with a late date of Nov. 13. Inland it is very rare as a transient within the same time frame as it occurs along the coast.

It has been less frequently observed from land in spring. Spring numbers are usually small, but hundreds could be seen in a day in mid- and late May, 1976, a year which also had unprecedented high numbers of Red Phalaropes at coastal locations during the spring migration.

The spring migratory period for the Arctic Tern is from early May until the end of May. In 1978, 15 were near Tillamook Bay, Tillamook Co., on April 9, with smaller numbers noted through that month. There are no acceptable inland records for spring.

Recent inland records include two at Sauvie I., Multnomah Co., on July 19, 1990; one at Wamic, Wasco Co., on June 30, 1991; and one at Mt. Vernon, Grant Co., on June 14, 1992.

Forster's Tern. *Sterna forsteri.*

Locally common near nesting colonies, but generally uncommon to rare summer resident and transient east of the Cascade Mts. Rare transient and non-breeding summer visitant west of Cascade Mts.

The Forster's Tern is a widespread summer resident east of the Cascades. Colonies are fairly common on the large, shallow lakes and marshes of Klamath, Lake, Harney, and southwestern Deschutes Cos. Small numbers are observed in summer on the Columbia R. from The Dalles Dam, eastward, but the only known breeding colony on the river is at Three Mile I., Morrow Co. Elsewhere east of the Cascades small colonies are widely scattered on large marshes and lakes. During summer, non-breeding birds are often observed over large bodies of water where no colonies exist. In some recent years they have been observed west of the Cascades at Fern Ridge Res., but there is no evidence of nesting.

Migration southward is first observed in early July. In mid-August as many as 3,000 may gather at Malheur N.W.R., where some remain through mid-September. Fall transients are fairly common and widespread over bodies of water east of the Cascade Mts. The latest Oregon record is one observed Oct. 20, 1971, at Malheur N.W.R., though late fall records are suspect due to possible confusion with migrant Common Terns.

West of the Cascade Mts. the Forster's Tern is a very rare fall transient. Individuals and small flocks are most frequently observed in the southern Willamette and Rogue Valleys. In some years a few transients are recorded in the northern Willamette Valley, on the lower Columbia R., or along the coast.

Spring migration peaks in Oregon from late April through mid-May. The earliest arrival dates are April 14 in the Klamath Basin and April 15 at Malheur N.W.R. Spring migrants and transients are widespread east of the Cascade Mts.

Spring transients are very rare in inland valleys west of the Cascades. Most are recorded in late May and early June, but records extend through June. Some reports from western Oregon may pertain to similar *Sterna* tern species.

Least Tern. *Sterna antillarum.*

Vagrant.

The endangered West Coast population of the Least Tern breeds as far north as San Francisco Bay, California. There are three Oregon records: two were collected near the S. Jetty of the Columbia R., Clatsop Co., on May 21, 1964; one was photographed there on May 31, 1976; and four were at the S. Jetty of the Siuslaw R., Lane Co., on Aug. 19, 1973.

Black Tern. *Chlidonias niger.*

East of the Cascade Mts. a locally common summer resident and uncommon widespread transient. Very rare summer visitant and transient west of the Cascades.

Black Terns nest singly and in loose colonies in marshes and marsh-bordered lakes and rivers east of the Cascade Mts. They are locally common summer residents in the large marshes of Harney, Lake, and Klamath Cos., and are locally fairly common in smaller marshes elsewhere east of the Cascades. On the east side of the southern Cascades Mts. many lakes and marshes at over 4,000 ft. are used for nesting.

Very small numbers of transients occur almost annually during summer in inland valleys west of the Cascade Mts., and in some years a few are observed on the coast in May and June. Nesting has been suspected several summers at marshy ponds in Benton Co., at Fern Ridge Res., and along the Willamette R. near Salem in 1981. Nesting was confirmed at Fern Ridge in 1992, and several pairs were present there in 1993.

In late July and August Black Terns leave the breeding marshes and during this time are observed widely east of the Cascade Mts. Many migrants are probably transients from breeding grounds north of Oregon. By late September migrants are very rare, though a few are recorded into late October.

In fall they are very rare transients through inland valleys west of the Cascade Mts. There are three fall records for the coast: five Oct. 1, 1977, flying over the ocean along the Lincoln Co. coast; one Nov. 23, 1979, at Meares L., Tillamook Co.; and one Dec. 16, 1979, on a beach in northern Clatsop Co.

Black Terns return to their nesting marshes in late April and May, and transients are widespread east of the Cascades at this time.

Family Alcidae

Common Murre. *Uria aalge.*

Abundant at coastal colonies and near shore in summer. Fairly common near shore and uncommon offshore in winter.

In summer the Common Murre is abundant on the ocean and fairly common in larger estuaries along the Oregon coast. It is by far the most common seabird nesting in Oregon, with the population estimated in 1988 to be about 715,000, constituting about 60 percent of all the seabirds breeding in the state (Lowe pers. com.). The 60 known Oregon colonies, located on the barren tops and ledges of rocky islands and headlands, are distributed fairly evenly over the length of the coast. The estimated 220,000 that nest on Three Arch Rocks, Tillamook Co., is the largest concentration of Common Murres in the Pacific south of Alaska. Additionally, 23 other sites host colonies numbering in the thousands (Varoujean and Pitman 1979).

Murres begin nesting primarily in late May and early June. From this period into late July and August, when the single young fledge, they are very uncommon more than 5 miles from shore. After fledging many disperse offshore. However, even following this dispersal in August and September, the bulk of the population remains near shore.

From mid-July through October, and in some years earlier, there is a gradual migration north along the coast. Many of these northbound migrants apparently winter in the Strait of Juan de Fuca, Washington.

The population is much reduced in winter, yet murres are still fairly common near shore and in estuaries. Although there is little offshore winter data, it appears that Common Murres are uncommon over the continental shelf in winter and early spring. Migrants return from late March through April, staging on the ocean adjacent to breeding rocks.

Away from colonies Common Murres usually occur singly or in flocks of less than 10 individuals, but during migration they may fly in long lines, often of 20 or more birds. Occasionally they penetrate more than three miles up the larger estuaries, but there are no truly inland records. Large die-offs occur almost annually, especially in late summer when dozens to hundreds may be found dead in a single mile of beach. Die-offs may be triggered by storms or by food shortages during the fledging period.

Thick-billed Murre. *Uria lomvia.*

Three records.

The Thick-billed Murre has been recorded three times in Oregon: a winter plumaged male found dead and collected on a beach near Mercer, Lane Co., Jan. 30, 1933; a female collected near Depot Bay, Lincoln Co., on Jan. 14, 1933; and a badly decomposed specimen, a portion of which was collected, found near the S. Jetty of the Columbia R., Clatsop Co., on Sept. 15, 1972. The normal winter range in the Pacific extends south to northern British Columbia.

Pigeon Guillemot. *Cepphus columba.*

Fairly common along the coast in spring and summer. Very rare in winter.

The Pigeon Guillemot is fairly common in estuaries and on the ocean near shore from early spring through summer. Breeders in their nuptial plumage first return in early March and numbers build into April. Nesting takes place on rock ledges, in crevices, and in rock piles on rocky islands and headlands the length of the Oregon coast. The supporting structures of bridges are also utilized.

Guillemots are not colonial breeders, but aggregations occur where suitable nesting habitat is available. Lowe (pers. com.) estimated in 1988 that about 4,800 nest in the state and found that the majority of sites support fewer than 20 birds. In summer Pigeon Guillemots are rare beyond three miles from shore. Wahl (1975) observed them more than three miles from shore in Washington on only three occasions during 42 pelagic excursions.

Pigeon Guillemots depart the Oregon coast primarily in late August and September, with a few seen into December. Where local birds winter is not known, but it is thought to be far offshore. In winter they are rare near shore, with one or more sightings in most years. Dead birds are seldom found on beaches.

Marbled Murrelet. *Brachyramphus marmoratus.*

Nests in forests along the coast. Uncommon near shore in all seasons except winter, when rare.

Over the length of the Oregon coast the Marbled Murrelet is an uncommon resident within one mile of shore in all seasons but winter, when it is rare. Prior to 1961 a Marbled Murrelet nest had never been found, yet there was much evidence that the species nested in forests. In recent years a few nests have been found high on tree limbs, generally within 30 miles of salt water. There is some evidence that nesting can take place even farther from the ocean, depending on the availability of remnant old-growth forests.

Varoujean and Pitman (1979) suggested that Oregon's breeding population may be on the order of 1,000 pairs. That number is still considered valid, but the continuing loss of old-growth forest near the ocean is considered a long-term threat to the species in Oregon (*Oregon Birds* 18(4):120).

No distinct migratory movement has been observed, however, there is a decrease in numbers in late October and an increase in April. Pairs are occasionally recorded on coastal CBCs. Marbled Murrelets are most frequently observed in pairs or singly, but small flocks of usually five birds or less are also encountered, especially from July through autumn. Young birds, first observed in July, are usually solitary but also are often accompanied by adults or other young. Waters off sandy beaches and estuary mouths are favored, but the species also occurs off rocky shorelines. It is rare in estuaries and more than a mile or so offshore.

Xantus' Murrelet. *Synthliboramphus hypoleucus.*

Very rare or erratic visitant offshore.

The Xantus' Murrelet has been observed in Oregon about 10 times. A pair, one of which was captured, was observed diving behind a research vessel on Nov. 19, 1969, 60 miles west of Newport, Lincoln Co.; an immature male flew onto the deck of a research vessel 120 miles west of Cape Falcon, Tillamook Co., on July 28, 1970; a pair was seen Sept. 1, 1970, 140 miles west of Cape Falcon; and one was captured and photographed in June 1973, about 175 miles west of Newport, Lincoln Co.

The fall of 1985 saw a flurry of records, starting with a pair 12 miles off Lane Co. August 31. They were also seen off Tillamook, 18 miles out on September 14 and two miles out September 15. Finally, four were seen off Cape Meares, Tillamook Co., on September 27. Additional records include one at Boiler Bay State Wayside, Lincoln Co., from Nov. 7-8, 1987, and one seen 10 miles off Lincoln City, Lincoln Co., Sept. 9, 1989.

The northern race of the Xantus' Murrelet, *E. h. scrippsi*, breeds on the Channel Is. off southern California, and the southern race, *E. h. hypoleuca*, nests on Guadalupe I. and the San Benitos Is. off Baja California. The northern race is the form that occurs regularly on the West Coast, while the southern race is rare. There are two Washington records and one Oregon record, the June 1973 bird, of the southern race.

Following breeding the Xantus' Murrelet disperses northward, beginning in July. The species prefers the warm waters that typically occur beyond 30 miles from shore during summer and fall. From July to October this warm water some years is less than 20 miles from shore. There are more than 20 Washington records ranging from early August to early December, with most falling in October. The paucity of Oregon records is no doubt due to the poor coverage by observers of waters beyond 20 miles from shore.

Ancient Murrelet. *Synthliboramphus antiquus.*

Fairly common fall and spring transient offshore and rare offshore in winter. Very rare in summer.

The Ancient Murrelet is a fairly common fall migrant along the Oregon coast. The first migrants are occasionally noted in early September, but October and November are the peak months, and the migration sometimes extends well into December. It often occurs singly or in pairs, but occasionally flocks of as many as 30 are observed. Most migration probably occurs offshore out of sight of land, and migrants have been seen 35 miles from shore off Washington (Wahl 1975). In October, November, and March there are few observers offshore to document migration. Many apparently linger in Oregon waters during this autumn period. The species appears to prefer water temperatures below 50° F., but temperatures of the principal wintering waters in central and northern California do not usually drop below 50° F. until mid-November (Ainley 1976). In 1976 and in the early 1990s much larger numbers were seen during the winter in Oregon.

In winter (after December) it is probably rare well offshore, there being a few sightings and dozens of beached specimens. The northbound migration is more direct, most birds passing in March with smaller numbers through mid-April. There are a total of only about 15 records extending from May through August, which suggests that a few may summer off the Oregon coast. Young Common Murres are sometimes incorrectly identified as Ancient Murrelets during the late summer.

There are at least 10 inland records in fall for Oregon, ranging from late September to early December. The only record from an inland location in spring was one captured at Medford, Jackson Co., on March 3, 1966.

154

Cassin's Auklet. *Ptychoramphus aleuticus.*

Rare breeder on offshore rocks. Rare near shore except in fall when fairly common. Common offshore in fall and spring and uncommon offshore in summer and winter.

The Cassin's Auklet is rare near shore during summer, and even from land adjacent to the four known Oregon island nesting colonies it is seldom observed due to its nocturnal habits. Varoujean and Pitman (1979) established that at least 120 pairs nest on various islands off Curry Co. Browning and English (1972) reported additional colonies on Haystack Rock, Clatsop Co., and Conical Rock, Lane Co. The total Oregon breeding population is currently estimated at about 240 (Lowe, pers. com.). Cassin's Auklet is uncommon during the summer from about six miles offshore and extending over the continental shelf, but seldom is it found beyond the continental shelf. The majority of these offshore birds are probably non-breeders.

In August numbers offshore begin to increase as migrants arrive. Throughout September and into October the species is common offshore, with pelagic excursions typically viewing more than 50 and occasionally counting several hundred. It is during this August to November period that they are most frequently seen near shore. Observations from land and presumably the numbers offshore decrease in November as migrants move south. El Niño water conditions can radically disrupt this pattern.

Throughout the winter they are very rare near shore. The little data available indicate that offshore in winter Cassin's Auklets are uncommon over the continental shelf, but rarely occur beyond it. Dead birds are found regularly on beaches throughout the winter.

Spring migration occurs primarily in March and early April, and during this period the species likely is common offshore. Unlike the autumn migration, abundance near shore does not increase in spring migration.

Cassin's Auklets nest in burrows and rock crevices on the tops and slopes of rocky islands. On the ocean they usually occur singly or in flocks of five or fewer. During migration, however, larger flocks of up to 50 birds are sometimes found offshore.

There are three inland records, but the first two birds, found Oct. 4, 1921, and Jan. 13, 1948, near the ship docks along the Willamette R. in Portland, are believed to have been brought inland by ships. The third record is of a bird seen Feb. 12, 1974, 35 miles up the Columbia R. at Westport, Clatsop Co.

Parakeet Auklet. *Cyclorrhynchus psittacula.*

Only four recent records. More often recorded early in the century.

The Parakeet Auklet has been recorded in Oregon only four times since 1940: a pair well-observed off Cape Lookout, Lincoln Co., on Aug. 13, 1977; single beached birds found Dec. 3, 1977, at Bayocean, Tillamook Co. and near Newport, Lincoln Co., on April 18, 1982; and four off Garibaldi, Tillamook Co., on Sept. 7, 1986.

Gabrielson and Jewett (1940) reported nearly 20 records for the state, all of birds found dead on beaches in January or February between 1913 and 1935.

Rhinoceros Auklet. *Cerorhinca monocerata.*

Very uncommon in summer at seven coastal breeding colonies. Rare elsewhere in summer near shore and very uncommon offshore. Uncommon to fairly common near shore and offshore from late August through early November. Rare near shore in winter and uncommon offshore. Very uncommon near shore in March and April and uncommon to fairly common offshore.

The Rhinoceros Auklet breeds or is suspected of breeding at only seven localities on the Oregon coast and at these sites it is very uncommon in summer. Varoujean and Pitman (1979) report that Goat and Hunters Is., Curry Co., each support approximately 50 pairs. Nesting is suspected at several other locations, all on the mainland. The total population was estimated at 1,000 in 1988 (Lowe, pers. com.). At least 15 pairs are believed to nest on the inaccessible slopes of Sea Lion Caves, Lane Co. From Yaquina Head, Lincoln Co., as many as 25 birds have been observed at dusk in "evening passing flights," a typical behavior exhibited at breeding colonies prior to entering the burrow. At Otter Crest and adjacent Cape Foulweather, Lincoln Co., and at Cape Meares and Cape Lookout, Tillamook Co., small numbers of breeding plumaged adults (not more than five), have been observed several times, and occasionally these have been engaged in evening passing flights.

Away from these colonies the species is rarely seen from land before late August. Offshore however it is very uncommon as far as the edge of the continental shelf about 75 miles from land (Wahl 1979), with summer pelagic excursions typically viewing from one to 10. Many of these offshore birds in summer are probably non-breeders.

Numbers begin to increase along the coast and offshore in August, as the young from the large colonies farther north fledge and the population moves south. From late August through October, and in some years extending into November, Rhinoceros Auklets are uncommon to fairly common near shore and offshore, ranging over the entire continental shelf. At their migratory peak in late September and early October, pelagic excursions usually view more than 30. By November most have departed to wintering areas off California.

During winter they are rare near shore, and the little data available suggest they are uncommon over and beyond the shelf. Many are washed up dead on beaches annually. From March through early May numbers again swell as transients and local summer residents return. In late March and April, the migratory peak, Rhinoceros Auklets are very uncommon along the coast and uncommon to fairly common over the shelf. Flocks of migrants have been observed flying north over 100 miles from land.

Rhinoceros Auklets nest in burrows on the tops and slopes of islands and on protected mainland slopes, often in association with Tufted Puffins. At most breeding colonies adults return to feed young almost exclusively at night, but at Goat I., Curry Co., and Sea Lion Caves, Lane Co., feedings often occurs during daylight. On the water they usually occur singly, but in migration and in the breeding season pairs are also frequently encountered. Occasionally flocks of 50 or more are seen on the ocean during the migration period. Migrants often travel in lines of five to 20 birds. Following storms they are more frequently observed from land. On occasion during the fall and winter they even occur in estuaries, usually near the mouth.

Tufted Puffin. *Fratercula cirrhata.*

Locally fairly common in summer at island and headland breeding colonies. Generally uncommon offshore in summer. Very rare in winter within sight of land, apparently wintering far offshore.

The Tufted Puffin is locally a fairly common burrow nester on the slopes of offshore rocks and headlands along the Oregon coast. Varoujean and Pitman (1979) estimated 3,300 pairs nest in the state, of which 2,100 pairs breed on Three Arch Rocks, Tillamook Co. They found that four other sites, Haystack Rock, Clatsop Co., Haystack Rock, Tillamook Co., Island Rock, Curry Co., and Goat I., Curry Co., each host colonies of more than 150 pairs, and that there are some 26 smaller colonies, each supporting fewer than 75 pairs. Estimates of the population made in 1988 were similar (Lowe pers. com.).

During the breeding season Tufted Puffins can be seen at the entrances to their burrows and on the water near colonies. Most foraging, however, appears to take place beyond sight of land. During the breeding season they occur throughout the offshore zone and even beyond the continental slope, 75 miles from land. Many of the birds found at sea may be non-breeders, as maturity is not attained until the fourth or fifth year. They are most abundant offshore on the northern Oregon coast, which corresponds with the distribution of breeders. Even in the north seldom are more than 10 observed during pelagic excursions, these usually seen singly or in pairs.

In August and early September adults abandon their single chicks and move offshore. The chicks then remain in the burrow for a week or so, after which, flightless, they paddle out to sea. From mid-September through winter Tufted Puffins are extremely rare within sight of land, and are not recorded in most years. They apparently winter far at sea, there being several observations for over 60 miles from shore. Dead birds are found annually on beaches in winter. They return to the nesting colonies primarily during early and mid-April, but in some years small numbers are seen in late March.

Horned Puffin. *Fratercula corniculata.*

Very rare along the coast and offshore in summer. Rare offshore in winter.

The Horned Puffin is currently very rare in summer on the Oregon coast. Prior to 1953, nearly all West Coast records, and all for Oregon, were in winter. But since 1953, the majority of West Coast occurrences have been in summer. It has been hypothesized that broad-scale changes in oceanic conditions are responsible for this turnabout in seasonal abundance patterns (Hoffman, Elliot, and Scott 1975).

There are about 23 Oregon summer records (several of dead birds on beaches) spanning from May 14 to August 23; all since 1968. Observations range from shore to 38 miles at sea, but most have been made in waters adjacent to rocks or headlands that support seabird colonies. Summer birds in Oregon near potential breeding sites are thought to be non-breeders, probably immatures, which are known to occupy burrows before they reach maturity at five years.

There are many winter records of dead birds found on beaches. In most cases only one or two birds were found in a given year, but hundreds were found in the winter of 1932-33 (unprecedented numbers of other seabirds also died that year) and at least 16 were found in 1980. Horned Puffins are known to winter on the open ocean across the North Pacific (Hoffman, Elliott, and Scott 1975), and their presence on Oregon's coast is likely linked to the periodic occurrence of favorable oceanic conditions nearer shore.

Order COLUMBIFORMES
Family Columbidae

Rock Dove. *Columba livia.*

Introduced. Common throughout Oregon in urban areas, towns, and agricultural lands.

The Rock Dove, is a native of Eurasia and an introduction to North America and widely elsewhere. It has become established throughout Oregon in urban areas and towns and on farms and ranches, where it nests primarily on man-made structures. In these habitats it is generally common year round, and very large populations exist near ship docks and railroad yards where grain is available. It is a locally fairly common breeder on cliffs east of the Cascades, where some colo-

159

nies exist far from agricultural land and are abandoned during winter. The species generally does not frequent forested mountains, though homing pigeons can be seen anywhere. While many birds closely resemble their wild Eurasian ancestors, most feral populations are highly varied in coloration and pattern.

Band-tailed Pigeon. *Columba fasciata.*

West of the Cascade crest, fairly common summer resident in forests and fairly common transient through forests and agricultural lands. In winter, locally rare to uncommon in the interior valleys of western Oregon and very rare along the coast. Very rare east of the Cascades from March to October.

The Band-tailed Pigeon is a fairly common summer resident and transient in dense coniferous and mixed coniferous-deciduous forests from the coast to the west slope of the Cascades to about 4,000 ft. Populations have declined drastically in recent decades, probably due to hunting pressure.

In July and August flocks form which forage widely for berries and nuts, and often congregate at mineral springs where they ingest salts. During this period birds are occasionally noted above timberline. Outside of the breeding season flocks often utilize agricultural lands where they feed on grains and occasionally fruit crops. Most migrate south in September, but some migrants are noted through October.

In winter, flocks may be locally uncommon in the interior valleys some years and absent others. On the coast individuals are very rare in winter. Winter birds are often sustained by food either intentionally or inadvertently supplied by humans. At locations where food is offered they are often present winter after winter. Spring migrants generally first arrive in late February and numbers build through April.

East of the Cascades the species occurs as a vagrant in riparian habitats and at desert oases, from late March to October. Occurrences at the well-birded Harney Co. oasis sites are typically in late May and early June.

White-winged Dove. *Zenaida asiatica.*

Vagrant.

The White-winged Dove has been recorded three times in Oregon: at the S. Jetty of the Columbia R., Clatsop Co., on Aug. 25, 1976; at Newport, Lincoln Co., on Oct. 28-30, 1979; and near Tillamook, Tillamook Co., on Dec. 20, 1986.

Mourning Dove. *Zenaida macroura.*

Common summer resident from the interior valleys of western Oregon eastward. Along the coast, fairly common in the south grading to rare in the north. In winter, generally rare at lower elevations east of the Cascade Mts. and along the coast, and fairly common in the interior valleys of western Oregon.

The Mourning Dove is a common summer resident in the interior valleys of western Oregon and their surrounding foothills, in the Cascades in open forests at low to moderate elevations (to about 5,500 ft. on the east slope), and east of the Cascades in open country and open forests to moderate elevations. Breeders inhabit agricultural land, chaparral, hills and canyons in grasslands and sagebrush country, and open forests including edges in Douglas-fir forests, and forests of juniper and ponderosa pine. Along the coast it is a fairly common summer resident in Curry Co., uncommon in Coos Co., very uncommon in Lincoln Co. and rare in Tillamook and Clatsop Cos.

In July and August after breeding, Mourning Doves form flocks. Occasionally small numbers are noted at timberline during this period. The migration peaks from late August through mid-September, and by early October most have left areas east of the Cascades. More occur on the north coast in fall than at other seasons, but it remains rare then as well.

In winter east of the Cascades, the Mourning Dove is rare to uncommon (varies annually) in agricultural lands at lower elevations. It is fairly common in winter, often occurring in flocks, in agricultural lands of the interior valleys of western Oregon, and rare along the coast, where it is typically absent from the northern counties.

Spring migrants first return to Oregon in March and early April. The migration continues through April.

Order PSITTACIFORMES
Family Psittacidae

Monk Parakeet. *Myiopsitta monachus.*

Introduced in the Portland area. Not certainly established.

Small numbers of this hardy cage bird are found in the Portland area. Breeding has been successful for a number of years but the total population is only a few dozen. The species is not included on the official list of the birds of Oregon as maintained by the Oregon Bird Records Committee. Whether the population that now exists will increase and prove self-sustaining in the long run is uncertain.

Order CUCULIFORMES
Family Cuculidae

Yellow-billed Cuckoo. *Coccyzus americanus.*

Very rare or possibly only a vagrant during late spring and summer in riparian areas and at oases east of the Cascade Mts. Vagrant in summer in the Willamette Valley.

Gabrielson and Jewett (1940) considered the Yellow-billed Cuckoo "not common anywhere in Oregon" but found it with greatest regularity in the willow bottoms bordering the Columbia and Willamette Rivers, where in some years it was fairly common. They reported three records east of the Cascades, including a nest observed by Bendire in 1876 along the Snake R. Between 1940 and 1970 there were only two records, both from La Grande, Union Co., where one was found dead Nov. 28, 1943 and one was collected during the 1950s.

Since 1970 there have been more than 35 records, all between May 20 and September 12. At least 20 of these records are for east of the Cascades, where most have been observed in Union, Harney, and Malheur Cos., and one or more in Klamath, Deschutes, Jefferson, Umatilla, Wallowa, Baker, and Lake Cos.

West of the Cascades there have been only four records since 1970, all from the Willamette Valley: one near Lebanon, Linn Co., July 29, 1970; one near Sandy, Clackamas Co., July 5, 1976; and two at different bottomland locations on Sauvie I., Multnomah Co., between Sept. 2 and Sept. 28, 1977. The species has never been recorded on the coast or in southwestern Oregon.

Yellow-billed Cuckoos are most frequently observed in Oregon during June and July. Although most observations are from locations where nesting undoubtedly does not occur, pairs have been noted in Baker City, Baker Co., and La Grande, Union Co., and at several sites birds have been seen repeatedly during a summer. At a few locations, such as along the Owyhee R. near Adrian, Malheur Co., they have been noted in several years, and nesting at La Grande, Union Co., was observed (Marshall 1992). Also, a female with a brood patch struck a window in Bend, Deschutes Co., on June 18, 1990. These records suggest that the species nests very locally east of the Cascades. In addition, there seems to be an increasing trend in the very small number that are found at the well-worked vagrant spots in Harney Co. (Fields, Malheur N.W.R. Headquarters), but even at these locations there have not been more than two records in a spring, and none at all some recent springs. Much is unknown about the current status of the Yellow-billed Cuckoo in Oregon.

Dense cottonwoods and willows bordering watercourses, such as occur along the Grande Ronde, Umatilla, Columbia, Owyhee, and Snake Rivers, appear to be preferred.

Order STRIGIFORMES
Family Tytonidae

Barn Owl. *Tyto alba.*

Common permanent resident in lowlands west of the Cascades. Locally common to very uncommon permanent resident at lower elevations east of the Cascades.

The Barn Owl is a fairly common permanent resident of the interior valleys of western Oregon and in agricultural areas along the coast. It is an uncommon permanent resident in the foothills, usually associated with agricultural lands. East of the Cascades, Barn Owls are common permanent residents in the grain-producing regions and grasslands of north-central Oregon, and are especially common along the Columbia R. in Sherman, Morrow, and Umatilla Cos. In Union, Baker, Malheur, Deschutes, and Klamath Cos. they are locally fairly common permanent residents where there are extensive cultivated lands and meadows.

In Harney Co., where they are uncommon, numbers have increased in recent years but cold weather may be limiting abundance, as many have been found dead in winter at Malheur N.W.R. Barn Owls are very uncommon throughout the year in sagebrush-juniper country and in agricultural areas within the ponderosa pine zone, and rarely occur higher. In such areas canyon walls and rimrock are utilized for nesting.

In fall when young disperse, individuals are occasionally observed at odd locations, including at timberline. The species regularly inhabits residential and industrial areas in large cities. Tree cavities, crevices in cliffs, nest boxes, and buildings are utilized for nesting.

Family Strigidae

Flammulated Owl. *Otus flammeolus.*

Fairly common summer resident east of the Cascades, and a rare summer resident in southwestern Oregon.

The Flammulated Owl is a fairly common summer resident east of the Cascades in forests of ponderosa pine and mixed forests of ponderosa pine, Douglas-fir, grand fir, and western larch. Often in such forests it is the commonest owl, but its soft call and retiring habits make detection difficult. Cavities in pine snags or aspens are usually utilized for nesting. Both old growth and younger forests are inhabited, and nests are often located near clearings or in riparian areas where aspens occur. At Blue Sky, a small isolated ponderosa pine forest on Hart Mt., Lake Co., nocturnal mist netting found the Flammulated to be the commonest owl in May and June, and present in mid-September.

Flammulated Owls return from wintering areas in Mexico and Guatemala during May and early June, the earliest record for Oregon being April 30. The apparent migration peak occurs in late May and early June. Fall migration peaks in September. The latest fall record is Nov. 13, 1991 at Long Mt., Harney Co.

In western Oregon there are scattered summer records for Jackson, Josephine, and Douglas Cos., including a flightless juvenile that was found in Josephine Co. in August, 1983. It is probable that the species is a regular breeding bird in the ponderosa and Jeffrey pine forests in those counties.

Western Screech-Owl. *Otus kennicottii.*

Common permanent resident west of the Cascades in the interior valleys and fairly common on the coast and in the mountains. East of the Cascades, uncommon permanent resident at lower elevations.

This screech-owl is a permanent resident at lower elevations throughout Oregon. In the interior valleys of western Oregon it is common and frequently occurs even in suburbs and city parks. It is fairly common on the coast, in the Coast Range, in the Siskiyou Mts., and on the west slope of the Cascades to 4,000 ft., frequenting coniferous and deciduous forests. In southwestern Oregon it is fairly common in chaparral and oak woodlands.

In the lowlands east of the Cascades Western Screech-Owls are uncommon, primarily inhabiting areas with deciduous trees, such as towns, orchards, desert oases, and riparian areas. In ponderosa pine and white fir/Douglas-fir forests east of the Cascades they are very uncommon, occurring most frequently near water. Large juniper stands support bigger populations. There may be some movement to lowlands in winter.

Great Horned Owl. *Bubo virginianus.*

Common permanent resident throughout the state.

The Great Horned Owl is a common permanent resident throughout Oregon, from sea level to timberline and from the driest deserts to the most humid old growth forests along the coast, though it generally avoids the few remaining large areas of unbroken old-growth evergreen forest. In winter birds descend from higher elevations, and there is probably some southward migration.

Cliffs or trees are required for nesting, but Great Horned Owls often forage over open country far from the nest site. They are common in agricultural areas and even occur in suburbs, at which time even house cats and small dogs are not entirely safe.

Snowy Owl. *Nyctea scandiaca.*

Irregular rare winter visitant, occasionally very uncommon during invasions.

The Snowy Owl is generally a winter vagrant to Oregon from the Arctic. One or more are observed, usually on the north coast and occasionally elsewhere in northern Oregon, on the average about every other year. Periodic invasions of southern Canada and the northern United States occur every three to five years, but during most invasions significant numbers do not reach Oregon. These periodic southward incursions are precipitated by population crashes in the owl's prey, principally lemmings.

Major invasions reaching Oregon in this century occurred in the winters 1916-17, 1917-18, 1950-51, 1966-67, 1971-72, 1973-74, and 1993-94. During major invasions hundreds of Snowy Owls may be scattered in open country throughout the state. They occur most frequently in the Willamette Valley, in northeastern and north-central Oregon, and along the coast, where they may be locally fairly common on sandspits. Individuals also occasionally reach southwestern and southeastern Oregon.

Snowy Owls have occurred in Oregon in early November, but generally arrive later in the month. Most depart the state in March, but there are a few April observations and a May 5 record.

Western Screech-Owl

Northern Hawk Owl. *Surnia ulula.*

Two records.

There are two Oregon records for this species: one was seen on Sauvie I., Multnomah Co., from Nov. 4, 1973, to early January 1974; and one at Palmer Junction, Union Co., was seen and photographed on Jan. 12-13, 1983.

Northern Pygmy-Owl. *Glaucidium gnoma.*

Uncommon to common permanent resident in forests throughout.

The Northern Pygmy-Owl is an uncommon to common permanent resident of coniferous and mixed forests throughout Oregon. Open forests and edges appear to be preferred, and in southwestern Oregon chaparral is inhabited. It occurs to timberline, but is more common at lower elevations. Juniper forests and isolated aspen stands east of the Cascades are not inhabited in summer, but serve as habitat in winter, when there is some dispersal to lower elevations.

Burrowing Owl. *Athene cunicularia.*

Uncommon and declining summer resident east of the Cascades. Rare winter visitant west of the Cascades

This partially-diurnal owl is found locally in open habitats east of the Cascades. Numbers are declining considerably. Nest locations are generally tied to existing mammal burrows though the owl is reputed to dig its own.

The earliest arrival date for Harney Co. is February 18. Family groups around nesting burrows are more regularly sighted, though the species can be also be seen out and foraging in the daytime. Most leave the Harney Basin in September and early October.

West of the Cascades, the Burrowing Owl appears as a rare winter visitant, with some occupying favorable locations for several years. Records are widely scattered, mostly in the interior valleys with a few on the coast. The species formerly bred in the Rogue Valley.

Spotted Owl. *Strix occidentalis.*

Fairly common permanent resident in the remaining dense old-growth coniferous forests and very rare in younger coniferous forests in western Oregon, and on the east slope of the Cascades.

The Spotted Owl is a permanent resident in coniferous forests throughout the mountains and foothills of western Oregon and on the east slope of the Cascades at least as far east as Badger Butte, Hood River Co., Abbot Butte, Jefferson Co., and Swan Lake Point, Klamath Co. (Forsman 1976). The edge of its range on the east slope of the northern Oregon Cascades appears to coincide with the eastern limits of the true fir zone, while in southern Oregon their range extends east beyond the Cascades in mixed forests of white fir, Douglas-fir, and ponderosa pine to south-central Klamath Co. There are also records for the Warner Mts. in extreme northeastern California, indicating possible occurrence in the Warner Mts. of Lake Co.

Spotted Owls are uncommon in old-growth coniferous forests. They have been found from sea level to 6,000 ft. in the southern Oregon Cascades, although in the northern Oregon Cascades they rarely occur above 4,000 ft. These high altitude extremes roughly correspond with the elevation at which trees become smaller and forests more open. Predation by Great Horned Owls appears to be the primary limiting factor. In western Oregon a wide variety of coniferous forest types are inhabited while on the east slope of the Cascades they are confined primarily to forests of true firs, which often include lesser elements of Douglas fir, ponderosa pine, and other conifers. Breeding is limited to mature forests.

As each breeding pair requires about one square mile of old-growth forest, this species is the subject of much political controversy between the environmental movement and the timber industry. The Oregon population as estimated by various federal agencies in 1992 consisted of 2,070 pairs and 970 unpaired birds.

Barred Owl. *Strix varia.*

Uncommon to rare permanent resident, expanding statewide.

The Barred Owl's range in Oregon has rapidly expanded since it was first detected in the state on June 18, 1974, in the Wenaha R. drainage, Wallowa Co. During the mid-1960s Barred Owls were reported extending their range south-westward from eastern British Columbia. After the first two Oregon sightings, which were pairs in Wallowa and Umatilla Cos. during the summer of 1974, small but increasing numbers have been detected in many parts of the state. Records now exist for virtually the entire length of the Cascade Mts., as well as for various areas in the Blue and Wallowa Mts. By the early 1990s it had become established in Coos and Curry Cos. near the coast, and in 1993 birds were found at Finley N.W.R. in Benton Co. The species might be expected almost anywhere in the state where sufficient forest habitat exists.

Barred Owls are permanent residents in a variety of forest habitats including mixed conifer and deciduous, Douglas fir, and ponderosa pine. They usually occur in old-growth forests and at low to moderate elevation. There is some dispersal or altitudinal migration to lower elevations in winter, when birds have been observed in deciduous trees in open country.

The range of the Barred Owl now overlaps that of the closely related and slightly smaller Spotted Owl in the Cascades. It seems doubtful that two species so similar in habitat requirements and foraging behavior can coexist for long (Taylor and Forsman 1978). Hybrids have been noted at several locations in Oregon and Washington. As those birds show intermediate traits both vocally and morphologically, care should be taken with identification.

Great Gray Owl. *Strix nebulosa.*

Uncommon to rare permanent resident in the Cascades and the mountains of northeastern Oregon.

The Great Gray Owl is an uncommon to rare permanent resident on the east slope of the Cascades and very locally regular on the west slope. In the mountains of

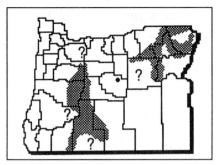

northeastern Oregon it is an uncommon permanent resident, extending south to northern Harney Co. and west to Crook Co. There are few records for the Cascades north of about the forty-fifth parallel, perhaps due to the limited meadow habitat available.

Nesting was first confirmed west of the Cascade crest in 1982, when an adult and two young were observed east of Ashland, Jackson Co. Forests of lodgepole pine, ponderosa pine, and mixed conifers are inhabited, and territories usually include large meadows. In recent years the Great Gray Owl has been found increasingly on the west slope of the Cascades, where clear cuts approximate their preferred meadow hunting habitat, and large old-growth forests are nearby for nesting habitat. Goggans and Platt (OB 18(2):35, 1992) found six pairs and four single males on 46 square kilometers of the Willamette National Forest in Lane and Linn Cos. in the spring of 1991.

During winter there is some dispersal to lower elevations, and every few years a bird is observed in the interior valleys of western Oregon or in the valleys and open country of northeastern Oregon.

Long-eared Owl. *Asio otus.*

Locally uncommon permanent resident in lowlands east of the Cascades. Rare in the Willamette Valley in summer; very uncommon in western Oregon interior valleys during winter.

The Long-eared Owl is a fairly common permanent resident in open country east of the Cascades, where it frequents juniper forests and wooded riparian areas. At lower elevations on the east slope of the Cascades it is locally uncommon in pine forests. In northeast Oregon it is a very uncommon summer resident in coniferous and mixed forests near open lands at low to moderate elevations. Migration appears to occur in March and in October. There are no winter records for Wallowa and Union Cos. Elsewhere east of the Cascades in winter, groups of 10 or more often roost together in streamside thickets or dense juniper stands. Migrant birds from north of Oregon may winter in the state.

In western Oregon the Long-eared Owl is a rare summer resident in the Willamette Valley, there being fewer than five nesting records. In winter it is very uncommon in the Willamette and Rogue Valleys. There are a few coastal records, mostly from Coos and Curry Cos., with one at Tillamook on Dec. 19, 1987, and one at Astoria, Clatsop Co., on Jan. 5, 1993.

Short-eared Owl. *Asio flammeus.*

Locally common to rare during summer and winter in open country throughout Oregon. Widespread in migration.

The Short-eared Owl occurs year-round in open country throughout Oregon. East of the Cascades it is a fairly common summer resident in the large meadows and marshes of Klamath, Lake, and Harney Cos., and a locally fairly common to rare summer resident in cultivated areas, grasslands, and smaller marshes in other counties. In western Oregon it is a very uncommon summer resident in the interior valleys.

Spring migration occurs in March and April. In August observations of Short-eared Owls increase as young disperse and migration begins. Through early November migrants are noted in odd habitats throughout the state, including sagebrush deserts, and mountain meadows to timberline. During this period the number utilizing marshes and cultivated lands may increase noticeably, and along the coast they may be fairly common. There are even several records of Short-eared Owls approaching birding boats miles at sea.

The winter status is extremely variable both east and west of the Cascades. This fluctuation is apparently in response to prey abundance. East of the Cascades they are typically very uncommon, not being recorded on most Christmas Bird Counts in a given year, although nearly all counts have recorded them at some time. West of the Cascades they are usually fairly common in the interior valleys during winter, occurring in a wide variety of open habitats. The extent to which the numbers in winter vary is illustrated by the Sauvie I. CBC, which has recorded between 0 and 30. On the coast they are uncommon in winter. Short-eared Owls occasionally roost communally in trees and brush during winter.

Boreal Owl. *Aegolius funereus.*

Permanent resident of the high Cascade, Blue, and Wallowa Mts.

The Boreal Owl was known to the state from only two old specimen records until the late 1980s. One specimen taken on Jan. 20, 1881 was labeled "Oregon Cascades;" the other record is a specimen taken at Fort Klamath on March 21, 1902.

The first modern records were made during the winter of 1987-88 when eight Boreal Owls were found at various locations in northeastern Oregon. Since then, it has been found in the central Cascades in Deschutes and Lane Cos. and at various locations in the Wallowa and Blue Mts. Almost all of the records have been above 5,000 ft. This species may prove to inhabit most of the forested areas above that elevation, where deep snow restricts observer presence during the season the species is the most vocal. Preliminary evidence suggests that it may be a fairly common species in its restricted habitat within the state.

Northern Saw-whet Owl. *Aegolius acadicus.*

Common permanent resident of forests west of the Cascades. East of the Cascades fairly common summer resident in forests and very uncommon in lowlands during winter.

The Saw-whet Owl is a fairly common summer resident in coniferous and deciduous forests from sea level to timberline throughout Oregon. Conifers appear to be preferred, and dry oak woods, chaparral, and junipers are rarely inhabited. Although Saw-whets are invariably found near trees, open country is also utilized during foraging (Forsman and Maser 1969).

In winter they remain common west of the Cascade crest, but east of there they are apparently very uncommon, being reported only from lower elevations, especially in dense riparian growth or deciduous trees around farms and towns. A shift in winter to lower altitudes probably occurs throughout Oregon. Northern and local birds may migrate south out of the state or winter here.

Spring migrants are rare at desert oases east of the Cascades from late March to mid-May, with most sightings in early May. Migrants appear at oases in fall slightly more frequently than in spring. Fall records extend from early September through early November, with an October peak.

Order CAPRIMULGIFORMES
Family Caprimulgidae

Common Nighthawk. *Chordeiles minor.*

Common to fairly common summer resident and transient throughout the state.

The Common Nighthawk is a fairly common summer resident throughout Oregon. It occurs in a wide variety of habitats, including coastal dunes, chaparral, grassy hills, sagebrush and juniper deserts, and forests high into the mountains. In forests it usually nests in clearings or where there is little undergrowth, but it often feeds over dense timber. It rarely nests in cultivated lands but regularly feeds over such areas. The Common Nighthawk is most common in grass- and sagebrush-covered hills and canyons east of the Cascade Mts. In flat sagebrush country it rarely nests away from rimrock, canyons, and outcroppings. This species also nests on the gravel-covered roofs of buildings, and until recent years did so even in downtown Portland. There has been a general decrease in the species in the Willamette Valley over the past fifteen years.

The southward migration begins in late July and peaks in early September. There are a few records as late as early October. Migrants are often seen in loose flocks of less than 50 birds, but flocks of over a hundred have been noted. Common Nighthawks have never been recorded in Oregon during winter.

This species is one of the last Oregon breeders to arrive in spring, usually appearing in the last days of May or the first days of June. The earliest record is April 17, though this and other April and early May records possibly pertain to vagrant occurrences of the Lesser Nighthawk (*C. acutipennis*), a species which arrives much earlier than the Common Nighthawk in northern California. The earliest certain record of the Common Nighthawk for Oregon is May 20 in Harney Co. (Littlefield, 1990).

Common Poorwill. *Phalaenoptilus nuttallii.*

Locally fairly common summer resident east of the Cascade Mts. and in Jackson and Josephine Cos. of southwestern Oregon.

East of the Cascade Mts. the Common Poorwill is a fairly common summer resident in hilly and rocky sagebrush country, juniper-covered hills, and open forests of ponderosa pine, especially where there are sagebrush clearings and rock outcroppings. Occasionally it is found in clearcuts and on rugged slopes within fir forests. There is some evidence that the habitat provided by clearcuts has enabled the Poorwill to expand its range on the east slope of the Cascade Mts. as far north as Mt. Hood (Horn 1975).

In Jackson and Josephine Cos., poorwills are fairly common on oak and chaparral-covered hills. There are a few summer records for Curry Co., where they may breed in the mountains. Recent records from the west slope of the Cascades in Douglas Co. and isolated buttes in the southern Willamette Valley north to Linn Co., show the species may be a regular summer resident. This may represent a fairly recent northward range extension, possibly associated with an increase in suitable habitat caused by clearcutting.

The migratory period of this nocturnal species is poorly known. Few birds are detected after early September. There is an Oct. 26 record from Klamath Co. There are no mid-winter records for Oregon. Spring migrants have been detected from late April through mid-May. One found at the Hermiston Airport, Umatilla Co., on March 30, 1992, may have been at a normal arrival date.

There are a few records for birds out of the species' breeding range in the state. Spring vagrants have reached Portland several times, as well as other locations in the northern Willamette Valley. Coastal records include a specimen obtained in Tillamook Co. on Oct. 27, 1933, and a bird found dead at Langlois, Curry Co., on Nov. 25, 1982. The last bird may have been attempting to hibernate locally.

Order APODIFORMES
Family Apodidae

Black Swift. *Cypseloides niger.*

Very local summer resident. Rare transient statewide.

The Black Swift is known to breed in Oregon only at Salt Creek Falls, Lane Co., at 4,100 ft. in the Cascade Mts. It is a regular summer resident in forested mountains to the north and south of Oregon, and its apparent absence in the seemingly ideal habitat of the Oregon Cascades and Blue Mts. remains an enigma. There are summer records which suggest it may breed at other spots in the Cascades such as Santiam Pass, Linn Co., and Mosier, Wasco Co.; as well as the Summit Ridge area in the Wallowa Mts., Wallowa Co.

Black Swifts are rare spring and fall migrants throughout the state. Spring migration occurs from mid-May through early June. Fall transients pass through Oregon in late August and September, and in some years as late as mid-October. Transients can occur almost anywhere in the state, but perhaps are most regularly noted along the coast in fall. The species typically flies high while migrating, and except during inclement weather is hard to detect despite regular passage. For example, live birds have never been reported from Harney Co., but in two separate years dead individuals have been found in the same yard in Frenchglen following storms in late May.

Vaux's Swift. *Chaetura vauxi.*

Uncommon to locally common summer resident from the Cascade Mts. west and in the Blue and Wallowa Mts. Migrates statewide, arriving in mid-April and departing in September and early October.

The Vaux's Swift is an uncommon to locally common summer resident in western Oregon from sea level to around 4,500 ft., occurring in cities, open country, and mixed and coniferous forests. East of the Cascades it is a rare to locally common summer resident in open forests and interlying valleys of the Blue and Wallowa Mts., and in lower elevation forests on the east slope of the Cascades east to the Warner Mts.

Vaux's Swifts normally arrive in Oregon from mid- to late April, but have appeared as early as March 2 at Ashland, Jackson Co. Fall migrants are usually gone by early October, but occasionally persist until mid-October. During April and May and again in late August and September migrants in flocks may be locally abundant, often over cities. During these periods hundreds or even thousands roost communally in chimneys, especially in fall. Migrants regularly occur over desert oases and occasionally high in the mountains.

White-throated Swift. *Aeronautes saxatalis.*

Locally uncommon summer resident east of the Cascade Mts.

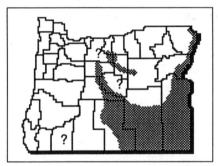

The White-throated Swift is a locally uncommon summer resident east of the Cascades where it nests on high cliffs, usually in open country. Suitable cliffs occur in a variety of habitats including the Columbia R. Gorge east of The Dalles; Wallula Gap, Umatilla Co.; Hell's Canyon, Wallowa Co.; Gearhart Mt., Klamath Co.; Steens Mt., Harney Co.; Hart Mt., Lake Co.; the moderate elevation Smith Rocks, Deschutes Co.; and Succor Creek, Malheur Co. Dozens of other localities are known. Dry escarpments surrounded by coniferous forest, high desert fault blocks, and river canyons are favored.

Summer observations from heavily forested sites on the east side of the Cascades like Davis Lake, Deschutes Co., and Crater Lake, Klamath Co., may be of locally nesting birds. A summer report from the Kalmiopsis Wilderness, Curry Co., suggests breeding in that region. The few reports from elsewhere west of the Cascades include four at Port Orford, Curry Co., April 25, 1979, and recent several reports at Table Rock, Jackson Co.

White-throated Swifts generally arrive in the first half of April. Fall migrants depart Oregon in September and early October.

Family Trochilidae

Black-chinned Hummingbird. *Archilochus alexandri*.

Fairly common to rare summer resident and transient east of the Cascade Mts. Vagrant to western Oregon.

The Black-chinned Hummingbird is a fairly common summer resident in many areas east of the Cascades, including the valleys and lower foothills associated with the Blue and Wallowa Mts., the oak and scrub areas of Wasco Co., the Snake and Owyhee Valleys. It inhabits open woodlands, riparian areas, and towns. Migrants occur at desert oases and in towns in southeastern and south-central Oregon. As with other hummingbirds, males wander and migrate early, making it necessary to find nesting evidence to confirm breeding in a given area.

Most Black-chinned Hummingbirds return to Oregon from the latter half of April through May, with the peak in mid- to late May. The timing of the migration is variable depending on the weather in the particular spring. There are however at least three late March records, all from west of the Cascades: March 22, 1980 and March 28, 1981 at Coos Bay; and March 26, 1969 at Shady Cove, Jackson Co. By early August most males have left Oregon, and the latest records of females and immatures are for late August. There are no acceptable winter records.

West of the Cascades, Black-chinned Hummingbirds have occasionally been reported from the Rogue Valley, where dates range from March 26 to Aug. 15. There is, however, no certain evidence of nesting. There are about 11 coastal records, the dates ranging from March 22 to Aug. 2, and including Coos, Lincoln, Tillamook, and Clatsop Cos. Six were on Saddle Mt., Clatsop Co., on July 3, 1985, which might indicate local breeding. There are a few records from the Willamette Valley and one from the Cascades at Blue R., Lane Co, on May 11, 1992.

Anna's Hummingbird. *Calypte anna*.

Common to locally rare summer resident and uncommon to fairly common during winter along the coast and in the interior valleys of western Oregon. Locally uncommon summer resident in the Klamath Basin and in Deschutes, Crook, Jefferson, Hood River, and Wasco Cos.

The Anna's Hummingbird was not recorded in Oregon until 1958, when a male was at Ashland, Jackson Co., on December 21. There were several records by 1966, after which its abundance and range began expanding rapidly. In the interior valleys and foothills of western Oregon, along the Columbia R. east to The Dalles, and along the coast, it is a rare to locally uncommon summer resident in open woodlands, agricultural land with scattered trees, towns and suburbs. Anna's increase in these areas, while withdrawing from the foothills, during September and October, and through winter they are uncommon to locally fairly common and apparently are largely dependent on feeders.

East of the Cascade Mts., the first record was a specimen taken at Heppner, Morrow Co., on Nov. 19, 1972. Today it is locally fairly common in the Klamath Basin (recorded north to Chiloquin) and in Deschutes, Crook, and Jefferson Cos., inhabiting open woodlands and towns. It usually arrives in these areas in late April and early May, and departs by mid-October (though a few have wintered at Bend). One at Ukiah, Umatilla Co., on June 22, 1992, provided an unusual record for that locale.

Costa's Hummingbird. *Calypte costae.*

Very rare visitant.

Since the first record in 1972, the Costa's Hummingbird has become a very rare visitant. It has been found at various coastal locations and both east and west of the Cascades in the interior, usually at hummingbird feeders. There are about 24 records for Oregon. A feeder in Bend, Deschutes Co., hosted what may have been the same or different birds for five consecutive years in the mid 1980s. Most records are from April through June, but some have persisted around feeders at other seasons. The earliest spring record was April 4. One bird remained to July 26. Fall records begin in early November. There have been four winter records, both on the coast and in the Rogue Valley.

Of considerable interest is a nesting attempt at Harbor, Curry Co., far from the species' nearest normal nesting areas in the San Joaquin Valley of California. A female found on June 15, 1991, was apparently mated with an Allen's Humming-

179

bird. She constructed a nest and laid two eggs, but the nest was destroyed by a passing car and the possible outcome of this liaison remains unknown.

Calliope Hummingbird. *Stellula calliope.*

Fairly common summer resident in the Cascade Mts. and in the mountains east of the Cascades. Locally uncommon in the Siskiyou Mts. and Rogue Valley. Uncommon transient outside breeding areas east of the Cascades; rare transient west of the Cascades.

The Calliope Hummingbird is a fairly common summer resident of the east slope of the Cascades, the Siskiyous, and the various mountain ranges of eastern Oregon, including isolated desert mountains such as Steens and Hart Mts. Habitats include open forests, the edges of meadows, riparian areas and others that produce abundant flowers. The Calliope Hummingbird mainly inhabits middle elevations, but also breeds near timberline and at the lower margins of mountain forests (such as suburban Bend and locations in the Grande Ronde Valley). The only verified record of nesting in the interior valleys of western Oregon was at Medford in 1967, but the species is regular in *ceanothus* habitat elsewhere in the Rogue Valley.

There appears to be some movement to higher elevations in late summer, and probably most migrants move south high in the mountains. Fall migrants are occasionally noted in valleys and desert oases east of the Cascades. Most adult males have left the state by early July. Females and immatures depart in numbers in the latter half of August and early September. A few have been noted to late September. Fall transients are very rare (not recorded most years) in the interior valleys of western Oregon. The only winter record is of one that stayed through the 1980-81 winter at Eugene.

Calliope Hummingbirds return to Oregon in the latter half of April and the first half of May. The earliest spring record is April 4. Transients have been noted at Malheur N.W.R. headquarters in late May. Spring migrants are rare to locally uncommon at lower elevations east of the Cascades, and rare in the Umpqua and Willamette Valleys and the Coast Range. There are recent spring records from Coos, Lincoln, and Clatsop Cos.

Broad-tailed Hummingbird. *Selasphorus platycercus.*

Occasional visitant and probable local summer resident, primarily in the south-eastern part of the state.

Evaluation of the status of this species in Oregon is difficult, due partly to questions regarding the identification of some birds reported.

Gabrielson and Jewett cited several sight records from various locations in eastern Oregon. An expedition to Mahogany Mt. in June of 1978 by two of the editors located two male Broad-tailed Hummingbirds in a six hour period. It is perhaps probable that the species breeds locally in the mountains of southern Malheur Co., just as it does in nearby Idaho.

Birds proven by photograph have also been found in July and August near Ukiah, Umatilla Co., in several recent years. Males, and some carefully observed females, have been found on a few occasions in the past ten years in the towns of Fields and Andrews, in southern Harney Co., typically during periods of unusually inclement weather, in mid- and late May. There have also been several reports of males seen in the Little Blitzen canyon on Steens Mt.

Evanich (1992) describes the Broad-tailed Hummingbird as an occasional spring and fall migrant and summer resident in Union and Wallowa Cos. of northeastern Oregon. He speculates that it probably breeds there.

Other spring reports that seem valid are from John Day, Grant Co., and near Chiloquin, Klamath Co. Additional other reports may also be valid. The species has occasionally been reported from various areas west of the Cascades, and some of these reports may be correct. None however have been satisfactorily proven, and some may pertain to young male Anna's Hummingbirds that have developed gorgets, but not yet fully developed red areas of the forecrown.

Rufous Hummingbird. *Selasphorus rufus.*

In the Cascade Mts. and west, uncommon to locally abundant summer resident from the coast to timberline. East of the Cascades, rare summer resident in arid country, uncommon to fairly common in the Blue and Wallowa Mts. of northeast Oregon.

Migrating Rufous Hummingbirds first arrive in Oregon along the coast, where a few males usually are noted in Coos and Curry Cos. by early February. In the interior valleys of western Oregon the earliest migrants usually appear in early March. The spring migration peaks west of the Cascades from mid-March through early May, and during this period they are locally abundant along the coast. They are common summer residents along the coast and generally common in the interior valleys; nesting commences in these areas in April. In the Coast Range, Siskiyou Mts. and the Cascades, breeders are uncommon to locally abundant in open forests and meadows up to timberline. At higher elevations nesting may begin as late as June or even early July. In all areas the local abundance appears to be largely dependent on the availability of certain flowers, most of them red, including salmonberry, currants, penstemons, paintbrushes, columbines and others.

Most males migrate to higher elevations, principally in the Cascades, in June and July, and then move southward in the mountains during these months. Dozens may sometimes be seen in flowering meadows at this time. Small numbers of males migrate at lower elevations, especially along the coast. Few males remain in Oregon by early August. Females and immatures migrate in lowlands and mountains from July through early September, with the peak in August. Few are noted after mid-September, but there are some October records. There are more than 10 winter records of *Selasphorus* hummingbirds for the coast and the interior valleys of western Oregon, and although some of these reports may pertain to misidentified Anna's Hummingbirds, at least some are probably referable to the Rufous Hummingbird.

East of the Cascades spring migrants are generally uncommon, and are usually first observed during the first half of April and continue to be noted, in areas where breeding does not occur, through May. In arid sagebrush country and grasslands the Rufous Hummingbird is a rare, local summer resident only occurring where there is ample water and flowers. In the Blue and Wallowa Mts. it is generally uncommon to locally fairly common, from the semi-open valleys to timberline. Males gather and migrate at higher elevations in June and July, but not in as large numbers as in the Cascades. Fall migrants are noted in the lowlands beginning in late June. The fall migration peaks from mid-July through mid-August, a few are noted in early September. The latest record is for Bend, on Oct. 27, 1987.

Allen's Hummingbird. *Selasphorus sasin.*

On the coast, a common summer resident north to southern Coos Co. and rarely in summer north to Douglas Co.

The Allen's Hummingbird is a common summer resident along the coast of Curry Co. and Coos Co. at least as far north as Bandon. Further north on the coast in summer, it is very uncommon at Coos Bay (may breed) and rare at Reedsport, Douglas Co. A male was netted, measured, and photographed at Astoria, Clatsop Co., on March 10, 1988.

Like the similar Rufous Hummingbird, spring migrants arrive on the coast early, first appearing in late February and early March. By late March most have returned. Fall migration peaks in July and after early August there are few records. This is probably due to the great difficulty of separating female and immature Rufous from Allen's Hummingbirds. Since *Selasphorus* hummingbirds are noted on the south coast into September, Allen's may remain in the state longer than records indicate.

Because of this species' similarity to some first year male Rufous Humming-birds, most of the several inland observations in northwestern Oregon are viewed with caution. One recorded at Corvallis, Benton Co., on March 28, 1979 was well described, and there is also a specimen of a male from Corvallis, found injured in April 1983.

In the Rogue Valley it is a very rare summer visitant with about 10 records distributed fairly evenly between April 1 and Aug. 14. There is a record from Crater Lake National Park, Klamath Co., on July 6, 1964.

Order CORACIIFORMES
Family Alcedinidae

Belted Kingfisher. *Ceryle alcyon.*

Uncommon to fairly common permanent resident.

Throughout most of Oregon the Belted Kingfisher is a fairly common summer resident, but is rather rare in some areas such as Malheur N.W.R. Availability of cutbanks for nesting sites limits its presence in areas that would be otherwise suitable. Breeding occurs near streams, rivers, lakes, and estuaries from the coast to high in the mountains.

In winter, it is uncommon to fairly common near fresh and salt water west of the Cascade Mts., and rare to locally fairly common at lower elevations east of the Cascades.

Order PICIFORMES
Family Picidae

Lewis' Woodpecker. *Melanerpes lewis.*

Locally fairly common to rare summer resident and widespread transient, except along the coast and the Willamette Valley where it has been nearly extirpated. In winter, fairly common in Jackson and Josephine Cos., rare in the Willamette and Umpqua Valleys.

Gabrielson and Jewett (1940) described the Lewis' Woodpecker as an exceedingly familiar sight in Oregon from timberline on the highest peaks to the straggling growth of willows and cottonwoods along the stream beds of the eastern part of the state. Since the mid-1960s this species has suffered a drastic decline and has been extirpated as a summer resident in many areas where formerly it was common. Breeding Bird Survey data indicate the Oregon population is declining at an alarming rate. The decline is likely related to the establishment and increasing abundance of the European Starling, which competes effectively for nesting cavities, and the destruction of lowland oak habitats in the interior valleys of western Oregon.

In Jackson and Josephine Cos., Lewis' Woodpeckers are locally fairly common summer residents in the chaparral-oak community and in open mixed conifer forests at lower elevations. Wintering concentrations in this region vary annually, but generally the species is fairly common in oaks in Jackson and Josephine Cos., and uncommon and declining in Douglas Co. In late August through October, with the peak in mid-September, there is an influx of transients throughout Oregon east of the Coast Range. Most of these migrants winter south of the state. Spring migrants return to Oregon breeding sites in late April and May. The local abundance of migrants varies greatly from year to year. Most years many are noted in late August and early September at timberline, where they feed on insects and berries.

In the Willamette Valley the Lewis' Woodpecker was formerly a fairly common summer resident and transient and uncommon to fairly common winterer. Breeding occurred in the Tillamook Burn of the northern Oregon Coast Range. In some autumns and winters large numbers from outside the area appeared in the Willamette Valley. A general decline was obvious by the late 1960s, and by the mid-1970s it had become rare as a breeder and very uncommon as a transient and winterer. The last breeding record known for the northern Willamette Valley was near Scappoose, Columbia Co. in 1977. Today it is a very rare spring and fall transient, and very rare winter visitant in the Willamette Valley.

On the coast it is a very rare spring and fall transient and winter visitant in Curry and Coos Cos.

East of the Cascades it is a fairly common to rare local summer resident in open forests, usually at lower elevations. Ponderosa pines and cottonwoods along watercourses are frequently utilized for nesting, as are snags in burns. Areas of particular importance in summer include Hood River, Wasco, Union, Wallowa, Baker, and Grant Cos. Smaller numbers are found as breeders in many other areas east of the Cascades. Oaks in Wasco and Hood River Cos. are used year-round, and individuals can be found in oak habitats elsewhere with less regularity. Other occasional winter records east of the Cascades are from the Grande Ronde Valley, Union Co., and the Klamath Basin. During migration east of the Cascades it often occurs along watercourses and where there are a few trees in arid open country.

Acorn Woodpecker. *Melanerpes formicivorus.*

Common permanent resident of the interior valleys and hills of southwestern Oregon. In the Willamette Valley, locally common in the south, local and uncommon in the north.

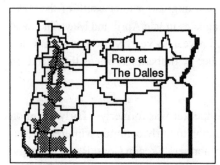

The Acorn Woodpecker is a common permanent resident of the valleys and foothills of Jackson, Josephine, and interior Douglas Cos. It is an uncommon permanent resident in the valleys within the Siskiyou Mts. of Curry and Coos Cos.

Gabrielson and Jewett (1940) reported only one Lane Co. record, but today it is a common resident of oaks in the southern Willamette Valley, and a fairly common resident northward in the Willamette Valley to Washington Co., where it is uncommon and local. Generally, greater numbers occur in the dryer western half of the Valley. It is absent from the northeastern portion, occurring regularly only to central Marion Co. Acorn Woodpeckers have only twice been recorded on Sauvie I., perhaps due to the habitat barrier created by the evergreen-dominated forests of the Tualatin Mts.

Acorn Woodpeckers were observed in The Dalles, Wasco Co., in the early 1960s, and a few have been found to be resident there since the late 1970s. Gabrielson and Jewett (1940) cite an 1883 record of three birds from Upper Klamath L., Klamath Co., and currently they are locally common residents in oak woodlands within the Klamath R. canyon, Klamath Co. One at Summer Lake, Lake Co., on May 27-28, 1989 was extralimital.

Acorn Woodpeckers form loose colonies where there are oak trees. They remain with their colony and store acorns throughout the year, although occasionally birds stray from established breeding areas. European Starlings compete with this species for nesting cavities, but this aggressive woodpecker has fared far better than the Lewis' Woodpecker in the face of such competition.

Yellow-bellied Sapsucker. *Sphyrapicus varius.*

Vagrant.

This highly-migratory eastern species has been recorded about seven times in Oregon. As it has been variously lumped and split with the following species, some records are not well-documented. Records include a male and a first year female at Scoggins Valley Park, Washington Co., on July 9, 1976; an adult male at La Grande, Union Co., on July 11, 1980; an adult female photographed at Gilchrist, Klamath Co., on July 5, 1983; individuals at Malheur N.W.R. on Oct. 4, 1987 and Oct. 14, 1990; a young male at Brookings, Curry Co., Feb. 24-25, 1991; and an adult male at Silver Lake, Lake Co., from Oct. 6-11, 1991.

Red-naped Sapsucker. *Sphyrapicus nuchalis*

Common summer resident and transient from east slope of Cascade Mts. eastward. In winter, rare in Klamath Co. and very rare elsewhere. Very rare west of the Cascade summit.

The Red-naped Sapsucker is a common summer resident from the eastern slope of the Cascades eastward throughout the Blue Mts., Wallowa Mts., and lesser mountains such as Mahogany Mt., Malheur Co.; Steens Mt., Harney Co.; and Hart Mt., Lake Co. It is also a common spring and fall transient through these mountains and at lower elevations along rivers, in towns, and at desert oases. Migrants have been noted in late March, but more typically arrive in mid-April, and occasionally into May. Fall migrants have been noted at Malheur N.W.R. as early as August 18 and as late as October 18. The peak of migration takes place in September.

The Red-naped Sapsucker is rare in winter at lower elevations in Klamath Co., where single birds have been noted on the Klamath Falls Christmas Bird Count. It is very rare in winter elsewhere east of the Cascades.

Vagrants have occurred in spring, summer, and fall to various locations west of the Cascades, along the coast and at inland sites. The species bred in eastern Jackson Co. in 1992.

187

Red-breasted Sapsucker. *Sphyrapicus ruber.*

Fairly common permanent resident from the western slope of the Cascade Mts. westward and in Klamath Co.; also locally in Lake Co. Rare summer resident along the eastern slope of the Cascade Mts. and a rare summer visitant in the Blue Mts. and Wallowa Mts. Rare transient in Harney Co.

The Red-breasted Sapsucker is a fairly common permanent resident from the western slope of the Cascade Mts. west to the ocean. Altitudinal and possibly southward migration occurs in winter, when the species increases in number in the inland valleys and foothills. It is a fairly common permanent resident in Klamath and Lake Cos.

The Red-breasted Sapsucker is a rare summer resident on the east slope of the Cascade Mts. north of the Klamath Basin. In recent years it has been found to be a rare summer visitant in the Blue Mts. and Wallowa Mts., but nesting has not been confirmed. There are several recent September records and only one May record for the Harney Co. deserts.

The Red-breasted Sapsucker utilizes deciduous and mixed forests and woodlands. Wintering birds are often found at localities that do not support nesting.

Williamson's Sapsucker. *Sphyrapicus thyroideus.*

Uncommon to common summer resident on east slope of the Cascade Mts., and in the Blue, Wallowa, and Warner Mts. Rare in winter in the Klamath Basin and very rare elsewhere east of the Cascade summit.

The Williamson's Sapsucker is an uncommon to common summer resident on the east slope and near timberline in the Cascade Mts., and in the Blue Mts., Wallowa Mts., and the Warner Mts. It nests in coniferous forests, and occasionally in deciduous riparian habitat within coniferous forests.

Migrants arrive in mid-March and April, and depart from late August through mid-October. Transients are occasionally noted at isolated mountains where breeding does not occur, at desert oases, and in other habitats.

Williamson's Sapsucker is a scarce winter resident in Klamath and Lake Cos. and only a very rare winter resident elsewhere in Oregon. There is a Dec. 1 record from Lake Co. (Gabrielson and Jewett 1940), and a Jan. 8, 1980, record from Union, Union Co. Evanich (1992) mentions an additional winter record from northeastern Oregon.

Gabrielson and Jewett (1940) mention at least one occurrence in the Siskiyou Mts. south of Ashland, Jackson Co., (date not mentioned), and one was seen near the town of Siskiyou on May 30, 1960. It may prove to be a rare summer resident of the Siskiyou Mts.

The species occasionally crosses the Cascade crest to the west slope, especially after the breeding season. Most such records have been from the southern part of the state, though there are at least three spring records from Mary's Peak, Benton Co. One photographed at Ashland, Jan. 15, 1982, is the only confirmed winter record west of the Cascade Mts.

Nuttall's Woodpecker. *Picoides nuttallii.*

Vagrant.

Until recently the only two records are those of a male collected Feb. 3, 1881, and a female collected Feb. 4, 1881, near "Ashland, Og'n" by H.W. Henshaw. The specimens are in the British Museum. One reportedly taken in the Umpqua Valley in August, 1855, is doubtful regarding the locality of collection (Gabrielson and Jewett 1940). Some question exists as to whether the Ashland birds were properly labeled as to location, but the record is accepted by the OBRC.

One was picked up dead in 1991 near Shady Cove, Jackson Co., and is now a specimen in the collection at Southern Oregon State College (M. Ralph Browning, in press).

Downy Woodpecker. *Picoides pubescens.*

Common permanent resident at moderate to low elevations throughout the state.

The Downy Woodpecker is a common permanent resident at moderate to low elevations throughout the state. In Oregon this small woodpecker inhabits deciduous and mixed woodlands and occasionally coniferous forests. Riparian areas grown in willows, alder, or cottonwood are particularly favored. It also inhabits cities where there are sufficient trees available.

Hairy Woodpecker. *Picoides villosus.*

Common to uncommon permanent resident throughout the state.

The Hairy Woodpecker is a permanent resident in evergreen, mixed, and to a lesser extent deciduous forests throughout Oregon. This species occurs from sea level to timberline. It is often very common in burns and alder woodlands which harbor many dead trees.

It is common in the Cascade, Blue, Wallowa, Coast Range and Siskiyou Mts., and generally uncommon in the interior valleys of western Oregon. It is fairly common along the coast.

White-headed Woodpecker. *Picoides albolarvatus.*

Fairly common to rare permanent resident of ponderosa pine forests in the Cascade, Blue, Wallowa, Warner, and Siskiyou Mts.

The White-headed Woodpecker is a fairly common permanent resident of ponderosa pine forests on the eastern slope of the Cascade Mts. Similar forests in the Blue Mts. have been so degraded by logging practices that it is now quite scarce. In the vicinity of Crater L., Klamath Co., its range crosses the Cascade summit to the western slope, where it is very uncommon in forests dominated by ponderosa pine. It is generally an uncommon permanent resident of ponderosa forests in the Wallowa Mts., and in the Siskiyou Mts. of southern Jackson, Josephine, and eastern Curry Cos. Smaller numbers occur at higher elevations within these mountain ranges where ponderosa pines mix with other conifers.

Rarely during winter individuals occur in deciduous trees in open country east of the Cascades. Vagrants have reached Lincoln and Clatsop Cos.

Three-toed Woodpecker *Picoides tridactylus.*

Uncommon to rare permanent resident of the Blue and Wallowa Mts. and locally in the Cascades.

The Three-toed Woodpecker is an uncommon permanent resident in the Wallowa Mts. and the Blue Mts., at least as far west as Crook Co. It is a rare permanent resident in the Cascade Mts., south into Klamath Co. In the Cascades it almost exclusively inhabits high elevations. It is also very rare in central Lake Co., and has occurred once on Hart Mt. It is generally more local and irregular on the southern edge of its range. West of high Cascades there are only two sight records: one on Roxy Anne Butte, Jackson Co., on Dec. 28, 1962; and one at Mt. Ashland, Jackson Co., on May 18, 1962 (Browning, 1975).

This species and the Black-backed Woodpecker are often sympatric, but the Three-toed tends to occur at higher elevations. It occurs in a variety of subalpine forest types and also invades recent burns and areas of insect outbreaks. In winter it is rare in lower elevation forests.

Black-backed Woodpecker. *Picoides arcticus.*

Uncommon resident of forests in eastern Oregon.

The Black-backed Woodpecker is generally an uncommon permanent resident in lodgepole pine and other moderate to high elevation coniferous forests in the Cascade, Blue, Wallowa, and Siskiyou Mts. Ponderosa pines are less frequently inhabited, at least where there has been a fairly recent burn. It occurs from 4,000 to 7,800 ft. in elevation in southern Oregon (Short 1982). In the Cascade Mts. it is far more numerous near the summit and on the eastern slope than on the western slope, and is fairly common in the extensive lodgepole pine forests of Deschutes, Klamath, and Lake Cos.

Black-backed Woodpeckers often breed and winter in increased abundance in areas with large numbers of dead trees and high insect densities, such as result from burns, insect epidemics, and blow-downs. Distribution within its range is often spotty and depends on the availability of these conditions.

Northern Flicker. *Colaptes auratus.*

Common permanent resident throughout the state.

The Northern Flicker is a common permanent resident throughout Oregon, and nests from sea level to timberline. There is some vertical migration from high elevations in fall. Small flocks often form in winter.

A wide variety of habitats are utilized, but woodland edges bordering open country, and open forests are preferred. Dense forests are generally avoided. Buildings and even large sage brush are used for nesting in grasslands and deserts east of the Cascades. Flickers are common in farmland and in towns, especially during the winter.

The Red-shafted Flicker (*C. a. cafer*) is the usual subspecies found in Oregon. The Yellow-shafted Flicker (*C. a. auratus*) is found rarely as a winter visitant and transient from September through April. The two subspecies hybridize freely where their ranges overlap in the Rocky Mts. and Great Plains, and birds showing intermediate characteristics are not unusual in Oregon.

Pileated Woodpecker. *Dryocopus pileatus.*

Uncommon permanent resident in forested areas throughout the state.

The Pileated Woodpecker is an uncommon permanent resident in forested areas throughout the state. It utilizes various forest types, including those dominated by conifers, maples, oaks, and cottonwoods. Pileated Woodpeckers are absent in open country, juniper forests, and isolated pine and aspen stands east of the Cascade Mts.

192

This species is somewhat nomadic in winter, when individuals occasionally occur away from breeding areas. Pileated Woodpeckers are often associated with large, undisturbed forests, but also inhabit woodlands within cities, such as areas in Portland's West Hills. The greatest densities occur in mature coniferous forests, a forest type that is fast disappearing.

Order PASSERIFORMES
Family Tyrannidae

Olive-sided Flycatcher. *Contopus borealis.*

Fairly common to common summer resident in areas of evergreen forests and an uncommon transient elsewhere throughout the state.

The Olive-sided Flycatcher breeds throughout Oregon in coniferous forests from sea level to near timberline. It is fairly common to common in coniferous forests with snags or trees with high dead branches. Breeders seldom inhabit dense young stands of trees of uniform height or small isolated groves. Numbers appear to have declined in the last fifteen years.

Transients appear in a variety of habitats where breeding does not occur, including juniper and oak woodlands, riparian areas, and oases. The spring migration peaks in mid- and late May, but there are early May records and very few late April records. Transients are regularly noted at desert oases into early June. The fall migration peaks in late August and early September, and there are a few late September records.

Western Wood-Pewee. *Contopus sordidulus.*

Common summer resident and transient throughout Oregon, except on north coast where uncommon.

The Western Wood-Pewee is the most widespread and adaptable flycatcher in Oregon, breeding throughout the state in a variety of habitats from sea level to timberline. Breeders are common in open deciduous and coniferous forests and woodland edges, at low and moderate elevations. Orchards, streamside woodlands and many residential areas are also inhabited. It is only a local and uncommon summer resident on the north coast. In the Cascade and Blue Mts. it breeds to timberline, but is generally local and uncommon above 5,500 ft. In arid open country east of the Cascades breeders are common in aspens to over 6,000 ft., in deciduous growth along watercourses and around homesteads and springs. Summer residents are locally uncommon in dense stands of juniper and mountain mahogany.

Transients, which appear in many habitats where breeding does not occur, are common throughout Oregon except along the north coast where they are rare. The fall migration peaks in late August and early September. By mid-September pewees are very uncommon, and there are a few late September records.

Spring migrants first appear in late April and early May (very rarely mid-April) and generally peak in mid- and late May. Migratory movements are often detected into early June east of the Cascades.

Eastern Wood-Pewee. *Contopus virens.*

Vagrant.

An individual was seen and heard calling and singing at Malheur N.W.R. on May 28-30, 1994.

Yellow-bellied Flycatcher. *Empidonax faviventris.*

Vagrant.
A calling bird was at Malheur N.W.R. on June 10-11, 1983, for the only Oregon record.

Willow Flycatcher. *Empidonax traillii.*

Uncommon to locally common summer resident and transient statewide.

The Willow Flycatcher is a common to uncommon summer resident west of the Cascade crest and a locally common summer resident east of the Cascades, inhabiting willow thickets bordering streamside lakes, woodland edges, young alder forests, and tall brush at the margins of fields. It usually occurs near water and is primarily a lowland species, although it is occasionally found breeding at up to 5,000 ft. in the Cascades, the Blue Mts., and on desert mountains.

A note of caution is necessary about the breeding status of this species in the state. Due to its late spring arrival, singing birds in early June may still be transients and not breeders at that site. Because of this the exact breeding distribution of this flycatcher is still somewhat unclear.

The Willow Flycatcher is an uncommon to common transient throughout the state. Spring migrants typically begin arriving in mid-May, but in some years they first appear in late May. There may be a few valid late April and early May records, but special care should be exercised in identifying this species before mid-May. Transients are noted into mid-June. The fall migration peaks in late August east of the Cascades and in early September west of the Cascades. Small numbers are noted into late September and rarely the first days of October. Concentrations sometimes occur during fall such as 32 on Cape Blanco, Curry Co., on Sept. 14, 1974 and 51 banded at a Medford, Jackson Co., banding station on Sept. 6, 1971.

The very closely related Alder Flycatcher, *E. alnorum,* is on the list of Oregon birds compiled by the Oregon Bird Records Committee on the basis of several records from Malheur N.W.R. Others have been reported elsewhere, usually in Willow Flycatcher nesting habitat. Identification by sight is virtually impossible. Although these birds have made vocalizations apparently identical or very similar to songs of the Alder Flycatcher in its normal range, some think they may be Willow Flycatchers as call notes are not totally consistent with those expected of Alder Flycatcher. Until this situation is resolved, we prefer not to give Alder Flycatcher full standing on the Oregon list.

Least Flycatcher. *Empidonax minimus.*

Rare migrant and vary local summer resident.

195

The Least Flycatcher is a rare migrant or vagrant at southeastern Oregon oases in late May and early June, though identification problems obscure its status. Several have been mist-netted or photographed at Malheur N.W.R. and Hart Mt., Lake Co. There are two records of territorial birds in western Oregon: a June 26, 1983 record from Glide, Douglas Co., and one on Sauvie I., Multnomah Co., from June 2 to July 4, 1991. A coastal vagrant was at Cape Blanco, Curry Co., on Sept. 1, 1985. A calling bird was in a residential area of Tillamook, Tillamook Co., on Dec. 20-28, 1992.

There is also an isolated breeding location, first discovered in 1982, at Clyde Holliday State Wayside, Grant Co. The resident pair was observed feeding a fledgling Brown-headed Cowbird on July 4, 1983 to confirm breeding at the site. These birds were present intermittently through the late 1980s and early 1990s.

Hammond's Flycatcher. *Empidonax hammondii.*

Uncommon to common summer resident of all mountain areas of the state. Rare summer resident along north coast. Uncommon transient in lowlands statewide.

The Hammond's Flycatcher is a common summer resident in the Cascade and Siskiyou Mts. It is uncommon to fairly common throughout the various ranges of the Blue Mts., and to a lesser extent on Steens Mt., Hart Mt., and in the Warner Mts. It is generally an uncommon summer resident in the Coast Range. In recent years a few presumed breeders have been found in the coastal lowlands of Lincoln, Tillamook, and Clatsop Cos.

As a summer resident the Hammond's Flycatcher is a bird of the dense, usually humid, coniferous forests, typically at middle to high elevations. Similar conditions exist at spots along the north coast where breeding is suspected. Occasionally it can be found during breeding season in somewhat more open forests east of the Cascades.

This flycatcher is a fairly common transient in the lowlands of interior western Oregon in spring, and uncommon in fall. It is also occasionally reported in transit along the coast. It is a fairly common transient east of the Cascades away from breeding areas.

The spring migration takes place from mid-April through late May, and transients are sometimes still seen into early June at oases in Harney Co. The fall migration has been noted from mid-August through mid-September. A well-described bird Dec. 19, 1992 near Roseburg, Douglas Co., is the only acceptable winter record.

Dusky Flycatcher. *Empidonax oberholseri.*

Uncommon to common summer resident in the Siskiyou Mts., Cascade Mts., and all mountain areas to the east. Uncommon to fairly common transient in the Cascades and eastward. Rare transient west of the Cascades.

The Dusky Flycatcher is a common summer resident in the Siskiyou Mts. of Jackson, Josephine, and eastern Curry Cos. It also occurs in the southern portions of inland Coos and Douglas Cos. Several territorial birds, presumed breeders, were found near Gales Peak, Washington Co., in 1983 and several years since.

The Dusky Flycatcher is also a common summer resident the entire length of the Cascade Mts., although habitat is limited on the western slope north of Lane Co., where this species becomes much less common. It nests in montane chaparral and open coniferous forests in the Siskiyous and Cascades.

It is also a common summer resident throughout most mountain areas east of the Cascades, except in the northeastern corner of the state (Union and Wallowa Cos.) where it is an uncommon breeder. In addition to montane chaparral and open coniferous forests, it nests in higher sage brush areas (usually near aspen groves), in mountain mahogany stands, and juniper forests.
Although transient records are hard to judge due to the difficulty in identifying *Empidonax* flycatchers in migration, this species is considered an uncommon to fairly common transient east of the Cascades.

Gray Flycatcher. *Empidonax wrightii.*

Uncommon to fairly common summer resident in south-central and southeastern Oregon, locally uncommon summer resident in north-central Oregon, and locally uncommon summer resident in the Blue Mts. Vagrant to western Oregon.

The Gray Flycatcher is an uncommon to fairly common summer resident east of the Cascade Mts. in the general region south of the Blue Mts. and in the Bend area. In north-central Oregon north of Bend and the Blue Mts., and in valleys within the Blue Mts., it is a local and uncommon summer resident.

Open sagebrush country, juniper forests and mountain mahogany woodlands up to at least 6,000 ft. are inhabited. Areas with large sagebrush are utilized most frequently. Breeders are locally common in open forests of ponderosa pine, and occasionally lodgepole pine, which have a ground cover of sagebrush and bitter-brush. In such areas Gray and Dusky Flycatchers may be sympatric.

Migrants arrive on the breeding grounds in late April and early May. The earliest record is April 16, 1972 at Bend. They generally depart by mid-September, but there are a few late September records.

Gray Flycatchers are rare spring migrants in western Oregon with records ranging from April 14 to May 14. Records have come from Jackson, Benton, Curry, Josephine, Lane, Linn, Clackamas, and Douglas Cos.

Pacific-slope Flycatcher. *Empidonax difficilis.*
Cordilleran Flycatcher. *Empidonax occidentalis.*
Formerly: **Western Flycatcher**

Common summer resident and transient west of the Cascade Mts. Locally common to very uncommon summer resident and transient east of the Cascades.

Note: The Western Flycatcher was separated into two species in the late 1980s by the American Ornithologists Union. Some of the research was done in Oregon. That research indicated that the Cordilleran Flycatcher is the species generally found east of the Cascade summit, and the Pacific-slope Flycatcher is the species found to the west. Controversy regarding the decision to split the former Western Flycatcher into separate species continues. Because of this, and the great difficulty with which the two species are identified (at least away from nesting sites) we have decided to treat them as one for the purpose of this account.

The Western Flycatcher is a common summer resident and transient from about 4,000 ft. on the west slope of the Cascades to the coast. Breeders inhabit moist, well-shaded coniferous and deciduous forest. In the Cascades it is locally fairly common in moist canyons and occurs nearly to timberline.

On the east slope of the Cascades and in mountains to the east it is a locally common to very uncommon summer resident in well-shaded forests, usually in valley bottoms or along watercourses.

During migration, Western Flycatchers appear in a variety of habitats not utilized for breeding, including open forests and deciduous brush. Spring migrants arrive in mid-April and early May and breeders are common west of the Cascades by mid-May. East of the Cascades, transients are generally uncommon but locally fairly common at oases in arid country. Migrants first arrive east of the Cascades in late April and early May, but peak in the latter half of May and early June, and a few are sometimes noted into mid-June. Statewide, the fall migration peaks in late August and early September, and by mid-September the species is very uncommon. There are a few early October records, with a late date of Nov. 8. There are also a few winter reports, with a well-described bird at Grants Pass, Josephine Co., on Dec. 29, 1991.

Eastern Phoebe. *Sayornis phoebe.*

Vagrant.

There is one certain record for this species, one at Falls City, Polk Co., from June 5-23, 1992.

Black Phoebe. *Sayornis nigricans.*

Uncommon to locally fairly common summer resident and rare in winter in the Rogue Valley and its tributary valleys. Local fairly common permanent resident in coastal Curry Co., and an uncommon winter visitant north to at least the lower Coquille Valley. Vagrant elsewhere in Oregon.

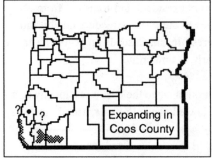

Expanding in
Coos County

Although unreported by Gabrielson and Jewett (1940), the Black Phoebe has been a regular resident of the Rogue Valley area since at least the early 1930s (Richardson 1964). It is now regarded as uncommon to fairly common local summer resident and as a locally uncommon winter resident. It is usually found near its preferred nesting sites, bridges over water. It has nested at least as far north as Evans Creek, just north of Wimer, Jackson Co., and at least twice at Myrtle Point, Coos, Co.

In recent years the Black Phoebe has been found regularly at all seasons along the Curry Co. coast. Nesting has been noted from near the Winchuck R. mouth, near Harbor, near the mouth of the Pistol R., and at Ophir. During the 1990s as many as 35 have been reported in the Coquille Valley, Coos Co. in winter. There are four coastal records north of Coos Co.: one collected near Mercer, Lane Co., on June 1, 1936; single birds near Newport, Lincoln Co., on Jan. 3, 1976, and May 15, 1984; and one at Beaver Creek, Tillamook Co., in early April 1994.

Fall and winter vagrants have reached Klamath Co., Harney Co., inland Douglas Co., Gold Lake in the Lane Co. Cascades, and as far north in the Willamette Valley as Benton Co. There is also a spring record from Lake Co., two from Harney Co., and one from Oakridge, Lane Co.

Say's Phoebe. *Sayornis saya.*

Uncommon to common transient and summer resident and very rare in winter east of the Cascade Mts. Very uncommon transient and very rare winter visitant in interior valleys west of the Cascades. Rare transient and very rare winter visitant along the coast.

The Say's Phoebe is an uncommon to common summer resident east of the Cascades. It is often found at ranches, where buildings provide nesting sites, as well as in steep canyons where nests can be built on cliffs. The spring migration takes place from mid-February through March, with a few birds sometimes noted in early February. The fall migration takes place in late August and September, with rare stragglers remaining into October. It is very rare in winter east of the Cascades at lower elevations. Outside the breeding season it is often found along streams and near ponds.

Gabrielson and Jewett (1940) listed the Say's Phoebe as a breeding bird of the valleys of interior western Oregon. There have been no reported nesting attempts since then. It is now known only as a very uncommon transient and winter visitant in the Willamette, Umpqua, and especially Rogue Valleys. It is most often found in spring, from late February through April. There are a few May and June records. It is a rare to very uncommon fall transient, when it has been recorded from late August through early November. As a transient this phoebe has shown up in a variety of open or semi-open habitats, even at higher elevations.

On the coast the Say's Phoebe is a very rare transient, more often found in fall than spring. The majority of the few records are for the south coast but it has been recorded the entire length of the coast. Two seen near Port Orford, Curry Co., Dec. 27, 1981, and one at Harbor, Curry Co., on Jan. 16, 1988 are the only coastal winter records.

Vermilion Flycatcher. *Purocephalus rubinus.*

Vagrant.

There are two records of the Vermilion Flycatcher from Oregon. The first, an immature, was seen near Bend, Deschutes Co., from Oct. 10-25, 1992. An adult male was at Myrtle Point, Coos Co., Dec. 6-7, 1992.

Ash-throated Flycatcher. *Myiarchus cinerascens.*

Uncommon to fairly common summer resident east of the Cascade Mts. and interior southwestern Oregon. Vagrant in the Willamette Valley and along the coast.

The Ash-throated Flycatcher is generally uncommon east of the Cascade Mts., but is locally fairly common. It is mainly found in juniper woodlands but also

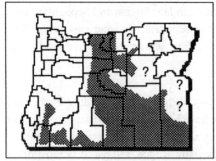

nests in cottonwoods, willows, and other deciduous trees in some canyons and river valleys. Oak woodlands, sometimes mixed with ponderosa pines, are used for nesting habitat in Wasco and Hood River Cos., where the species is common. There are only three records for the combined two-county area of Wallowa and Union Cos. (May, late June, and September records).

The Ash-throated Flycatcher reaches its greatest abundance in the state in the Rogue Valley and surrounding foothills, and in the lower Klamath R. canyon of southwestern Klamath Co., where it is a common summer resident. It is a fairly common summer resident in the Umpqua Valley of Douglas Co. In these areas it is found in oak woodlands and to a lesser extent in riparian woodlands.

This flycatcher is a vagrant in the Willamette Valley, where it has been recorded at least 20 times. The majority of the records are from Lane Co. and are from May or June. These probably represent spring overshoots from breeding areas just to the south. There are a few fall records starting in August, with a Nov. 22, 1952, record from Rickreall, Polk Co., being the latest record for the Willamette Valley. In addition to Lane and Polk Cos., it has been recorded in Clackamas, Marion, and Multnomah Cos.

It is a vagrant to the coast in spring, fall, and early winter, with an exceptionally late date of one at Florence, Lane Co., on Dec. 16, 1990. A pair may have nested near Brookings, Curry Co., in 1993.

The Ash-throated Flycatcher typically arrives in early May and departs by early September. A few birds may linger through September and rarely into October.

Tropical Kingbird. *Tyrannus melancholicus.*

Vagrant.

This species has been recorded only as a post-breeding dispersant from south of the United States border. All records are from the immediate coast; dates range from September 30 to November 17. To date there have been about 14 records.

Cassin's Kingbird. *Tyrannus vociferans.*

Vagrant.

The only record of this species is of one collected Aug. 4, 1935, at Mercer in Lane Co. (Jewett 1942).

Western Kingbird. *Tyrannus verticalis.*

Fairly common to common summer resident east of the Cascade Mts., and in the Rogue and Umpqua Valleys. Uncommon to very uncommon transient, summer resident, and summer visitant in the Willamette Valley. Uncommon to rare transient along the coast.

The Western Kingbird arrives by mid- to late April and departs the state by early to mid-September. It is a common summer resident east of the Cascades, and in the Rogue and Umpqua Valleys. It nests in open country near ranch houses, towns, isolated groves of trees, and cottonwood-lined stream courses.

It is a very uncommon spring (mostly May), rare fall transient, and rare summer resident in the Willamette Valley north of southern Lane Co. It is most frequently encountered as a breeder in Lane Co., but nesting has been recorded throughout the length of the Willamette Valley, and in Multnomah and Columbia Cos. along the lower Columbia R. It has bred irregularly in southeast Coos Co.

This kingbird is a very uncommon transient in spring (May and June) and rare in fall (August and September) along the coast. Several reports from coastal locations later in fall may actually have been occurrences of the Tropical Kingbird.

Eastern Kingbird. *Tyrannus tyrannus.*

Uncommon to locally common summer resident and transient east of the Cascade Mts.; rare transient in the Klamath Basin. Rare late spring to early summer vagrant to western Oregon.

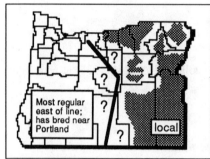

The Eastern Kingbird is generally distributed throughout eastern Oregon, excluding the Klamath Basin and Central Oregon. It arrives in late May, occasionally early May, and departs by mid-September. Its population centers are in the larger irrigated valleys of northeastern Oregon south to Malheur N.W.R., Harney Co. It is locally common in favored areas of Umatilla, Wallowa, Union, and Baker Cos., and along the lower Deschutes River. It is uncommon to rare in many areas east of the Cascades, especially in central and north-central Oregon.

In the Klamath Basin it is a rare spring and early fall transient recorded only two times on the Oregon side, but at least three times in the California portion of the Basin.

In western Oregon this kingbird is a very rare late spring and summer visitant. Since 1962 it has been recorded at least 25 times. All western Oregon records fall between late May and early September with the great majority in late May to mid-June. There are records from most western Oregon counties. Four birds at Powell Butte, Multnomah Co., in the summer of 1992 may have bred. The species was present at various locations in eastern Multnomah Co. in the summers of 1993 and 1994 as well. Breeding occurred near the mouth of the Sandy River, Multnomah Co., in 1993 (Oregon Birds, 20:56).

Scissor-tailed Flycatcher. *Tyrannus forficatus.*

Vagrant.

There are about eight records of this conspicuous flycatcher; most as uncon-firmed single-observer sight records. One at Davis Lake, Klamath Co., on June 14, 1978 was photographed, as was one at Devil's Punchbowl State Park, Lincoln Co., from Nov. 10-14, 1993. Others include singles at Cape Arago, Coos Co., on May 7, 1966; at Malheur N.W.R. June 27, 1973; near Burns, Harney Co., on Aug. 3, 1987; at Cascade Head, Tillamook Co., on May 16, 1992; at Portland May 25, 1992; at Cape Blanco, Curry Co., on June 26, 1992; and at the S. Jetty of the Columbia R., Clatsop Co, on Nov. 12, 1993.

Horned Lark. *Eremophila alpestris.*

Local and uncommon permanent resident and transient west of the Cascades. Common to abundant permanent resident and transient east of the Cascades. Locally uncommon summer resident above timberline in the Cascade, Wallowa, and Steens Mts.

East of the Cascades the Horned Lark is generally a common permanent resident and transient, where it inhabits open short grass habitats, areas of low and fairly sparse sage, grain producing areas, plowed fields, the edges of alkali playas, and other open, sparsely-vegetated habitats. It is one of the few species that has bene-fited from the extensive planting of exotic crested wheatgrass east of the Cas-cades (Littlefield, 1990). Transient and wintering flocks can number in the hundreds.

In the Willamette Valley the Horned Lark nests locally in small numbers in large open fields where very short vegetation or open ground is present. It has probably declined somewhat in recent decades, but may never have been common. A few transients and winter birds are also sometimes noted. The species is absent from most parts of the valley.

Along the coast it was formerly an uncommon and local summer resident on sand spits. The last nesting site that we aware of was at the S. Jetty of the Columbia R., where a particularly beautiful form of the species was present in very small num-bers. That site was abandoned in the mid-1980s. Its apparent elimination as a nesting species along the coast is evidently due to dune stabilization, which results in vegetation too tall for this species. It still occurs as an uncommon tran-sient along the coast in September. Autumn transients have on rare occasions been noted at open habitats on Coast Range mountain tops at various locations. The Horned Lark is a summer resident above timber line in the Wallowa and Cascade Mts., and on Steens Mt. Three were singing in possible breeding habitat in the Siskiyou Mts. near Vulcan Peak, Curry Co., on May 23, 1993.

Family Hirundinidae

Purple Martin. *Progne subis.*

Uncommon and local summer resident and an uncommon to rare transient in many areas of Oregon.

The Purple Martin is Oregon's least common swallow. It is a local summer resident in many scattered areas west of the Cascades. East of the Cascades it is a local summer resident in Klamath Co.

It is absent as a nesting species over the rest of the eastern two-thirds of the state, and only occurs there as a rare to very rare transient. Littlefield (1990) mentions three spring records from the refuge files for the Malheur National Wildlife Refuge, and we know of two additional sightings. All are for May, except an exceptionally early record from March 15, 1982.

West of the Cascades transients can occur about anywhere, but the species is generally uncommon to rare in migration away from its breeding sites, since the species is not numerous north of Oregon. The first migrants arrive in early April, and obvious transients are sometimes noted into early May. The fall migration is in August and the first half of September.

Nesting takes place where large snags are present with woodpecker holes of correct size are present. In Oregon these are usually made by Northern Flickers, and in some areas by Acorn Woodpeckers. Holes in old log pilings along watercourses are also used. Increasingly, the species is dependent upon nest boxes put up by dedicated volunteers along waterways especially for this species. Competition from the vile Starling for nesting sites in the past half-century has caused problems for the Purple Martin. Some areas that formerly supported this species are now without nesting populations. Although most nest sites that we know of are along watercourses, it also nests to some extent in other situations, including ridge tops at moderate elevations, or in snags left in clearcut areas of forest. Foraging is generally done over water or open country. It probably forages further afield from its nest sites than do other species of swallows.

Tree Swallow. *Tachycineta bicolor.*

Common summer resident and transient statewide.

The Tree Swallow is a common summer resident throughout the state. As a nesting bird it is almost always associated with bodies of fresh or brackish water. The only other requirements seem to be that there be sufficient foraging areas that are not overly obstructed by trees, and the presence of trees or snags with woodpecker holes, or man-made cavities of similar dimensions for nesting.

This is the hardiest swallow. It arrives earliest in spring. Occasionally the first presumed migrants west of the Cascades have been noted during the last days of January, especially in southwestern Oregon. More typically the vanguard is noted in early February. By early March it is usually present in good numbers west of the Cascades. Apparent transients headed further north are noted into early May. East of the Cascades it typically arrives in early March or the last days of February, and may not be common until April.

The autumn migration begins in August, and is most pronounced in September. Only a few birds remain by mid-October. Its migratory status is somewhat obscured by the fact that there are records for this species for every month of the year, on both sides of the Cascades. As a migrant it sometimes concentrates over watercourses in hundreds or even thousands of birds, especially during cold weather.

It is a very rare winterer west of the Cascades. Although most attempts at wintering lead to disaster, the occasional bird probably succeeds in surviving the winter during years with more mild temperatures. Small flocks have even been seen during the latter half of December in the Willamette Valley. No individuals are seen in December or January during the typical winter.

Violet-green Swallow. *Tachycineta thalassina.*

Common summer resident throughout most of the state, and a common transient statewide.

The Violet-green Swallow is a common summer resident throughout most of the state where it finds suitable nesting situations. These are found where rocky cliffs provide crevices of the correct size, in towns and agricultural lands where nest boxes and crevices in buildings exist, in more open woodland habitats, and the in other forests where suitable woodpecker holes are available. The species is not particularly attracted to water, and in some places is found miles from permanent water nesting on desert cliffs. In contrast, nesting also occurs in crevices on some rocky cliffs over the ocean. This handsome swallow is common in cities such as Portland. There it nests in cornices and eaves of buildings downtown as well as in the residential districts. It nests high in the mountains, almost to timberline.

The first migrants typically are noted at the end of February or early March, but the species is not common until late March or the early part of April. Obvious transients are noted into May. The fall migration begins in late July, and peaks in the latter half of August. Migrants are often noted into early October, but by the middle of that month only the odd stray is noted. Migration east of the Cascades is skewed a bit later in spring and a bit earlier in autumn. Records after September east of the Cascades are very rare. Two were near Forest Grove, Washington Co., on Dec. 20, 1992.

Northern Rough-winged Swallow. *Stelgidopteryx serripennis.*

Common to fairly common summer resident and transient statewide.

The Northern Rough-winged Swallow is a common to fairly common summer resident where it can find dirt banks suitable for its nesting holes. Such situations are usually along streams, but other circumstances are sometimes sufficient even when not in the immediate proximity of water. Unlike the superficially similar Bank Swallow, the Rough-winged Swallow is not a colonial nester. Small numbers may nest in a particular locale due to its suitability, but concentrations are seldom noted outside migration. While the species is never found in nesting con-

208

centrations like the Bank Swallow, it is certainly much more numerous statewide. It nests along some creeks immediately adjacent to where they enter the ocean, as well as in banks in the high desert of southeastern Oregon, and in many other situations in between. Nesting also occurs rather high in the mountains in some places, to 5,000 ft. in Douglas Co.

It typically arrives in numbers in early April west of the Cascades, and in the latter part of April east of the Cascades. Early migrants have been noted west of the Cascades in late February, and in early March east of the Cascades. The fall migration begins in July, and very few are still present by mid-September. Stragglers are sometimes noted into early October.

Bank Swallow. *Riparia riparia.*

Locally common to abundant summer resident. Rare transient west of the Cascades. Uncommon transient east of the Cascades.

The Bank Swallow in Oregon is primarily a bird found east of the Cascade Mountains. There it nests locally in colonies that are sometimes populated by hundreds of pairs. It burrows into the vertical sides of banks, usually those made by streams. Man-made bluffs and banks, such as the sides of road cuts and quarries, are also often used. Since this species must excavate its own burrows, banks with soft soils or sandy loam are required. This fact greatly restricts the species' opportunity to find nesting sites west of the Cascades. Only one small colony is currently known for western Oregon, along the Chetco R. in Curry Co. Gabrielson and Jewett (1940) also mention a small colony that Gabrielson found at Yachats, Lincoln Co., in July 1922. East of the Cascades there are many colonies, but large areas are uninhabited due to the restrictive nesting requirements.

The Bank Swallow is a very rare transient west of the Cascades in spring in late April and May, and a rare transient in the autumn from late July into September. It is generally an uncommon transient through most areas east of the Cascades in late April and May, and again from mid-July to the latter part of August and occasionally into mid-September.

Cliff Swallow. *Hirundo pyrrhonota.*

Common summer resident and transient throughout most of the state.

The Cliff Swallow is a common summer resident throughout most of the state, except along the coast where it is only locally common. This species is one that has benefited by changes created by man in the past 150 years. East of the Cascades it nests in colonies on rim rock and rock cliffs. On both sides of the Cascades it also uses man made structures, such as barns and bridges. Its only other requirements are sufficient numbers of flying insects to support a colony, the availability of some open water from which to drink, and a source of mud in spring to use in nest construction. When these factors coincide, there are likely to be Cliff Swallows. Some colonies number in the hundreds or even thousands. Small groups of several pairs are also encountered. Many areas are now used for nesting where the species must have been absent or very restricted as a breeder before the arrival of the white pioneers last century. The Willamette Valley, for instance, would have provided very few if any natural nesting sites. Now it is common there, and even nests along the river wall in downtown Portland.

Transients occur throughout the state where nesting does not take place. The first migrants usually appear in the last week of March west of the Cascades, and in the first half of April east of the Cascades. Exceptionally early birds have been recorded on both sides of the mountains in the last week of February. It is common in western Oregon by early April, and east of the Cascades by the end of April. The fall migration begins in July, and few birds remain after the end of August. It is very rare by October, but there are a few records west of the Cascades into early November.

Barn Swallow. *Hirundo rustica.*

Common summer resident throughout the state.

The Barn Swallow is a common summer resident from sea level to near timberline throughout the state. During its migrations, particularly in the autumn, flocks that number in the thousands are sometimes found at their evening roosts. Migrants generally first appear in early April, and obvious transients are often noted into May. The earliest spring migrants are sometimes noted in mid-March. The earliest date cited by Littlefield (1990) for the Malheur N.W.R. is Feb. 27. In autumn migrating birds are typically noted from mid-August to mid-October. A few late migrants are sometimes seen into November. There are several true wintering records for the interior valleys of western Oregon and along the coast.

This species is a bird of generally open country. As a nesting bird it requires places not too distant from water, where either naturally overhung cliffs, cutbanks, or man-made structures are present where it can affix its mud nest. Most use structures such as farm buildings and bridges. The clearing of forests, the construction of buildings, the creation of canals and irrigation projects, and similar activities over the past 150 years has without doubt allowed this species to increase greatly in numbers and nest in areas where nesting had formerly been impossible. In the past twenty years it has increased as a nesting species in residential areas of Portland, an area formerly dominated almost exclusively by the Violet-green Swallow.

Family Corvidae

Gray Jay. *Perisoreus canadensis.*

Fairly common to locally uncommon in coniferous forests of the mountains and along the coast.

The Gray Jay is a fairly common resident in the Cascade and Blue Mts. from the upper limits of the Douglas-fir zone to timberline. In lower elevation forests of Douglas-fir and lodgepole pine it is locally uncommon, although seldom found below 2,000 ft. in summer except on the north coast. During winter it descends into ponderosa pines and occasionally the foothills of western Oregon interior valleys. It is often common and tame around campgrounds where it feeds on handouts and refuse.

Gray Jays are uncommon and increasingly local residents of coniferous forests in the Coast Range and breed locally in older forests on the immediate coast south to about Lane Co. In winter they are locally fairly common in conifers along the north coast and often frequent bird feeders. Data of Gabrielson and Jewett (1940) suggest the species was historically more common in the Coast Range. They are also uncommon in the Siskiyou Mts.

There are single September and December records of wanderers for Malheur N.W.R., Harney Co.

Steller's Jay. *Cyanocitta stelleri.*

Common to uncommon resident of coniferous and mixed forests statewide.

The Steller's Jay is a resident of coniferous and mixed woodlands from sea level to timberline throughout Oregon. It is common in most areas where it is present. Small tracts of conifers within cities are often inhabited.

The species is absent or rare in the great desert areas of southeastern Oregon. It is rare during summer in pure juniper forests, and generally uncommon in winter in that habitat. The Steller's Jay is rare in summer and uncommon in winter on Hart Mt., Lake Co.

During late summer and fall it increases at higher elevations of the Cascades in forests of mountain hemlock and fir. During winter throughout the state there is a general withdrawal from higher elevations and some southward movement. During winter individuals occasionally occur in deciduous habitats. During extreme winters east of the Cascades large numbers may gather in lowland towns such as Baker City, Baker Co., and La Grande, Union Co.

Blue Jay. *Cyanocitta cristata.*

Vagrant throughout Oregon with most records in fall and winter.

There are about 25 records of Blue Jay scattered around Oregon, with several records of multiple individuals. Minor invasions in the winters of 1976-77 and 1990-91 account for about two-thirds of the total. With the exception of the one nesting record, the extreme dates of occurrence are Sept. 30 (Lake Co.) and April 14 (Umatilla Co.).

In 1977 a pair nested at the Ranger Station in Union, Union Co., where they were observed feeding three fledglings on July 11, 1977.

Scrub Jay. *Aphelocoma coerulescens.*

Common resident in the inland valleys of western Oregon and southern Lake and Klamath Cos. Uncommon along the southern coast, and in the Hood R. Valley. Expanding its range.

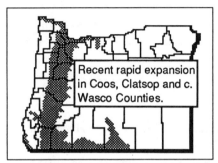

Recent rapid expansion in Coos, Clatsop and c. Wasco Counties.

The Scrub Jay has one of the most complex ranges of any Oregon species. In the Willamette, Rogue, and Umpqua Valleys it is a common resident in open deciduous habitats such as agricultural and residential areas, brushy hillsides, and especially oak woodlands. In the northern Willamette Valley it has increased markedly over the last three decades. A few also reach well into the Cascades, as at Oakridge, Lane Co. It has recently expanded its range down the Columbia R. to Astoria, where it occurs in small numbers year around. Breeding was confirmed there in 1992 and 1993. Wanderers are occasionally reported at other coastal locations south to Coos Co.

In coastal Curry Co. Scrub Jays are uncommon residents north to at least Sixes. They occur rarely in coastal Coos Co., mostly in winter. In the winter of 1993 at least 13 individuals were seen in the lower Coquille Valley, Coos Co.

East of the Cascades in southern Lake and Klamath Cos., Scrub Jays are locally common in juniper forests, residential areas, and on dry, brushy hillsides. In the Hood R. Valley, Hood River Co., they are uncommon residents in areas of mixed agricultural land and deciduous trees. There is a small population in central Wasco Co., and in 1992 and 1993 birds were found as far east as John Day, Grant Co. Elsewhere east of the Cascades there are scattered records, including three from Steens Mountain, Harney Co., where there may historically have been a resident population.

Pinyon Jay. *Gymnorhinus cyanocephalus.*

Fairly common permanent resident in central Oregon. Vagrant elsewhere.

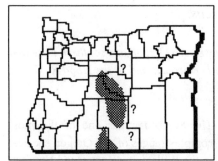

The Pinyon Jay is a fairly common summer resident in the juniper forests of central Oregon, and also breeds in the transition zone between yellow pines and junipers. In summer this bird nests colonially and is often difficult to find. It is most common in Deschutes, Jefferson, Crook, and northern Lake Cos. There are also records for Harney, Malheur, Wheeler, and Wasco Cos., but there is no evidence of breeding there. It is a local and uncommon permanent resident in Klamath Co. and in southeastern Lake Co.

In fall and winter, this species is very gregarious. Flocks of several hundred can be found foraging through the junipers. The semi-open country around and in the towns of Bend and Sisters, Deschutes Co., is perhaps the best area to find this species.

West of the Cascades, two specimens were taken at Salem, Marion Co., Dec. 21, 1910. The species also staged a mini-invasion of the west side in 1987, with records near Tiller, Douglas Co., on Sept. 16; Howard Prairie Res., Jackson Co., Oct. 4; and Lebanon, Linn Co., Oct. 15.

Clark's Nutcracker. *Nucifraga columbiana.*

Fairly common to uncommon resident of high mountain forests. In fall and winter fairly common to uncommon at lower elevations east of the Cascades. Has wandered to all areas of the state.

The Clark's Nutcracker is a fairly common to uncommon resident of high elevation forests in the Cascade and Blue Mts. Generally it nests above 4,000 ft. but east of the Cascades it occasionally nests lower in ponderosa pines and junipers.

Nutcrackers disperse in mid-summer and through winter east of the Cascades. Flocks and individuals are locally fairly common from timberline to the ponderosa pine zone and locally uncommon in junipers. During this period some disperse over open country. There are several records for Malheur N.W.R., Harney

214

Co., and many observations from the isolated pines and junipers of Hart Mt., Lake Co. The erratic winter distribution appears tied to the quality of local cone crops. Oregon winter populations appear to be augmented by northern migrants.

During fall and winter Clark's Nutcrackers occasionally wander west of the high Cascades, where there are records for about 20 widely-scattered locations in both the interior valleys and along the coast. There was a small irruption in the fall of 1986 to western Oregon, with sightings from five locations. During the fall of 1972 hundreds were noted between Bandon and Charleston in Coos Co. The only western Oregon summer record was two observed on Mt. Ashland, Jackson Co., on July 2, 1965.

Black-billed Magpie. *Pica pica.*

Common resident east of the Cascades. Rare visitant to western Oregon.

The Black-billed Magpie is a common permanent resident at lower elevations east of the Cascade Mts. It prefers open sagebrush-juniper areas and areas of agricultural intrusion with scattered deciduous growth. It tends to be less abundant in heavy juniper stands and typically is absent from the pine forests. Magpies also avoid areas with very few or no trees.

This species is most common in Deschutes, Jefferson, Klamath, and Lake Cos. Further east, populations are more scattered. Concentrations occur around irrigated areas, such as northern Malheur Co. There are substantial populations in the Alvord Basin and the Catlow Valley in Harney Co. Magpies are also quite common around Malheur N.W.R. In northeast and north central Oregon this species is found regularly in the irrigated lowlands and only occasionally in other habitats.

The Black-billed Magpie is a fairly regular visitant to the Rogue Valley of Jackson Co. Otherwise, it is rare visitant west of the Cascades in fall and winter. There are far fewer records for spring and summer, but this species has occurred in western Oregon in every month. The one coastal record was a small flock at Blaine, Tillamook Co., on Oct. 8, 1919. Many records are of more than one bird, such as a flock of seven at Portland in June 1967. Although there are no documented breeding records west of the Cascades, two juveniles and one adult at Medford, Jackson Co., on May 17, 1970, indicates probable nesting.

American Crow. *Corvus brachyrhynchos.*

Common resident west of the Cascade Mts. Locally fairly common in summer and very local and sporadic in winter east of the Cascades.

The American Crow is a very common resident in the interior valleys and urban areas of western Oregon and along the coast. Throughout the Coast Range and in the western foothills of the Cascades it is fairly common in agricultural lands and in forests near open country.

East of the Cascades American Crows are locally fairly common during summer in irrigated farmlands, towns and around ranches. During winter they are absent most years in nearly all areas east of the Cascades except the Ontario area, Malheur Co., the Klamath Basin, and the Bend-Redmond-Prinville area. Migrants return east of the Cascades in mid-March.

Northwestern Crow. *Corvus caurinus.*

Status uncertain. Possibly very uncommon in winter on the coast from Lincoln Co. north.

The status and identification of the Northwestern Crow in Oregon are uncertain. Voice, range, and slightly smaller size are the imprecise characteristics field guides use in differentiating this species from the small western forms of the American Crow, with which some authorities believe the Northwestern Crow is conspecific.

Gabrielson and Jewett (1940) report two specimens taken in Portland and from sight records regarded the species (subspecies at that time) as a very uncommon winter visitant to northwestern Oregon.

216

Common Raven. *Corvus corax.*

Common to uncommon permanent resident throughout the state, except in the northern portions of the Willamette Valley.

The Common Raven is a bird of mountains and open country. It can be regularly found throughout the state, except in the northern portion of the Willamette Valley, where it is locally rare.

In western Oregon, this species nests commonly in the Cascades and Coast Range. It is fairly common along the immediate coast throughout the year. Most Common Ravens along the coast during the breeding season are probably foragers from the breeding areas of the Coast Range. In the Willamette Valley, this species is a summer visitant from Salem southward, and it may nest occasionally in the valley. In the Umpqua and Rogue Valleys, Common Ravens are uncommon permanent residents.

East of the Cascades the Common Raven is common in all areas, but is most abundant in the southeast portion of the state. The cattle ranches and the great marshes of Harney and Lake Cos. provide a massive food resource for this scavenger/predator. Flocks of hundreds are sometimes noted even in summer.

In central Oregon, most birds nest at higher elevations and feed in the open sage-juniper areas. In northeast Oregon this bird is a common summer resident in the Blue and Wallowa Mts.

In winter Common Ravens gather in the lowlands. Flocks of 10 to 20 birds are not uncommon. The largest winter roost in the state is at Malheur L., Harney Co., where 7,800 birds were counted in 1977.

Family Paridae

Black-capped Chickadee. *Parus atricapillus.*

Common permanent resident west of the Cascade Mts. and locally east of the Cascades.

217

The Black-capped Chickadee is a common permanent resident from the foothills of the Cascades to the Pacific Ocean. It is most abundant in the Willamette and Umpqua Valleys where the deciduous woodlands that it prefers are widespread. Although it is sometimes found in almost pure stands of evergreens, that habitat is dominated by the Chestnut-backed Chickadee. It has adapted well to cities and towns, where deciduous ornamental and fruit trees provide it with suitable foraging habitat.

East of the Cascades it is a common, but local, permanent resident in many areas where deciduous woodlands and riparian areas that it prefers are present. In large areas east of the Cascades it is absent or only a rare winter visitant. These areas include most of Jefferson Co., and Deschutes, Lake, Crook, and Klamath Cos. In Malheur Co. it is found south into the Snake and Owyhee R. bottoms. In Harney Co. it is found regularly along streams north of Burns, but in the riparian habitats of the Blitzen Valley on the Malheur N.W.R. it is absent as a nesting species and occurs only occasionally in small numbers in the winter (Littlefield, 1990). Individuals are sometimes found far from nesting areas in fall and winter, but the species is generally very sedentary.

Mountain Chickadee. *Parus gambeli*.

Common permanent resident in mountainous areas (except the Coast Range) in many parts of the state. Wintering birds occur at lower elevations east of the Cascades in winter; and as irregular visitants in small numbers to the valleys west of the Cascades and along the coast.

The Mountain Chickadee is a common permanent resident in the Cascade, Blue, Wallowa, Warner, and Siskiyou Mts. It is also a permanent resident in small numbers on Hart Mt., Steens Mt., and other isolated mountain areas east of the Cascades. Nesting occurs to timber line in pines, true firs, mountain hemlock, and juniper. It is generally absent from the Douglas-fir zone of the Cascades. In winter there is considerable withdrawal from the highest elevations, and at that season it can be found in varying numbers in almost any forested area east of the Cascade summit. In the more moist conifer forests it is largely replaced by the Chestnut-backed Chickadee.

It most winters it is absent or very rare in the lowlands of western Oregon, but it does occur in small numbers irregularly, both in the valleys and along the coast. There are also a few winter records for the Coast Range.

Chestnut-backed Chickadee. *Parus rufescens.*

Common permanent resident from the Cascade crest westward, and locally uncommon permanent resident in the Blue and Wallowa Mountains.

The Chestnut-backed Chickadee is a common permanent resident of the Cascade Mts. west to the Pacific Ocean. On the eastern slope of the Cascades it is restricted to the more moist, dense coniferous forests. West of the summit such forests are the norm, and predominate to the floor of the Willamette Valley in the northern half of the state. The species is common almost anywhere to the west where lush evergreen habitat exists. City parks with Douglas-firs are often sufficient habitat. It also finds the dense forests of Sitka spruce and western hemlock along the coast much to its liking. In winter, small numbers sometimes wander miles from suitable nesting habitat.

It is also an uncommon permanent resident in the wetter, denser areas of evergreen habitat in the Wallowa and Blue Mts, west to at least Grant Co. Such habitat is most prevalent there at middle elevations. Some downslope withdrawal is occasionally noted in winter near these mountains and also on the east slope of the Cascades.

Plain Titmouse. *Parus inornatus.*

Common permanent resident of Jackson and Josephine Cos. Locally fairly common permanent resident in southern Klamath Co. and locally uncommon permanent resident in southern Lake Co.

The Plain Titmouse is a common permanent resident in the Rogue Valley, its tributary valleys, and in the surrounding hills of Jackson and Josephine Cos. It is primarily found in oak and associated chaparral habitats, and also in towns where oaks can be found. The race found west of the Cascades is *P. i. sequestrátus.*

219

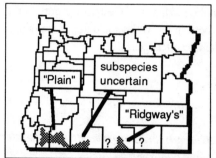

It also occurs locally as a fairly common permanent resident in southern Klamath Co. in junipers and associated brushy habitats. This is apparently the same form found west of the Cascades.

The race *P. i. zaléptus* is an uncommon local permanent resident of southern Lake Co. north into the Warner Valley. Two titmice of unknown form were reported from Table Rock, east of Silver Lake, on May 15, 1990. An individual of *zaléptus* was collected in the Blitzen Canyon, Steens Mountain, Harney Co., on Feb. 9, 1932. The reference to the species being a permanent resident to the Blitzen Canyon in the A.O.U. Check-list of North American Birds (Fifth Edition, 1957) is presumably made based on that one specimen. There is no evidence that the species now occurs anywhere in Harney Co., and we know of no other records from that area.

The distribution of the two races is mentioned because they may eventually be recognized as distinct species by the American Ornithologists' Union. If such a split is made, the likely name for the form found west of the Cascades is Plain Titmouse. Ridgway's Titmouse is the name likely to be used for the form found in Lake Co.

Family Aegithalidae

Bushtit. *Psaltriparus minimus.*

Common permanent resident west of the Cascades. Locally common to absent east of the Cascades.

The Bushtit is a common permanent resident from moderate elevations of the west slope of the Cascades west through the interior valleys, and into the moderate elevations of the Coast Range. Along the immediate vicinity of the ocean it is locally uncommon, and is absent in many areas. It is found in a wide variety of brushy habitats, including chaparral, riparian brush, forested areas with brushy understory, and in residential plantings in towns and cities. It has increased markedly during the past twenty years in parts of Portland devoid of native habitats.

East of the Cascades it is locally common to absent. In northeast Oregon it is a rare visitant for which there are only a few records. It is also rare to absent from the counties touching the Columbia R. east of Sherman Co. It is a fairly common permanent resident in the juniper lands and riparian habitats of central Oregon, and across the southern tier of counties east of the Cascades. It occurs north as a permanent resident into Wheeler and Grant Cos. It also occurs as a permanent resident in Hood River, Jefferson, and Wasco Cos. In addition to juniper habitats, the Bushtit east of the Cascades also inhabits riparian areas with brush, and some dry, brushy habitats in Klamath Co. There is some withdrawal from higher elevations in winter.

Family Sittidae

Red-breasted Nuthatch. *Sitta canadensis.*

Common permanent resident in coniferous forest habitats throughout the state. Occurs widely in migration and as a winter visitant and wanderer.

The Red-breasted Nuthatch is generally a common permanent resident in coniferous and mixed woodlands throughout the state. It nests from sea level to timberline. Numbers are variable from year to year at any given locality. Wintering birds may be found throughout the state. Wanderers and transients often occur during the breeding season at areas where nesting does not occur, and may show up in almost any forested or even brushy habitat. June and July occurrences at localities such as Fields, Harney Co., and at Mahogany Mt., Malheur Co., demonstrate the species' propensity to wander. This nuthatch is absent or in very small numbers in the immediate vicinity of the ocean, but at times is common.

White-breasted Nuthatch. *Sitta carolinensis.*

Common to uncommon permanent resident in open woodlands.

The White-breasted Nuthatch is a common to uncommon permanent resident in may parts of the state where it inhabits open woodlands. It is found from near sea level to middle elevations in the mountains. It is generally very sedentary, but occasional individuals are sometimes found far from nesting areas, such as at

Malheur N.W.R. It reaches its greatest abundance in the oak habitats of the interior valleys of western Oregon and in Hood River and Wasco Cos., and in the ponderosa pine forests on the eastern slope of the Cascades. It is also common in similar habitats of the Siskiyou Mts. and at lower elevations in the Blue and Wallowa Mts. This nuthatch is also found on the eastern foothills of the Coast Range, and in the drier valleys within the Coast Range, where suitable open woodlands exist. It is absent along the immediate coast and in large areas of forests that are too dense and moist for its requirements.

Pygmy Nuthatch. *Sitta pygmaea.*

Common permanent resident along the eastern slope of the Cascades, and eastward. Uncommon in Jackson County.

The Pygmy Nuthatch is a permanent resident in most parts of Oregon where substantial forests of ponderosa pine exist. It seems to use no other habitat within the state, unless adjacent to ponderosa pines. It is common along the eastern slope of the Cascades and in suitable habitat in the various mountains to the east. It is uncommon on the west slope of the Cascades in Jackson Co., and occasionally occurs in the Rogue Valley and Siskiyou Mts.

On rare occasions it is found many miles from its normal habitat, such as at Malheur N.W.R. Headquarters. There is also a coastal record at Cape Blanco, Curry Co., on Sept. 14, 1974, one at Salem, Marion Co., Dec. 19-20, 1991 and again there Feb. 20 and 26, 1993.

Family Certhiidae

Brown Creeper. *Certhia americana.*

Common permanent resident and transient throughout the state.

The Brown Creeper is a common but inconspicuous permanent resident throughout most of Oregon. It is typically absent or very scarce in the immediate vicinity of the coast. Nesting occurs from near sea level to high in the mountains. Both coniferous and deciduous woodlands are used, although pure stands of juniper are avoided. Migrants and winterers are sometimes found far from nesting areas, such as at Malheur N.W.R., where it is an uncommon spring and fall transient.

At Malheur N.W.R. spring records extend from March 5 to June 6, and autumn records from September 24 to November 13. The peak of the spring migration is from about April 25 to May 7 (Littlefield 1990).

Family Troglodytidae

Rock Wren. *Salpinctes obsoletus.*

Common in summer and very uncommon in winter east of the Cascade Mts. In summer, locally fairly common in the Cascades, locally uncommon in the Siskiyou Mts. Rare throughout the year in the Rogue Valley.

The Rock Wren is a common summer resident east of the Cascades, where it frequents outcroppings, rimrock, canyons, and even rocky scablands, and breeds regularly as high as 7,000 ft. on barren southeastern Oregon mountains. Along the Columbia R. it occurs sparingly at least as far west as Rooster Rock State Park, Multnomah Co. On the east slope of the Cascades and in the Blue Mts., rocky hillsides, talus slopes, cliffs, and outcroppings within forests are inhabited in summer. In recent years clearcuts have provided additional suitable habitat, which is widely utilized on the east slope of the Cascades and is very locally on the west side.

In southwestern Oregon, Rock Wrens are rare, local breeders north of the Siskiyou Mts. in Jackson Co. In the Siskiyous, including Josephine Co., they are locally uncommon and a pair probably nested along the Elk R. east of Port Orford, Curry Co., in 1979. In the Coast Range, they have been seen several times during nesting season on Saddle Mt., Clatsop Co., and bred near Hagg Lake, Washington Co., in 1983. The only breeding records in the Willamette Valley have occurred on Spencer Butte near Eugene in 1917, 1970, and 1979.

Most Rock Wrens migrate south out of Oregon in September and October. In winter they are very uncommon at lower elevations east of the Cascades and are rare in the Rogue Valley, Jackson Co. Most migrants return in late April and May.

Canyon Wren. *Catherpes mexicanus.*

Locally fairly common in summer and uncommon to rare in winter east of the Cascade Mts. Rare and local resident in eastern Jackson and Douglas Cos.

The Canyon Wren is a locally fairly common summer resident east of the Cascades on steep, rocky canyon walls and on rimrock in open country. It is often absent or very uncommon in seemingly ideal habitat. The Canyon Wren and the Rock Wren are sympatric in many areas, but unlike the Rock Wren, it seldom occurs on small rock outcroppings, in boulder fields, or in rocky areas within forests. In the arid, treeless mountains of the Great Basin in southeastern Oregon, Canyon Wrens have been observed during summer above 6,000 ft. elevation.

In late summer, apparently beginning in late July, there is some dispersal and through September individuals are found at odd locations from timberline in the Cascades eastward. In fall (as late as October 24), birds have occasionally been observed above 1,500 ft. in the Sandy and Zigzag R. canyons, Clackamas Co. Other similar canyons on the west slope of the Cascades may also be inhabited irregularly, and there are several records from Cougar Res. Dam, Lane Co. There is apparently some southward migration, for in winter Canyon Wrens are locally uncommon to rare east of the Cascades and they are absent from many of their high-elevation breeding areas.

The Canyon Wren is a rare permanent resident in eastern Jackson Co., where it frequents rocky canyons and rimrock. Elsewhere in southwestern Oregon, singing birds have been noted in June along the Rogue R. west of Merlin, Josephine Co., and along the North Umpqua R., Douglas Co. One was singing near Wedderburn, Curry Co., on June 28, 1970.

Bewick's Wren. *Thryomanes bewickii.*

Common permanent resident west of the Cascade Mts. and fairly common permanent resident in the Klamath Basin. Locally uncommon east of the Klamath Basin to the Warner Valley. Locally common permanent resident along the upper Columbia R. and its tributaries.

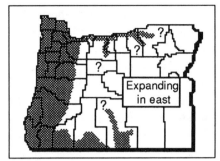

The Bewick's Wren is a common permanent resident throughout the lowlands of western Oregon, where it inhabits thickets, the edges of woodlands, and dense vegetation in residential areas. In southwestern Oregon it is a fairly common permanent resident in chaparral-covered hills. In the Coast Range, Siskiyou Mts., and in the foothills of the west slope of the Cascades to at least 2,000 ft., it is a locally fairly common summer resident in clearcuts and at forest edges.

In the Klamath Basin and the surrounding foothills Bewick's Wrens are fairly common permanent residents. They are locally uncommon at lower elevations in southern Lake Co. as far east as the Warner Valley.

In areas near the Columbia R. east of the Cascades they are locally common permanent residents. The species range extends up several of the tributary rivers in that area, east to central Umatilla Co. These areas represent range expansion in the past twenty years.

In late July, August and September there is some dispersal and during this period individuals are occasionally observed at timberline in the Cascades. Bewick's Wrens winter primarily in the valleys, where in western Oregon they are common. During mild winters they may be uncommon as high as 1,500 ft.

Wandering birds are occasionally found outside the species' breeding range east of the Cascades. Individuals have been found at Malheur N.W.R. and other Harney Co. locations during almost every part of the year, but most records are from September and early October. Other extralimital records are from Union and Deschutes Cos., and the species doubtlessly occurs at least occasionally in many other areas.

House Wren. *Troglodytes aedon.*

Common to very uncommon summer resident throughout the state. Possibly very rare in winter in southwestern Oregon.

The House Wren breeds throughout Oregon in a wide variety of semi-open habitats. Along the southern Oregon coast it is uncommon in open forests and brush, and occurs throughout the southern Coast Range. On the northern Oregon coast it is locally uncommon in lodgepole pine forests and in brush. It breeds sparingly in clearcuts on the west slope of the Coast Range. In the eastern foothills of the Coast Range, House Wrens are common in oak and mixed oak-fir woodlands, while in the Willamette Valley they are generally uncommon although they may be locally fairly common at forest edges, in oaks, and in residential areas. They also commonly inhabit cottonwood woodlands. In the western foothills of the Cascades they are uncommon, occurring primarily at edges and in clearcuts. In Douglas, Jackson, and Josephine Cos., House Wrens are fairly common in the valleys, and common in the chaparral-oak covered foothills and recent clearcuts.

On the east slope of the Cascades and in the mountains to the east House Wrens are common in aspen forests and in riparian areas in open Douglas-fir and ponderosa pine forests, locally breeding to over 6,000 ft. In the valleys and deserts east of the Cascades they are locally common in towns, around farmhouses, and in riparian areas.

In August and September there is some dispersal, and during this period individuals are occasionally observed at timberline in the Cascades. By mid-September most have migrated south, but occasionally birds are observed in October and there are even a few early November records. House Wrens are sometimes reported on Christmas Bird Counts, especially in the relatively warm southwestern portion of Oregon. There are few well-substantiated winter records. Spring migrants are occasionally observed in late March, but most arrive between mid-April and mid-May.

Winter Wren. *Troglodytes troglodytes.*

Uncommon to common summer resident in moist, forested areas throughout the state. In winter, common in lowlands west of the Cascade Mts.; uncommon and local at lower elevations east of the Cascades. Partial migrant.

The Winter Wren breeds throughout Oregon in moist coniferous and deciduous forests from sea level to timberline. On the coast and in the Coast Range it is a common summer resident. In the Willamette Valley summer residents are fairly common. In the Cascade, Siskiyou and Blue Mts., and on isolated forested mountains east of the Cascades it is a fairly common summer resident, although in drier forests and at high elevations it may be local, occurring most frequently near water. Ponderosa pine forests and aspen forests are not inhabited, but riparian zones within such areas may be utilized. Non-breeders are sometimes observed at desert oases in mid-summer.

There is some migration out of the state in fall. A few migrants are noted in early September, but most apparently migrate in October and November, when they are frequently observed at oases east of the Cascades. Higher elevations are abandoned in winter when Winter Wrens are very common in forests, woodlands, and thickets in the valleys of western Oregon, and in riparian areas at lower elevations east of the Cascades. They are usually fairly common during winter in the foothills of the west slope of the Cascades and in the Coast Range. The east slope of the Cascades and mountains to the east are rarely inhabited during winter. Most migrants apparently return in late March and April. By late April breeders are again common in the mountains.

Marsh Wren. *Cistothorus palustris.*

Common summer resident throughout the state. In winter, common on the coast and locally fairly common to very uncommon inland.

The Marsh Wren is a common summer resident in marshes and in aquatic vegetation at the borders of bodies of water and watercourses throughout Oregon. On the coast it is common in brackish as well as freshwater marshes, and in the mountains it is locally common to at least 4,000 ft.

By late September few remain in the mountains. During the latter half of August and in September migrants are occasionally observed at oases east of the Cascades, and birds appear throughout the state in wetland habitats not utilized for nesting. Numbers decline through November.

In winter Marsh Wrens are fairly common along the coast, but in the interior valleys of western Oregon their status varies with winter severity from locally fairly common to very uncommon. East of the Cascades numbers vary from locally uncommon in mild winters to rare in harsh winters. In the Klamath Basin and at Summer L. they remain at least uncommon even in the coldest years.

West of the Cascades migrants return in late March and April, while east of the Cascades most arrive between mid-April and early May.

Family Cinclidae

American Dipper. *Cinclus mexicanus.*

Locally common permanent resident.

The American Dipper is a common permanent resident of fast-flowing, rock-strewn streams and rivers throughout Oregon. Most such habitat is in mountainous areas, but nesting occurs to sea level on coastal streams where the conditions are correct. Dippers are found in all of the state's major mountain areas, and also in some isolated mountains such as Steens Mt., Harney Co., and Mahogany Mt., Malheur Co.

This species remains on territory nearly year round, though harsh winters will force some downward movement. It is found regularly at Malheur N.W.R. foraging in muddy rivers under those conditions.

Family Muscicapidae
Subfamily Slyvinae

Golden-crowned Kinglet. *Regulus satrapa.*

Fairly common to common summer resident. In winter, common at lower elevations in and west of the Cascade Mts., and generally uncommon to fairly common in mountains and at lower elevations east of the Cascades.

Throughout Oregon the Golden-crowned Kinglet is a fairly common summer resident in dense coniferous forests from sea level to timberline. East of the Cascades and in southern Oregon it generally breeds above the ponderosa pine zone.

In the Willamette Valley it is a fairly common summer resident in the localized remaining stands of conifers.

Deciduous forests, lowland riparian, and brush at lower elevations are also inhabited during winter. East of the Cascades migrants are occasionally noted in late August, but the migration peaks from late September through mid-October, when they are uncommon to fairly common at oases and in ponderosa pine and juniper.

In winter they are very uncommon to fairly common in coniferous forests of the mountains, where at higher elevations they are less common but do occur to near timberline. East of the Cascades, in ponderosa pine and juniper forests, they are very uncommon to locally fairly common, and in riparian areas and oases in open country they are rare to very uncommon. Wintering numbers east of the Cascades vary dramatically from year to year. West of the Cascades from late September to March, Golden-crowned Kinglets are common in lower elevation coniferous and mixed forests and less common in strictly deciduous habitat. They are especially abundant along the coast.

Ruby-crowned Kinglet. *Regulus calendula.*

Common summer resident of high elevations in the Cascade, Warner, Blue and Wallowa Mts. Winter visitant and transient throughout the state.

The Ruby-crowned Kinglet is a common summer resident at high elevations in the Cascade, Warner, Blue, and Wallowa Mts., where it breeds to timberline in true fir, mountain hemlock, and lodgepole pine forests. In migration it occurs almost everywhere in the state, and is at times abundant. In winter this kinglet is common in the lowlands and at moderate elevations west of the Cascade summit, and generally uncommon at lower elevations to the east.

Blue-gray Gnatcatcher. *Polioptila caerulea.*

Local and uncommon summer resident in the Rogue Valley, southern Klamath Co., southern Lake Co., and irregularly in southern Harney Co.

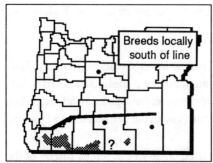

The Blue-gray Gnatcatcher is a local, uncommon summer resident in dense stands of buckbrush (*ceanothus* sp.) in the hills of the Rogue Valley. Nesting was first reported in 1962 on Roxy Anne Butte, Jackson Co. There are scattered breeding sites in the valley extending as far north as Merlin, Josephine Co. Rogue Valley breeders arrive during early April and depart in August.

It is an uncommon summer resident in mountain mahogany thickets on Stukel Mt., where the population was first recorded in 1983, and elsewhere in Klamath Co. The species breeds locally in the same habitat on Hart Mt., and on Winter Ridge, both Lake Co. Breeders have been located in some years since 1975 in southern Harney Co. (Page Springs, Cottonwood Creek, near Buena Vista Station). One or two pairs at Cyrus Springs, Crook Co., were suspected of nesting in the summer of 1992. In addition to the breeding populations there have been scattered summer sightings from Gilliam, Klamath, Harney, Lake, and Malheur Cos.

In western Oregon there are about 10 records, mostly from spring and fall, with two winter records away from the southwestern Oregon breeding area: one at Coos Bay, Coos Co., on Dec. 20, 1987; and one at Salem, Marion Co., on Dec. 22, 1979.

Subfamily Turdinae

Northern Wheatear. *Oenanthe oenanthe.*

Vagrant.

The only Oregon records are a single male photographed near Malheur N.W.R., on June 22, 1977, and one seen at Finley N.W.R., Benton Co., on Oct. 2, 1988.

Western Bluebird. *Sialia mexicana.*

East of the Cascade Mts., rare to locally fairly common summer resident and transient; very uncommon and irregular in winter. Fairly common permanent resident in Jackson, Josephine, and Douglas Cos. Local and uncommon permanent resident in the Willamette Valley and adjacent hills. Uncommon to common summer resident in clearcuts on the west slope of the Cascades. Locally uncommon permanent resident in Curry Co., rare and local elsewhere on the outer coast and in the Coast Range.

The Western Bluebird is a rare to locally fairly common summer resident east of the Cascades, where it occurs to at least 5,800 ft. in open forests of Douglas-fir and pine, in some agricultural lands, and sparingly in juniper forests. Most birds migrate south in fall, but small flocks occasionally remain through winter in the valleys, especially in mild years.

In Jackson, Josephine, and Douglas Cos. it is a fairly common summer resident in the open Douglas-fir and oak forest of the lowlands and foothills. There is a withdrawal to lower elevations in winter.

The Western Bluebird was formerly a common permanent resident throughout the Willamette Valley and adjacent hills. Currently it is a locally uncommon summer resident in open country with scattered oaks and conifers, including yards and orchards in the foothills, and less frequently in the valley bottom. Only one pair is now known to breed in Multnomah Co., where it was once common. The number that winter in the Willamette Valley fluctuates from year to year. Wintering birds usually occur at lower elevations.

In the western Cascades, it breeds in clearcuts with snags. Most retreat to lower elevations in winter. It is local in the Coast Range in similar habitat. Individuals or small flocks are rarely noted in the coastal lowlands north of Curry Co., usually in spring or fall, but there are also a few winter records.

In Curry Co., Western Bluebirds are uncommon summer residents in meadows and clearcuts throughout the foothills and mountains and in the lowlands near Wedderburn. In winter small flocks are uncommon in the lowlands along the Curry Co. coast.

The severe decline in population that has occurred in the Willamette Valley since the early 1950s is attributed to competition with starlings for nesting cavities. starlings have probably also caused a decline elsewhere in Oregon. The placement and maintenance of nest boxes unsuitable to starlings in bluebird habitat appears to have halted the decline of the Western Bluebird in a few areas. We hope such efforts will be expanded.

Mountain Bluebird. *Sialia currucoides.*

Common summer resident and usually uncommon in winter east of the Cascade Mts. Common summer resident in the Cascades and uncommon in the Siskiyou Mts. Rare visitant elsewhere west of the Cascades.

The Mountain Bluebird is a common summer resident in eastern Oregon and locally on the west side. It inhabits juniper woodland, and open pine forests at lower elevations east of the Cascades. Burns, clearcuts, and the edges of meadows throughout the true fir zone on both slopes of the Cascades are also used. Small numbers breed in the Siskiyou Mts. of Jackson, Josephine, and eastern Curry Cos.

In September and October many summer residents east of the Cascades migrate south, sometimes forming large flocks of as many as 200 birds. Large flocks are also observed in March when migrants return. West of the Cascades, individuals and less frequently small flocks are found rarely during the migration periods.

During some winters individuals and flocks of Mountain Bluebirds are fairly common at low elevations in ponderosa pine, juniper, and sagebrush areas east of the Cascades, while in severe winters they may be rare. They are very rare during winter in the valleys of Jackson and Josephine Cos.

Townsend's Solitaire. *Myadestes townsendi.*

Common summer resident on east slope of the Cascade Mts.; winters at lower elevations. Locally common summer resident on the west slope of the Cascades, in the Siskiyou Mts. and Coast Range. Rare in winter west of the Cascades.

The Townsend's Solitaire is an uncommon to fairly common summer resident in coniferous forests from timberline down into the ponderosa pine zone on the east slope of the Cascades and in the Blue Mts. On the west slope of the Cascades and in the Siskiyou Mts. of Jackson, Josephine, and Curry Cos., solitaires are uncommon to locally common in coniferous forests and accompanying clearcuts above 1,000 ft. Summer residents are uncommon but widespread in the Coast Range. Open forests and the edges of clearcuts and burns, especially in western Oregon, are the sites most frequently inhabited.

In winter solitaires are fairly common to abundant in juniper forests east of the Cascades, where they feed almost entirely on juniper berries. They are rare during winter in ponderosa pine forests with scattered junipers and seldom occur at higher elevations. West of the Cascades solitaires are rare during fall, winter, and spring in the interior valleys and along the coast. In these areas they are typically found near a berry source.

Veery. *Catharus fuscescens.*

Fairly common summer resident in the mountains and valleys of northeastern Oregon and Crook Co. Vagrant or possibly rare transient elsewhere.

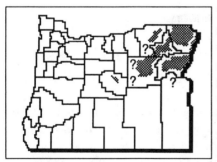

The Veery inhabits riparian areas in the mountains and valleys of northeastern Oregon. It breeds throughout Union and Wallowa Cos., at many sites in northern Baker Co., in eastern Umatilla Co. along the Umatilla R. east of Cayuse and along other watercourses that flow out of the Blue Mts. It also breeds locally in Grant Co., where small numbers have been found on the middle fork of the John Day R. near Bates, on Canyon Creek south of Canyon City, on Pine Creek east of John Day, and on upper tributaries of the Malheur R. in the Logan Valley. Veerys are locally fairly common in the Ochoco Mts. of Crook Co., where they occur along Ochoco Creek, McKay Creek and Mill Creek, and probably breed along other watercourses. The status in the region between the Crook and Grant Co. locations is unknown, though there are a few reports from this area. One was recorded in June 1898, at Fossil, Wheeler Co., and breeding may occur in this area, along with the Heppner area of Morrow Co.

The species is a rare transient at desert oases in Harney Co., mostly in June. One at Fields on June 2, 1993, was of the reddish eastern race. There are late May and early June records of individuals at Bend and at Indian Ford Campground, both Deschutes Co., and Hart Mt., Lake Co. There are a few reports for west of the Cascades, but none have been satisfactorily documented.

Veerys return to Oregon from mid-May to early June, and depart in late August and early September.

Gray-cheeked Thrush. *Catharus minimus.*

Vagrant.

There is one record for this species, one photographed at Fields, Harney Co., on Sept. 22, 1984.

Swainson's Thrush. *Catharus ustulatus.*

Common to uncommon summer resident. Common spring and fall migrant in forests throughout Oregon.

The Swainson's Thrush rarely arrives in Oregon as early as mid-April, but most spring migrants return in early and mid-May. It is a common summer resident in coniferous and mixed forests with dense undergrowth and in riparian thickets, from mid elevations on the west slope of the Cascade Mts. to the coast. It is especially common in the immediate vicinity of the coast. It is also uncommon in dense forests on the east slope of the Cascades, but generally does not occur in or below the ponderosa pine zone although it does occur in aspen groves and riparian areas within pine forests. In the mountains of northeastern Oregon and in the Ochoco Mts. of Crook Co., the Swainson's Thrush is an uncommon summer resident in fir forests up to timberline. On Steens Mt., Harney Co., and on other isolated mountains and mountain ranges east of the Cascades, breeding occurs in firs and in aspen woodlands.

The fall migration begins in late August, but the peak occurs in September, when migrants are fairly common to common in dense cover throughout the lowlands. A few migrants are usually noted into early October, especially along the coast. Migrants overhead are often detected at night by their call note.

Swainson's Thrushes are occasionally reported in mid-winter west of the Cascades, but details have been insufficient and these sightings may pertain to the Hermit Thrush. The latest certain date is November 8. There are no confirmed winter records for the state.

Hermit Thrush. *Catharus ustulatus.*

Fairly common to common summer resident in the Cascade, Siskiyou, and Blue Mts.; uncommon in the Coast Range. Fairly common transient throughout Oregon. In winter, fairly common along the coast, uncommon inland west of the Cascade Mts., and rare in most years east of the Cascades.

The Hermit Thrush inhabits coniferous forests from the foothills to timberline. It occurs sparingly, usually in riparian areas, in forests of ponderosa pine east of the Cascades, and is a rare summer resident in some high-elevation juniper forests. Fall migrants, many from north of Oregon, are common throughout the lowlands in late September and October. Many are transients that winter further south.

In winter Hermit Thrushes are fairly common in the lowlands and foothills along the coast. They are uncommon to very uncommon inland west of the Cascades, where Christmas Bird Counts rarely record more than 10 birds. In winter they inhabit coniferous and deciduous woodlands, usually with dense undergrowth. They are rare during winter east of the Cascades, occurring only at lower elevations, and in most areas usually only during mild years. Towns and ranches where berries are available are frequented.

Spring migrants are fairly common in the lowlands west of the Cascades from early April through early May and east of the Cascades from mid-April through mid-May. In many areas singing breeders have returned to their territories in the mountains by mid-May.

Wood Thrush. *Hylocichla mustelina.*

Vagrant.

There are two records of the Wood Thrush in Oregon: one at Pike Creek, Harney Co., on May 27, 1980; and one at Fields, Harney Co., on Oct. 14, 1989.

American Robin. *Turdus migratorius.*

Common to abundant permanent resident and transient throughout the state.

The American Robin is a common summer resident from sea level to timberline throughout Oregon. It inhabits urban areas, agricultural lands, chaparral in southwestern Oregon, juniper forests east of the Cascades, riparian situations in deserts, and most deciduous and coniferous forests.

Large flocks of migrants are observed in late September and October. Many migrants are northern breeders that winter in Oregon or pass through the state. Local summer residents migrate south or winter in the lowlands.

In the winter individuals and flocks, often numbering thousands, are usually common in the lowlands throughout Oregon. East of the Cascade Mts. large numbers winter in juniper forests, where they feed on the abundant berries. Roosts where many thousands of birds gather each night have been observed in juniper forests at a variety of eastern Oregon sites. The number that winter varies greatly from year to year in all parts of the state.

In late February and March flocks of migrants from the south return, many passing through Oregon to northern breeding areas. At this season large lawns and pastures, particularly along the coast, often host thousands. Breeding begins as early as February in the lowlands.

Varied Thrush. *Ixoreus naevius.*

Fairly common summer resident in the Cascade, Siskiyou, and Blue Mts., Coast Range, and along the north coast. In winter, common in foothills and valleys of western Oregon. Generally uncommon east of the Cascades. Transient statewide.

The Varied Thrush is a locally fairly common to rare breeder in dense coniferous forests in the mountains and foothills throughout Oregon. It is especially common in old growth. It does not breed in junipers and is rare in the dry pine forests east of the Cascades. Breeders are very uncommon to absent in coniferous forests at low elevations in all areas except along the northern coast, where they are fairly common in forests at sea level, especially forests of hemlock and spruce.

During winter Varied Thrushes are fairly common in the lowlands west of the Cascades, where they frequent suburbs and woodlands from October through April. In severe winters greater numbers occur in the lowlands, apparently as a result of birds from the Coast Range and Cascade foothills being forced out by snow cover. At such times they may be abundant in the coastal lowlands.

The winter status east of the Cascades varies from rare throughout to locally fairly common. This fluctuation is apparently related to the severity of the winter. Riparian areas, suburbs, juniper forests, and orchards are frequently inhabited.

Varied Thrushes return to the mountains in March and April. Transients from breeding areas north of Oregon pass through the state in late September and October, and again in late March and April. Many of the birds that winter in Oregon probably breed north of the state.

Subfamily Timaliinae

Wrentit. *Chamaea fasciata.*

Common resident in brush and chaparral along the Oregon coast and southern interior valleys of Western Oregon. Uncommon along west slope of southern Cascade Mts. Locally irregular or rare in southern Klamath Co.

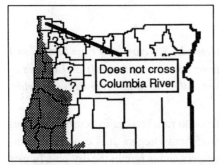

The Wrentit is a common resident in suitable habitat along the length of the Oregon coast, where its year-round singing reveals its presence even when unseen. They occur in areas of heavy brush, particularly evergreen huckleberry and salal. The Columbia R. is a formidable barrier to the species. Although regular at Fort Clatsop State Park at the mouth of the river, it has never been recorded in Washington.

In the Coast Range, logging of formerly unsuitable forests has created habitat in the form of dense Douglas-fir reproduction and brush. In the last 20 years Wrentits have spread up the western edge of the Willamette Valley as far as Yamhill Co. A few also occur locally in the western Cascades north to Linn Co.

In the Rogue and Umpqua Valleys, this species is also a typical inhabitant of dry, brushy habitats. It climbs the Cascades nearly to the crest in eastern Douglas Co. It is also rare but regular in the Klamath R. Canyon, Klamath Co.

Family Mimidae

Gray Catbird. *Dumetella carolinensis.*

Locally fairly common summer resident in valleys and foothills of northeastern Oregon. Vagrant elsewhere.

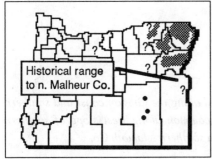

The Gray Catbird is locally fairly common along watercourses throughout Wallowa, Umatilla, Baker and Union Cos., occurring most commonly in the valleys. Tributaries in in the foothills are also inhabited. It breeds in suitable habitat along the Grande Ronde, Umatilla, and Powder Rivers. It may eventually be found breeding in Grant Co., and birds have been found in summer as far west as Wasco Co.

238

The Gray Catbird bred at Malheur N.W.R. in 1943, but currently it is a very rare visitant in Harney Co. One record is from Van in the extreme northeast of the county, and it is possible that Catbirds breed in this area. In Malheur Co., it occurred along Willow Creek in the early 1900s, but the present status there is unknown. There are scattered records elsewhere in eastern Oregon, mostly in May and June.

Catbirds arrive in Oregon in late May, the earliest record being May 19, and depart the state by late August, the latest record of a fall migrant being September 5. There is one winter record, a bird that ate berries in La Grande, Union Co, during the winter of 1988-89.

In Oregon the Gray Catbird typically inhabits deciduous riparian growth. Only rarely does it occur in suburban settings, a habitat in which it is fairly common throughout much of the eastern United States.

Northern Mockingbird. *Mimus polyglottos.*

Rare visitant in all seasons west of the Cascade Mts. Rare visitant east of the Cascades in spring, summer, and fall; three winter records. No Oregon breeding records.

The Northern Mockingbird is a rare visitant throughout the year west of the Cascades, occurring in both the interior valleys and the coastal lowlands. Most records are for fall and winter. It is much more regular in the southwestern part of the state, especially in Jackson and Curry Cos. East of the Cascades the Mockingbird is a rare visitant from spring through fall. There are three records of birds that may have wintered east of the Cascades: one in the Blitzen Valley, Harney Co., on Nov. 21, 1935; one on Steens Mt., Harney Co., on Feb. 9, 1936; and one at Lake Billy Chinook, Jefferson Co., on Dec. 23, 1980.

There are no confirmed Oregon breeding records, although pairs have summered at Port Orford, Curry Co., Medford, Jackson Co., Klamath Falls, Klamath Co., and Milton-Freewater, Umatilla Co., where six birds were present in 1972. Gabrielson and Jewett (1940) considered the Mockingbird a rare permanent resident on Steens Mt., based on five records between Aug., 1935, and Aug., 1936, which included a juvenile collected at 5,000 ft. elevation on Aug. 30, 1936. Mocking-birds have bred as far north as Siskiyou and Del Norte Cos. in California, and it is likely that someday they will be found breeding in Oregon.

Sage Thrasher. *Oreoscoptes montanus.*

Common summer resident east of the Cascade Mts.; not recorded every year in winter. Rare spring, summer, and fall vagrant in western Oregon.

The Sage Thrasher is a fairly common to common summer resident in sagebrush and greasewood plant communities east of the Cascades. It may be found in areas with scattered junipers but does not inhabit juniper forests. The southward migration occurs in late August and September. Individuals are occasionally observed east of the Cascades in winter. Spring migrants return in late March and April, with the earliest record February 27.

West of the Cascades it is a spring vagrant that is not observed every year. The earliest record is March 18 and the latest is June 5. There are fewer than ten summer records for west of the Cascades. Fall vagrants are even less frequent than in spring, with a late record of November 22.

Brown Thrasher. *Toxostoma rufum.*

Vagrant.

Single Brown Thrashers have been recorded about 15 times in Oregon, most of which have been verified by photographs or specimens. Records come from throughout the year and from a wide variety of locations. Several have wintered: at Malheur N.W.R. and Frenchglen, Harney Co., Molalla, Clackamas Co., Salem, Marion Co., and Sunriver, Deschutes Co.

California Thrasher. *Toxostoma redivivum.*

Vagrant.

A California Thrasher irregularly visited a feeder five miles west of Medford, Jackson Co., from July 24 through Oct. 20, 1967. This feeder was again visited Feb. 4-25, 1968, by what was presumed to be the same bird. A singing individual was seen near O'Brien, Josephine Co., on June 18, 1977.

The California Thrasher breeds in the Shasta Valley, Siskiyou Co., California, and has been recorded very close to the Oregon border.

Family Motacillidae

Black-backed Wagtail. *Motacilla lugens.*

One certain Oregon record.

The only accepted Oregon record of the Black-backed Wagtail was one at Eugene, Lane Co., Feb. 3 to March 26, 1974. It was photographed and during the observation period molted from first-winter to adult female plumage.

Two other Oregon wagtail sightings lack sufficient details to determine if they were Black-backed or White Wagtails (*M. alba*): one Feb. 9, 1975 at Umatilla N.W.R., and one June 4, 1980 at Harris Beach State Park, Curry Co.

American Pipit. *Anthus rubescens.*

Locally uncommon summer resident in alpine areas. Common migrant at lower elevations statewide. In winter, uncommon in agricultural lands west of the Cascade Mts. and rare east of the Cascades.

The American Pipit is a very local, uncommon summer resident in alpine areas of the Cascade and Wallowa Mts., and on Steens Mt., Harney Co. Southbound migrants are occasionally noted at lower elevations in the last days of August and by mid-September small numbers occur throughout Oregon. Fall migration peaks from late September through mid-October, during which it is often abundant at lower elevations statewide. The latest fall departure date at Malheur N.W.R. is November 7. In alpine areas breeders or transients are regularly noted into late

September, and occasionally into early October. Migrant and wintering American Pipits inhabit shores, fields and lawns.

In winter pipits are uncommon and erratic in the interior valleys of western Oregon and along the coast. Throughout Oregon wintering numbers fluctuate from year to year. East of the Cascades in winter they are usually rare, a few being recorded most years on one or more of the Christmas Bird Counts in central or northeast Oregon or in the Klamath Basin. Large flocks are occasionally noted.

Spring migrants begin to appear in early March, are common during the peak in April, and decrease steadily through May, and are rarely noted to early June (east of the Cascades).

Family Bombycillidae

Bohemian Waxwing. *Bombycilla garrulus.*

Erratic winter visitant statewide. In typical years fairly common in northeast Oregon and rare or absent elsewhere.

The Bohemian Waxwing is a fairly common annual winter visitor to the valleys of northeast Oregon (Baker, Grant, Umatilla, Union, and Wallowa Cos.), where it inhabits open woodlands, including junipers, and towns. Throughout the state numbers vary dramatically from year to year, and northeast Oregon is the only region where numbers appear annually. Elsewhere east of the Cascade Mts. it is rare in most years, but during irruption years may be fairly common. Visitants occur more frequently in north-central Oregon than elsewhere in the state except the northeast.

West of the Cascades they are usually very rare winter visitants to the interior valleys and along the coast, and may also be very rare in the Cascades, which are poorly covered by observers during this season. Most years only a few are reported from western Oregon, where they favor berries of cultivated shrubs. Irruptions this century to western Oregon include the winters of 1919-20, 1931-32, 1968-69, 1972-73, and 1981-82. Irruptions don't appear to occur in any pattern, but are seldom separated by fewer than ten years. Even in these years reports from the coast are very few.

Bohemian Waxwings generally arrive in Oregon in mid-November (earliest September 9) and depart in late March and April, with a few records extending into May. There is only one acceptable summer record, which is also the only Oregon breeding record: a nest was taken at Gearhart, Clatsop Co., on June 25, 1958 (Griffee 1960).

Cedar Waxwing. *Bombycilla cedrorum.*

Fairly common summer resident and migrant statewide. In winter, rare to uncommon east of the Cascade Mts., rare to fairly common in the interior valleys of western Oregon, and very rare along the coast.

Throughout Oregon the Cedar Waxwing is an uncommon to common summer resident from sea level to moderate elevations in deciduous and mixed deciduous-coniferous forests, including deciduous streamside trees in coniferous forests. It does not regularly breed in aspen stands, arid mountains or in stands of cottonwoods and willows along desert watercourses east of the Cascades.

The fall migration begins in late August and usually peaks in the latter half of September through late October, when it is common to locally abundant statewide, including along desert watercourses and at oases. In the interior valleys of western Oregon large numbers remain into November.

East of the Cascades in winter, flocks are rare to uncommon at lower elevations, inhabiting residential areas, open woodlands and juniper forests. West of the Cascades during winter, flocks are uncommon in woodlands, residential areas and near berry sources in the interior valleys, and very rare along the coast. Throughout the state winter abundance varies from year to year.

The spring migration begins in late April and peaks from the latter half of May through early June. The species is scarce before mid-May.

Family Ptilogonatidae

Phainopepla. *Phainopepla nitens.*

Vagrant.

The Phainopepla has been recorded five times in Oregon. One was seen May 17, 1957 at Malheur N.W.R. near Frenchglen and collected the following day. Other records include one observed at Medford, Jackson Co., March 15, 1961; one near Gold Hill, Jackson Co., from Dec. 22, 1988 to Feb. 8, 1989; one at Lakeview, Lake Co., on Jan. 26, 1991; and one at Fields, Harney Co., on April 27, 1992.

Family Laniidae

Northern Shrike. *Lanius excubitor.*

Very uncommon to fairly common winter visitant throughout Oregon.

The Northern Shrike is a winter visitant throughout Oregon and inhabits open country and areas with scattered trees at lower elevations. East of the Cascades it is uncommon to fairly common. West of the Cascades it is uncommon to rare along the coast and in the Willamette Valley, and very uncommon to rare in the Rogue and Umpqua Valleys. It arrives in Oregon during October (rarely late September) and departs in March (rarely mid-April).

Loggerhead Shrike. *Lanius ludovicianus.*

East of the Cascade Mts., fairly common summer resident and rare in winter. Very rare west of the Cascades in fall, winter, and spring.

The Loggerhead Shrike is a fairly common summer resident in open country and open juniper woodlands east of the Cascade Mts. In these areas during winter it is generally rare, but in some years it is very uncommon, especially in the lowlands of Klamath and Lake Cos. Most migrants return in March and depart by late September, but a few linger into November.

West of the Cascades, Loggerhead Shrikes are very rare (a few records annually) during fall, winter, and spring in open country along the coast and in the Willamette and Umpqua Valleys. In the Rogue Valley, it is rare in spring and fall, and very uncommon in winter.

Family Sturnidae

Eurasian Starling. *Sturnus vulgaris.*

Introduced. Common to abundant permanent resident throughout Oregon.

The Eurasian Starling is a native of Europe and Asia. In 1889 and 1892 the Portland Songbird Club released 70 starlings which became established for a short time and disappeared about 1901 or 1902. Oregon was then free of Starlings for about 40 years until one was observed at Malheur N.W.R. Dec. 10-24, 1943. Another was observed in early 1946 in Union Co. and a small flock was at Malheur N.W.R. later that year. The first western Oregon records were 100 at Eugene and 22 at Meadow View, Lane Co., on Dec. 26, 1947. Nesting was first noted east of the Cascade Mts. in 1950 near La Grande, Union Co., and west of the Cascades in 1958.

Populations grew rapidly and today the Starling is common to abundant year round in urban areas, towns and agricultural lands throughout Oregon. It also nests in open woodlands, usually near agricultural areas. In late summer, after nesting, large wintering flocks form which sometimes mix with blackbirds. In fall there appears to be some migration out of areas east of the Cascades, but many remain. Communal roosts, usually containing thousands and rarely hundreds of thousands of birds, occur erratically in many areas and are typically situated in dense trees and man-made structures.

Starlings are large, aggressive cavity nesters and compete directly with many native birds, such as Western Bluebird, Purple Martin and Lewis' Woodpecker, for a very limited cavity supply. There is much evidence linking the increase of European Starlings to the decline of these natives. Additionally, starlings consume millions of dollars worth of grain annually and cause damage to fruit crops and holly orchards.

Family Vireonidae

Bell's Vireo. *Vireo bellii.*

Vagrant.

245

There are two sight records for the species, single birds at Fields, Harney Co., on May 22-24, 1980, and at Malheur N.W.R. on May 4, 1991. The Bell's Vireo has not been physically documented for Oregon.

Solitary Vireo. *Vireo solitarius.*

Fairly common summer resident in mixed forests in most of the state; rare summer resident but common transient in southeastern Oregon, and rare in summer on the north coast.

The Solitary Vireo is one of the characteristic breeding birds found throughout the state, most typically in mixed coniferous-deciduous woodlands. Although this species is apparently absent as a summer resident from the lowlands of southeastern Oregon, it does breed in small numbers in aspen or pine groves on such high fault-block ridges as Hart and Steens Mts. It is much less common on the coast, especially the north coast, where breeding birds are mostly absent.

A few birds begin arriving in western Oregon in early April or even late March, but most spring movement is in the latter two-thirds of April and early May. East of the Cascades arrival dates are typically at least a week later, with peak movements at Malheur N.W.R. during the third week of May (Littlefield, 1990). Fall movements are more prolonged and less well known, but southbound birds are seen from late August through late September or even early October across the state. The peak at Malheur is in late September.

Note: This species may be split into two or three species by the American Ornithologists' Union. There are a few sight records of the more colorful eastern form and the "Plumbeous" (Rocky Mountain) form of this vireo from southeastern Oregon. One to several Plumbeous Vireos have been reported in recent years from Harney Co., with some photographed. It has also been seen during the breeding season in Umatilla and Wallowa Cos., with nesting a possibility.

Hutton's Vireo. *Vireo huttoni.*

Resident west of the Cascade crest, most common at lower elevations. Vagrant east of the Cascades.

This vireo is a fairly common but inconspicuous resident of lowland mixed forests in western Oregon. It is most common in the Coast Range, coastal forests, and the valley foothills of southwestern Oregon, and less common in the western Cascade foothills. Some occur in nearly-pure evergreen stands, but it is most common where trees such as Douglas-fir and western hemlock are intermixed with oak or madrone. It occurs in other associations as well, such as fir and maple dominated riparian areas, especially in winter. Although there is some seasonal movement, especially out of higher elevation areas, the extent and results of this movement are not well known.

It can often be found in winter foraging with flocks of chickadees, nuthatches and kinglets; its distinctive sounds help draw attention to it.

There have been a few sight records of Hutton's Vireo from Klamath Co. and southeastern Oregon, where it is extremely rare. Care should be taken to distinguish it not only from the Ruby-crowned Kinglet but from such species as Bell's Vireo, which may be just as likely to occur at oases in southeastern Oregon.

Warbling Vireo. *Vireo gilvus.*

Common summer resident throughout most of the state.

The Warbling Vireo breeds in forested areas throughout the state. It prefers deciduous trees, especially in riparian areas, and is absent from dense evergreen stands. It can also be found in open situations such as small riparian alder, maple or cottonwood groves, open oak forests, and residential areas. It is typically the most common vireo wherever it breeds in numbers, except perhaps for the northern Snake R. canyon and adjacent areas of northeastern Oregon, where the Red-eyed Vireo can be locally common. It is scarce as a breeder along at least some areas of the immediate coast.

This species arrives in western Oregon lowlands in late April (later than the first Solitary Vireos). Most arrive in eastern Oregon during May, and some birds are still moving north in the first few days of June. Fall migration is extended, with movement noticeable from August through late September. A few records extend into early October.

Philadelphia Vireo. *Vireo philadephicus.*

Vagrant.

There is one record of this species for the state: one photographed at Fields, Harney Co., on June 3, 1991.

Red-eyed Vireo. *Vireo olivaceus.*

Summer resident in northeastern Oregon and locally west to a few sites in western Oregon, may breed occasionally elsewhere in the state.

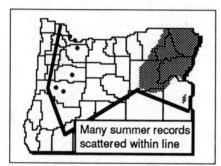

Many summer records scattered within line

This species is locally quite common in Wallowa Co., especially in the Imnaha R. Valley and along other tributaries of the Snake R., and fairly common in Union Co. and northern Baker Co. Summering birds can generally be found in Grant Co., in northeastern Malheur Co. (Snake and Owyhee Valleys) and in eastern Umatilla Co., where regular breeding is likely. Outside this area the species' summer distribution is patchy and irregular, with scattered records of singing birds and possible nesting throughout the northern half of eastern Oregon, and south along the eastern slope of the Cascades to Klamath Co. There are no confirmed breeding records in eastern Oregon south or west of eastern Grant Co.

This species is local west of the Cascades, with some favored sites supporting birds for several years at a time, then seeming to lose them. The more regular of these sites include the Columbia R. bottoms from Sauvie I. east to the Sandy R. in Columbia and Multnomah Cos.; the Middle Fork of the Willamette R. from Jasper to Oakridge, Lane Co.; and sites in eastern Linn Co. along Crabtree Creek and at Foster Res. The species has also bred at Fern Ridge Res., Lane Co., and has been reported with some regularity along the Sandy R., in Clackamas Co. There are a number of spring and summer records from Jackson Co., and a few records of birds reaching the coast in summer.

Gabrielson and Jewett note that they first found the species at Portland in 1924, but that they found it with "increasing frequency" thereafter; Shelton (1917) collected a male near Oakridge on June 22, 1916, so it is possible that the species has used some of the current breeding sites since the early part of the century.

Throughout its Oregon range it prefers riparian zones, especially extensive stands of very large cottonwood, but is also found in alder, willow, and aspen belts with large trees. Dense stands of Oregon ash have also been occupied in Lane Co.

This species typically arrives quite late (late May or early June) on the breeding grounds, but scattered migrants are seen in eastern Oregon after mid-May. Fall migration patterns are poorly known, but the peak at Malheur N.W.R. is mid-September (Littlefield, 1990). Migrants are quite rare in western Oregon at any season, but are occur in small numbers at southeastern Oregon oasis sites.

Family Emberizidae
Subfamily Parulinae

Blue-winged Warbler. *Vermivora pinus.*

Vagrant.

There are two records for the state, both single-person sight records: one 10 miles west of Burns, Harney Co., on May 18, 1992; and one at Page Springs Campground, Harney Co., on May 29, 1993.

Golden-winged Warbler. *Vermivora chrysoptera.*

Vagrant.

The two records of this species for the state are a male at Indian Ford Campground, Deschutes Co., on June 14, 1977, and a male at Malheur N.W.R. headquarters June 3-4, 1983.

Tennessee Warbler. *Vermivora peregrina.*

Very rare transient spring and fall. A few winter records.

The Tennessee Warbler is one of the more expected vagrant warblers to Oregon in spring. Most records are from Malheur N.W.R. and other oases in Harney Co., and from Hart Mt. N.W.R. There are also records from other scattered areas east of the Cascade Mts. such as Weston, Umatilla Co., near John Day, Grant Co., and Sycan Marsh, Lake Co. Numbers reported in Harney Co. in spring have varied over the last ten years from a maximum of seven to none. It is very rare in spring west of the Cascades where there are a number of credible reports from Douglas, Josephine, Marion, Multnomah, and Lane Cos. and possibly elsewhere. Some spring reports may pertain to misidentified Warbling Vireos.

Most spring records are from the latter third of May and the first half of June. The earliest date that the editors agree is beyond any significant doubt is May 20.

Two singing territorial males were found between July 2 and 5, 1982 near Canyon City, Grant Co., but no females or evidence of nesting was noted.

Fall vagrants have been less frequently reported than spring birds, and dates range from Aug. 20 to Dec. 29. The Dec. 29 bird was at Florence, Lane Co., in 1980 and was possibly a wintering individual. Another Tennessee Warbler was at Florence Dec. 27, 1987, but could not be relocated thereafter. Another late fall bird, which possibly attempted to winter, was photographed at Eugene, Lane Co., on Nov. 29, 1981. This bird remained for several days. The species was seen two consecutive winters at the Hatfield Marine Science Center, Lincoln Co.; one Jan. 4-14, 1992, and again Feb. 11, 1993.

Orange-crowned Warbler. *Vermivora celata.*

Common summer resident west of the Cascade Mts., and in winter rare to very uncommon. East of the Cascades, uncommon to fairly common local summer resident and very rare in winter. Common transient at lower elevations statewide.

The Orange-crowned Warbler is a common summer resident in brush and brushy understories of forests from about 4,000 ft. on the west slope of the Cascades down to the coast. It breeds locally at higher elevations on the west slope of the Cascades. In southwestern Oregon it also is common in dense chaparral and oak woodlands. Understory vegetation appears to be a necessary habitat component.

On the east slope of the Cascades and in forested regions to the east, it is a local, uncommon to fairly common summer resident in dense forests with a deciduous understory up to 6,000 ft. Such forests usually are found on north-facing slopes and along watercourses. It is a locally uncommon summer resident to about 7,000 ft. in dense aspen, willow, and mountain mahogany stands on isolated desert mountains. In late July and August there is some movement to higher elevations and timberline, where birds are occasionally seen through September.

Fall migrants are first noted in the last ten days of August, peak in early and mid-September, and a few are noted into mid-October. Migrants are common in deciduous and brushy habitats at lower elevations statewide.

In winter, Orange-crowned Warblers are rare to very uncommon at lower elevations west of the Cascades, where they are found most often in blackberry and other brush. They are very rare at lower elevations east of the Cascades, mostly along the Columbia R.

Spring migrants first appear west of the Cascades in mid-March, peak in mid- and late April, and some are noted into mid-May. East of the Cascades, spring migrants are first observed in early April, peak in mid- and late May, and a few are noted into early June.

Nashville Warbler. *Vermivora ruficapilla.*

Summer resident in southwestern and northeastern Oregon, and locally north through the Cascades. Migrants are seen throughout the state except for the northern coast. Very rare in winter.

The Nashville Warbler is a common breeding bird in roughly the southwestern quarter of Oregon, from Klamath Co. west to the higher elevations of eastern

Curry Co., and north through Douglas Co. The species occurs in natural brushy areas, especially those dominated by *ceanothus*, and can be found in such habitat north locally in the Cascades on both sides of the summit ridge. However, it is much less common north of the Calapooya Divide (roughly the Lane-Douglas Co. line) than in the drier areas south of the Willamette R. watershed. Although birds are found in summer north to Hood River Co., the species' breeding status in the Cascades from Lane Co. northward is poorly known, and it may be absent from some areas of the northwestern Cascades and foothills. It is fairly common in Hood River and Wasco Cos.

In the Willamette Valley, Nashville Warblers breed in dry brushy foothill areas of Lane Co., and have been reported in summer as far north as Finley N.W.R., Benton Co., and sparingly north to at least Yamhill Co.

The only known breeding site in Coos Co. is at Mt. Bolivar in the extreme southeast corner of the county. We are aware of no breeding records north of Douglas Co. in the coast range away from the edge of the Willamette Valley or on the coast, although Forest Service researchers have found the species in summer locally north to Lincoln Co. in very small numbers.

In the northern parts of its range, and in northeastern Oregon, it occurs in dense shrub cover of various types. Evanich (1992) notes that it breeds "in brushy wetland areas at moderate to high elevations" in Union and Wallowa Counties. The species breeds locally in the Blue and Ochoco Mts. to southern Umatilla and Morrow Cos. To the east, it is uncommon at higher elevations in the mountains of Lake Co. There are no other breeding records between Grant Co. and the Cascades, or in the Columbia R. counties east of Wasco Co.

Migrants appear state-wide except on the northern half of the coast, where the species is rare. Spring migrants begin arriving in numbers during the second week of April in southwestern Oregon, and during early May east of the mountains. In fall, this is one of the least visible migrants, in part because it appears to leave earlier than some other species and seems to avoid migrant traps frequented by observers. Late departure dates include November 19 in Douglas Co., though that bird may have been attempting to winter. At Malheur N.W.R., fall migration takes place mainly in August, with no reports later than September 15.

There are a few acceptable winter records for the state, mainly from the coast. However, caution should be used in distinguishing winter Nashville Warblers from the more gray-headed forms of the Orange-crowned Warbler, and from Common Yellowthroats; the former is regular in small numbers in winter, while the latter is rare but reported most years.

Virginia's Warbler. *Vermivora virginiae.*

Vagrant.

An adult, apparently non-breeding, female Virginia's Warbler was netted, banded, and photographed at Camp Creek on Hart Mt., Lake Co., May 29, 1977. Single birds were observed at Eugene, Lane Co., on Nov. 8, 1979; at Stukel Mt., Klamath Co., on July 27 and Aug. 3, 1980; in the Lane Co. Coast Range Aug. 9, 1988; and at Fields, Harney Co., on Sept. 17, 1988.

There is speculation that this species may breed on isolated mountain ranges in southeastern Oregon as it is present in similar habitat in southern Idaho and northern Nevada.

Lucy's Warbler. *Vermivora luciae.*

Vagrant.

There is one record, a bird seen repeatedly and photographed along the N. Fork of the Siuslaw R. near Florence, Lane Co., from Dec. 27, 1986 to Jan. 24, 1987.

Northern Parula. *Parula americana.*

Vagrant.

The Northern Parula has proven over the past 15 years to be one of the more regular vagrant eastern warblers to Oregon. There are now approximately 35 records from the state. Most are during the spring at Harney Co. oases except for one at Cascade Head, Tillamook Co., on Sept. 4, 1980; one at Klamath Falls, May 26, 1981; one at Charleston, Coos Co., on July 9-10, 1984; one at Davis L., Klamath Co., on June 18, 1986; one at Summer L., Lake Co., on June 11, 1988; one at Yaquina Bay State Park, Lincoln Co., on Aug. 28, 1991, and one at Harbor, Curry Co., in August 1993; and on at Sauvie I., Multnomah Co. on Aug. 5, 1993

Yellow Warbler. *Dendroica petechia.*

Fairly common to common summer resident and transient statewide.

The Yellow Warbler breeds statewide, primarily in riparian habitat of willows and cottonwoods. It is a fairly common to common summer resident in the interior valleys of western Oregon and locally in the surrounding foothills to about 4,000 ft. Numbers in this region have declined, apparently due to nest parasitism by the Brown-headed Cowbird. Along the coast and in the Coast Range it is a very local, uncommon summer resident. On the east slope of the Cascade Mts. and in the Blue and Wallowa Mts. breeders are common to abundant in riparian growth and locally fairly common in aspen groves; above 5,000 ft. in this region, breeders are very local. In arid, open country east of the Cascades, it breeds commonly in deciduous thickets along watercourses, and occurs locally in willows and aspens. Breeding also occurs on a limited basis in shade trees in some towns.

The Yellow Warbler migrates throughout Oregon. Spring migrants are occasionally noted in early and mid-April (earliest, April 2), but generally first arrive in late April. The migration builds through May, and peaks in the latter half of the month. The fall migration peaks in the second half of August and early September, and the species is fairly common through mid-September. By late September, it is very uncommon, with only a few early October records along the coast and at desert oases. There are several verified winter records to at least late December in the Willamette Valley.

Chestnut-sided Warbler. *Dendroica pensylvanica.*

Vagrant.

The Chestnut-sided Warbler is one of the more regular "eastern" vagrants in late May-June and September in Harney Co., with scattered records from elsewhere in the state. There are about 25 total records. These include coastal records for May, July, and September, one in Douglas Co. in August, and one in Jackson Co. in late September. Spring records in southeastern Oregon range from April 25 to June 30; fall records from September 8 to October 12.

Magnolia Warbler. *Dendroica magnolia.*

Vagrant.

There are now about 30 records of this bird in Oregon. The first record was an immature found in an "island" of trees separating Tillamook Bay from the Pacific on Bayocean sand spit, Tillamook Co., on Oct. 25, 1964. Many of the records are from the well-birded Malheur N.W.R. and Fields, Harney Co. Most of the rest are from western Oregon, especially the coast. Spring records generally span from May 27 through June 14, and fall records span from September 19 through October 25. One on the Blue R. Ranger District, Lane Co., on May 5, 1988, was inexplicably early.

Cape May Warbler. *Dendroica tigrina.*

Vagrant.

This species was first confirmed in Oregon with a juvenile at Bayocean Spit, Tillamook Co., on Oct. 19, 1980, and another was on the coast at Harris Beach State Park, Curry Co., on May 30, 1992. The remaining records are from Harney Co.: four in autumn (extreme dates September 13 to October 7) and four in spring (extreme dates May 22 to June 7).

Black-throated Blue Warbler. *Dendroica caerulescens.*

Vagrant.

There are about 32 records of this species, mainly in Harney Co, but with sightings in Clackamas, Coos, Clatsop, Jackson, Jefferson, Tillamook, Sherman, Lake, Deschutes and Lincoln Cos. Most records are from late September to mid-October with a few in June, but a Medford, Jackson Co., bird lingered from Jan. 9-30, 1986; one was at Bayocean Spit, Tillamook Co., on Dec. 11, 1985; and one in Powers, Coos Co, stayed most of January 1989. A territorial male spent June 23 to July 10, 1979, on the Mt. Hood National Forest, Clackamas Co.

Yellow-rumped Warbler. *Dendroica coronata.*

Common summer resident in the Cascade and Siskiyou Mts. eastward, and an uncommon summer resident west of the Cascades. Common transient statewide. In winter, uncommon to common west of the Cascades and rare to uncommon east.

The "Audubon's" Warbler (*D. c. auduboni*) breeds in coniferous and mixed coniferous/deciduous forests from sea level to timberline. It is a common summer resident in the Cascades and Siskiyou Mts. and in eastern Oregon, and generally an uncommon summer resident in the interior valleys of western Oregon, the Coast Range, and along the coast. In late July and August there is some movement to higher elevations where flocks often mix with other species. Most depart the higher areas in early September.

Migrating Yellow-rumped Warblers (mostly *auduboni*) are common to abundant at lower elevations statewide and utilize deciduous thickets and trees as well as conifers. The fall migration peaks west of the Cascades from mid-September through October, and some movement continues through November. East of the Cascades, the fall migration peaks from mid-September to mid-October, with a few transients noted into early November.

In winter, Yellow-rumped Warblers usually inhabit deciduous brush and trees at lower elevations. Numbers fluctuate widely from year to year. Wintering flocks are generally common on the coast north to Lincoln Co., and generally uncommon (but some years fairly common) on the north coast and in the interior valleys of western Oregon. East of the Cascades in winter, they are rare or absent most years in most areas, but occasionally uncommon especially in the lower elevations of Umatilla and Morrow Cos. Survivorship is low among those that attempt to winter in eastern Oregon.

The spring migration is noticeable west of the Cascades in mid-March, peaks from early April through early May, and a few migrants are observed through mid-May. East of the Cascades, spring migration begins in mid-April, peaks from late April through mid-May; small numbers are sometimes noted into early June.

The "Myrtle" Warbler (*D. c. coronata*) is a common transient west of the Cascades (peaks in April and mid- through late October) and an uncommon transient east of the Cascades (peaks mid-May and early October). In winter it is generally fairly common west of the Cascades and rare east of the Cascades.

Black-throated Gray Warbler. *Dendroica nigrescens.*

Fairly common to common summer resident in lower and mid-elevation deciduous and mixed forests west of the Cascade Mts. East of the Cascades, local, rare to uncommon summer resident in oak and juniper woodlands except in northeast Oregon where absent. Very rare in winter.

The Black-throated Gray Warbler is a fairly common to common summer resident in deciduous and mixed deciduous-coniferous forests, including regenerating clearcuts, from the west slope of the Cascade Mts. (generally to about 4,000 ft.) west through the interior valleys, the Siskiyou Mts. and the Coast Range to the coast. It is generally absent as a nester in spruce and hemlock forests very near the ocean. East of the Cascades it is a local, rare to uncommon summer resident in oak woodlands of Hood River and Wasco Cos. It is a rare transient through Lake and Klamath Cos., and may breed in very small numbers. It is an uncommon transient in Harney Co., where it breeds in small numbers in juniper habitats. Generally it is absent east of Sherman Co. and north of Grant Co.

Transients occur in deciduous and coniferous trees throughout the breeding range, and are fairly common along the immediate coast, common elsewhere in western Oregon, and rare to uncommon east of the Cascades. The fall migration peaks in the last half of August and the first half of September, with small numbers regularly noted into early October and rarely through late October. West of the Cascades spring transients are occasionally noted in late March, but generally first arrive in early April and peak in late April and the first half of May. East of the Cascades spring transients are first noted in early May.

Since 1972 there have been about 15 winter records from the coast and the interior valleys of western Oregon.

Townsend's Warbler. *Dendroica townsendi.*

Common summer resident in the mountains of northeastern Oregon. Uncommon summer resident from the central Cascade Mts. northward. Fairly common transient statewide. Uncommon to very uncommon at lower elevations west of the Cascades in winter.

The Townsend's Warbler is a common summer resident in moderate and high elevation fir forests in the Blue, Ochoco, and Wallowa Mts. of northeastern Oregon. In similar forests on the east slope of the Oregon Cascades, it is uncommon in summer and also probably nests locally above 4,500 ft. on the west side. It is also present in the Warner Mts. of Lake Co. There are a few widely scattered summer records for coniferous forests west of the Cascades and in the southern Cascades, and breeding has been confirmed in Linn and Lane Cos. Another breeding record was at Rockaway (not Garibaldi as previously published), Tillamook Co., where a pair was found feeding two young on July 12, 1967.

It is a fairly common transient in varied woodland types statewide in spring and fall. Fall migrants are first noted in mid-August. East of the Cascades, the migration peaks in late August and the first half of September, and small numbers are seen into mid-October. In western Oregon the migration peaks in mid-September to early October.

During winter, Townsend's Warbler is uncommon in inland western Oregon, and uncommon along the coast; their status varies from year to year and geographically. There are several records from east of the Cascades as late as the latter half of December, but these may pertain to late migrants rather than wintering birds.

258

Spring migration west of the Cascade crest begins in early April and peaks from mid-April through early May, with a few migrants noted through May. East of the Cascades, spring migrants are occasionally observed in late April, but generally arrive in early May, peak in mid-May, and are rare into mid-June.

Hermit Warbler. *Dendroica occidentalis.*

Common to locally uncommon summer resident in coniferous forests from the west slope of the Cascade Mts. to the Pacific Ocean. On the east slope of the Cascades, locally common summer resident in the more moist coniferous forests. West of the Cascades, uncommon spring and fall transient outside of breeding habitats, and very rare in winter.

The Hermit Warbler breeds in a variety of young and old coniferous forest types, reaching its greatest numbers where there is Douglas-fir. In the Coast Range and along the west slope of the Cascades it is abundant in old-growth and even second-growth, sometimes occupying plantations as little as 20 years old. Along the immediate coast, it is locally fairly common in western hemlock and Sitka spruce forests. In the Siskiyou Mts., it is a fairly common summer resident, preferring Douglas-fir.

This warbler is a fairly common summer resident in the fir zone on the east slope of the Cascades, and locally from low to high elevations in southern Klamath Co. In the Cascades, this species inhabits dense forests of western hemlock, Douglas-fir, true firs, and high-elevation forests of lodgepole pine. It is more scarce within the mountain hemlock zone. On the lower east slope of the Cascades, it may breed very locally in isolated dense stands of firs. In July and August there is some movement to higher elevations and timberline, where the Hermit Warbler often joins flocks of other species. There are several summer sight records from moderate elevation forests in the Blue and Wallowa Mts., where the it is possibly a rare local summer resident.

In Oregon, migrating Hermit Warblers primarily frequent conifers, but occasionally are noted in deciduous trees and brush. Spring migrants first arrive in Oregon in late April and are well established in breeding areas by mid-May. In the interior valleys of western Oregon and along the coast, spring migrants are very uncommon in non-breeding habitats. At lower elevations on the east slope of the Cascades, spring and fall migrants are rare. Statewide the fall migration occurs primarily at higher elevations and birds are rarely noted in the lowlands. Most depart in the last week of August and the first weeks of September, but probable transients have been recorded as late as October 22.

During winter, they are very rare in coniferous forests of the interior valleys of western Oregon and along the coast.

Transients have only been observed at Malheur N.W.R.'s well-birded headquarters four times; three times during spring migration, and once in late September. There is also a June 2 record for Fields in southern Harney Co.

Hermit X Townsend's Warbler hybrids are sometimes found, and should be considered when reporting an occurrence of either species in an unusual time or place, or in identifying the Black-throated Green Warbler, a vagrant to Oregon.

Black-throated Green Warbler. *Dendroica virens.*

Vagrant.

There are five records of this warbler, scattered around the state, all individual birds: at Pike Creek, Harney Co., on May 21, 1983; Cape Blanco, Curry Co., on June 19, 1982; Corvallis, Benton Co., Sept. 21, 1985; Malheur N.W.R., Harney Co., June 16, 1986, and again June 4-5, 1990.

Blackburnian Warbler. *Dendroica fusca*

Vagrant.

There are seven records for the Blackburnian Warbler in Oregon, one immature at Malheur N.W.R. on Sept. 18, 1986; a male that wintered at Nehalem, Tillamook Co., with sightings from Nov. 15, 1987 to at least March 12, 1988; an adult male at Malheur N.W.R. on May 29, 1988; a male at Page Springs Campground, Harney Co., on June 1, 1990; a male at Malheur N.W.R. headquarters on May 23, 1994; and one near Krumbo Res. on Malheur N.W.R. on May 24, 1994.

Yellow-throated Warbler. *Dendroica dominica.*

Vagrant.

The first record of this species for Oregon was found at Malheur N.W.R., Harney Co., and observed by many June 9-11, 1985; one was also seen at North Bend, Coos Co., on May 26, 1989.

Pine Warbler. *Dendroica pinus.*

Vagrant.

The sole observation of the Pine Warbler in Oregon was a single immature found at Harbor, Curry Co., on Oct. 23, 1986. The species has not been physically doc-umented for the state.

Prairie Warbler. *Dendroica discolor.*

Vagrant.

This species has been recorded four times, all in fall from the immediate coast: one immature at Newport, Lincoln Co., on Sept. 27, 1981; one at Bandon, Coos Co., Aug. 24-Sept. 3, 1989; one seen on a boat off Brookings, Curry Co., on Sept. 28, 1991; and one at Harris Beach State Park, Curry Co., on Sept. 21-23, 1993.

Palm Warbler. *Dendroica palmarum.*

On the coast, rare fall migrant, rare to very rare in winter, and very rare in spring. Vagrant to inland western Oregon and east of the Cascade Mts.

Since the second state record in 1966, the Palm Warbler has been a regular rare migrant along the coast in autumn. In some years its status has been uncommon or very uncommon, when as many as 30 reports were received from mid-September though early November as was the case in 1987. The autumn of 1993 produced exceptional numbers in Oregon and elsewhere on the Pacific coast. A total of 97 were found in Curry Co. alone during the season. Migrants first appear in the latter part of September (earliest, September 9, Curry Co.). Some presumed transients are noted well into November.

The Palm Warbler has been found along the coast annually in recent winters, typically several being noted from mid-December through March. There is also a winter record for eastern Oregon, one at the mouth of the Deschutes R., Sherman Co., on Feb. 7, 1992. The species is very rare after March, with records of presumed transients extending into early May.

There are about eight records for the Willamette Valley, which include fall, winter, and spring occurrences. There are about 10 records for east of the Cascades in spring and fall, with records ranging from early May to June 7 in spring, and in fall from mid-September to mid-October in addition to the February 7 record.

A bird of the eastern race (*D. p. hypochrysea*) was seen at Malheur N.W.R. on June 7, 1985.

Bay-breasted Warbler. *Dendroica castanea.*

Vagrant.

There are about 10 records of the Bay-breasted Warbler, all from eastern Oregon oases except for the first record, a male collected near Upper Klamath Lake, Klamath Co., on July 6, 1963, and one near Howard Prairie Reservoir, Jackson Co., on June 22, 1976. Unusual among vagrant warblers is an August record, one at Hart Mt., Lake Co., banded Aug. 2, 1987 and recaptured on August 23 at the same location.

Yellow-rumped Warbler

Blackpoll Warbler. *Dendroica striata.*

Vagrant.

The Blackpoll Warbler has proven in recent years to be one of the more regular vagrant warblers to the state. Most records are from Malheur N.W.R. and elsewhere in Harney Co., where it has been found from mid-May through early June, and from mid-August to early October. One or two have been recorded there some springs, but the species has been missed other springs. There are also two spring records from Cape Blanco, Curry Co. One to four per fall is about typical for Harney Co.; eight were seen during the fall of 1987. It has also been noted with somewhat similar regularity at Hart Mt. N.W.R., Lake Co., when that area has received regular coverage.

There are nine western Oregon records, all but one from the coast: Sept. 15, 1988, at Fern Ridge Res., Lane Co. The coastal records all fall between September 30 and October 10. These few records contrast with the large numbers seen on the coast of California each fall.

A most unusual but well-verified occurrence was that of two adults feeding three young in a woodlot of Douglas-fir, grand fir, and other trees on Sauvie I., Multnomah Co., July 24-26, 1976. The adults were in basic plumage. The young birds, although out of the nest, were begging and were regularly fed. It is presumed that nesting took place at that location, at least 500 miles from the nearest known breeding areas in the Canadian Rockies.

Black-and-white Warbler. *Mniotilta varia.*

Vagrant.

There are now more than 55 records of this species for Oregon. About two-thirds are from the spring. Most are from desert oases of southeastern Oregon such as the Malheur N.W.R. headquarters and the town of Fields, Harney Co., but there are records from throughout Oregon. Spring records extend from early May to late-June, with most in the last week of May and the first days of June.

About one-third of the records are from the fall, from mid-August to late October, with the majority in the latter half of September. As in the spring, the occurrences are widespread and most are from the oases of southeastern Oregon. Fall vagrants have also occurred on the coast, the inland valleys of western Oregon, and from scattered locations east of the Cascades.

There are two well-documented winter records: one at North Bend, Coos Co. from Dec. 17, 1977 to at least Jan. 22, 1978; and one at Eugene, Lane Co., from Feb. 25, 1989 to the end of the winter.

American Redstart. *Setophaga ruticilla.*

Locally uncommon to rare summer resident in the Blue Mts. and Wallowa Mts; breeds or formerly bred locally on the east slope of the southern Cascade Mts. Rare transient generally east of the Cascades. Vagrant west of the Cascades.

The American Redstart is a locally uncommon summer resident below 5,500 ft. on the east slope of the southern Oregon Cascades and in the Blue and Wallowa Mts. It inhabits the deciduous woods that occur along watercourses and lake edges, often within coniferous forests of ponderosa pine and Douglas-fir. On the east slope of the southern Cascades probable breeding sites have included the Little Deschutes R., Deschutes Co., Crescent Creek, Klamath Co., and Davis L., Deschutes and Klamath Cos. Recent records have been few at these sites. There are also a few records for the Salt Creek area of Lane Co., on the west slope of the Cascades. It is a summer resident in Union, Wallowa, Umatilla and Baker Cos., and there are occasional summer records from Grant, Wheeler, Crook, and northern Malheur Cos. Other counties encompassing portions of the Blue Mts. may also support small populations. The only breeding record west of the Cascades was at Shady Cove near Medford, Jackson Co., in 1970, and the only other western Oregon mid-summer record was a male near Foster Res., Linn Co., in July 1982.

Migrants are rare east of the Cascades and are seen most frequently at oases in open country. Fall migration occurrences begin in mid-August, and peak during the first three weeks of September, and few have been noted after early October. The latest fall departure date at Malheur N.W.R. is November 14. Spring transients east of the Cascades are generally rare. The spring occurrences peak in the last days of May and the first week of June, but non-breeders occasionally linger at oases throughout the summer.

Fall vagrants west of the Cascades have been noted from late August to the end of September, mostly along the coast. Spring vagrants, also mostly coastal, have been recorded in late May and early June.

There are two winter records: two immatures at Coos Bay, Jan. 13, 1980, and one at Eugene, Dec. 28, 1987.

Prothonotary Warbler. *Protonotaria citrea.*

Vagrant.

There are four records for the state: one at Charleston, Coos Co., on Oct. 19, 1974; one at Hart Mt., Lake Co., on Aug. 19, 1976; one at Malheur N.W.R. headquarters on Oct. 11, 1987; and one at Malheur N.W.R. headquarters from May 30 to June 2, 1993. The fall birds were immatures and the spring record was a singing adult male.

Worm-eating Warbler. *Helmitheros vermivorus*

Vagrant.

There is one Oregon record for the Worm-eating Warbler, one at Malheur N.W.R. on Sept. 16, 1990.

Ovenbird. *Seiurus aurocapillus.*

Vagrant.

The Ovenbird is one of the more regular "eastern" warblers, especially in Harney Co. in late May and June. Fall records are from early September to early October. There are over 35 records of the species for the state. Scattered records of singing birds around the state are of interest, including one at Wolf Creek, Josephine Co., June 20-22, 1983 and three reported from different locations in the central Cascades in the summer of 1992.

Northern Waterthrush. *Seiurus noveboracensis.*

Rare transient and very local summer resident.

This species maintains a small breeding population in riparian thickets along Crescent Creek and the Little Deschutes R., Klamath Co., and Salt Creek, Lane Co. There is also a record of a singing bird at Lost Lake, Linn Co., in the summer of 1990. Summer birds have also been found on at least two occasions along Clear Creek, Wasco Co.

It is a vagrant elsewhere in the state, most often found in Harney Co. vagrant traps. Records there average about two per year. Most are found in the last ten days of May or the middle two weeks of September. Extreme spring dates range from May 9 to June 11. Autumn records in Harney Co. range from August 2 to October 3. It has been found with similar frequency at Hart Mt. when that area has been covered. There are a few records elsewhere east of the Cascades Mts.

Vagrants to western Oregon include individuals at Beaver, Tillamook Co., on Aug. 26, 1931; Cape Perpetua, Lincoln Co., on Sept. 5, 1988; and Astoria, Clatsop Co., on Oct. 2, 1988. There is a winter record, a bird that hit a window in Coos Bay, Coos Co., on Jan. 7, 1978.

Kentucky Warbler. *Oporornis formosus*

Vagrant.

The Kentucky Warbler was first recorded at Fields, Harney Co., on June 16, 1989 and again at Frenchglen, Harney Co., on June 8, 1990.

Mourning Warbler. *Oporornis philadelphia.*

Vagrant.

There are four records of the Mourning Warbler for the state: an immature at Malheur N.W.R. on Sept. 26, 1982; near Corvallis, Benton Co., on Sept. 4, 1983; a male in breeding plumage near Oakridge, Lane Co., on July 12, 1984; and one at Brothers, Deschutes Co., on June 3, 1990. The species has yet to be unequivocally documented in Oregon.

MacGillivray's Warbler. *Oporornis tolmiei.*

Common summer resident throughout most of the state.

The MacGillivray's Warbler is a common summer resident from near sea level to near timberline throughout most of Oregon. It generally does not nest in the immediate vicinity of the ocean along the north coast. Nesting occurs in dense brush of a wide variety, including waterside deciduous brush, forest understory, chaparral, and the emergent growth of clearcuts and burns. It does not nest in sage habitats or on the immediate coast.

Spring transients are fairly common away from breeding locations in dense vegetation in lowlands, and at higher elevations in autumn. Spring migrants are first observed west of the Cascade Mts. during the latter half of April (very rarely early April) and the migration peaks in early and mid-May. East of the Cascades, migrants are rare in late April (earliest at Malheur N.W.R., April 15), generally first arrive in early May, peak in mid- May, and are sometimes noted away from breeding sites through the first third of June. Fall migration takes place mainly from mid-August through mid-mid-September, with some migrants typically noted into early October. There one mid-winter record, at Eugene, Lane Co., on Dec. 31, 1967. Observers should consider the more northerly gray-headed forms of the Orange-crowned Warbler, scarce even as transients in western Oregon, when identifying possible MacGillivray's Warblers in winter.

Common Yellowthroat. *Geothlypis trichas.*

Locally common summer resident through most of Oregon. Very rare in winter.

The Common Yellowthroat is a common summer resident in marshes and areas of damp lush grass, especially when interspersed with willows or brush, through most of Oregon from sea level locally to about 5,500 ft. It is much less common in northeast Oregon. Transients occur in dense brush and weedy fields as well.

Spring migrants first appear in late March, and are widespread by early April. West of the Cascade Mts., the fall migration begins in late August, birds are often present into October, but are rarely found in the latter part of October.

The Common Yellowthroat is very rare in winter along the coast and in the interior valleys of western Oregon. There are about 20 records from mid-December through February. One at John Day, Grant Co., on Dec. 8, 1987, represents the only winter record for east of the Cascades of which we are aware.

Hooded Warbler. *Wilsonia citrina.*

Vagrant.

There are eight records of this species, including two of singing males defending apparent breeding territories: one at Washburne Wayside, Lane Co., on July 20, 1974; and one along a small creek south of John Day, Grant Co., on July 11, 1982. Other records include one at Malheur N.W.R. on May 20, 1977; one at Portland, Multnomah Co., Oct. 12, 1978; one near Pendleton, Umatilla Co., on Oct. 21 and Nov. 8, 1983; one at Harbor, Curry Co., from Aug. 29 to Sept. 28, 1985; one at Malheur N.W.R. May 31, 1992; and one near Beaverton, Washington Co., on May 20, 1994.

Wilson's Warbler. *Wilsonia pusilla.*

Common summer resident west of the Cascade summit, and locally common to uncommon summer resident east of the Cascade summit. Very rare in winter.

The Wilson's Warbler is a common summer resident from the west slope of the Cascades near timberline to the coast. Coniferous and deciduous forests with dense deciduous understory are preferred. In forests on the east slope of the Cascades and elsewhere in eastern Oregon, it is a locally common to uncommon summer resident in dense deciduous brush, which usually is found along watercourses in this region. Breeding does not occur in aspen or willow stands on isolated desert mountains or along desert streams. In August, post-breeding birds also occur in coniferous habitats and often mix in flocks with other small birds.

Migrants are common in deciduous brush at lower elevations statewide, including desert oases. Throughout Oregon the fall migration begins in early August and peaks in the last half of August and the first half of September. Small numbers are regularly noted through late September, and it is rare into late October. West of the Cascades, spring migrants are occasionally noted in early April, but generally first arrive in mid-April, and peak in the first half of May with smaller numbers noted through late May. East of the Cascades, the earliest record is April 19, but most years it is first noted in early May and peaks in the second half of May. A few transients are sometimes noted into mid-June at locations where breeding does not occur.

In winter, the Wilson's Warbler is very rare in the interior valleys of western Oregon, and on the coast (where most records occur). One at Weston, Umatilla Co., on Jan. 14, 1990, is the only winter record for east of the Cascades.

Canada Warbler. *Wilsonia canadensis.*

Vagrant.

There are four records for Oregon: an immature mist-netted and photographed at Malheur N.W.R. headquarters on Sept. 25-26, 1982; one at the same location on Sept. 2-4, 1988; one at Seaside, Clatsop Co., from Oct. 29-31, 1989; and a window-killed specimen recovered at Gold Hill, Jackson Co., on Sept. 17, 1990.

Yellow-breasted Chat. *Icteria virens.*

Locally common to uncommon summer resident and transient on the southern coast, in the interior valleys of western Oregon and east of the Cascades.

The Yellow-breasted Chat is a locally common summer resident in the Rogue Valley, the Umpqua Valley, and the drier valleys that extend into the coastal ranges of Curry and Coos Cos. On the immediate coast it is a local summer resident only in Curry Co., with a few records of migrants further north. In the Willamette Valley it is a locally uncommon summer resident, more regular on the western edge and in the southern half of the valley. East of the Cascades it is a locally common summer resident at lower and mid-elevations, though mostly absent from the Klamath Basin and Lake Co.

The fall migration peaks in late August and early September. East and west of the Cascades the latest known departure dates are in the first week of October. There are two winter records: one observed eating pears in the Rogue Valley, Jan. 11, 1956; and one at Bandon, Coos Co., on Dec. 29, 1991.

Spring migrants first arrive west of the Cascades in mid- and late April (earliest April 5) and peak in the first half of May. East of the Cascades the first arrivals appear in early May and the peak is in the latter half of May.

Dense willows and brush along watercourses and in bottomlands are the habitats most frequently used, but dense brush in open country or beneath open deciduous and mixed woodland is also inhabited. The cleaning of waterside habitats for development or through livestock grazing has caused a decline in this species, although it remains common in many areas.

Subfamily Thraupinae

Summer Tanager. *Piranga rubra.*

Vagrant.

There are six Oregon records: a male at Hart Mt., Lake Co., June 14, 1979; a female (photo) at Fields, Harney Co., June 13, 1982; an immature at Charleston,

Coos Co., Nov. 10, 1981; a first year male at Malheur N.W.R., June 9, 1987; one at Malheur N.W.R. Sept. 30, 1988; a second-year bird at DeMoss Springs County Park, Sherman Co., on May 24, 1992; and one at Frenchglen, Harney Co., on May 27, 1994.

Scarlet Tanager. *Piranga olivacea.*

Spring vagrant.

There are four Oregon records of this species, all from desert oases in Harney and Lake Cos. in spring. All have been verified by photograph. They include a male at Malheur N.W.R., May 31, 1979; a male at Hart Mt., Lake Co., June 13-14, 1979; a male at Trout Creek, 15 miles southeast of Fields, Harney Co., May 28, 1980; and a female at Pike Creek, Harney Co., May 31, 1987.

Western Tanager. *Piranga ludoviciana.*

Common summer resident throughout the state in coniferous and mixed forests, and common transient in deciduous habitats at lower elevations.

The Western Tanager is a common summer resident in coniferous and mixed coniferous/deciduous forests throughout Oregon from sea level to timberline. It does not breed in juniper country, but breeders are common at Blue Sky, the isolated ponderosa pine stand on Hart Mt., Lake Co.

Migrants are common at lower elevations, often in deciduous habitats. West of the Cascade Mts., spring migrants usually first arrive in late April (very rarely early April), peak in mid-May, and a few are noted in non-breeding habitats into early June. East of the Cascades, spring migrants are first noted at the end of April and in early May, peak in the last week of May, and are noted in small numbers at desert oases through mid-June.

Statewide, fall migrants are first noted in non-breeding habitats in late July, and peak in the second half of August and the first week of September. Small numbers are regularly noted into late September and early October with latest dates in late October. It is extremely rare in winter, with one record Dec. 30, 1973, near Eugene, Lane Co, and one on Sauvie I. on Jan. 18, 1976. Another apparently wintered successfully in Grants Pass, Josephine Co., as it was seen three times from Feb. 28 to March 25, 1975.

Subfamily Cardinalinae

Rose-breasted Grosbeak. *Pheucticus ludovicianus.*

Vagrant.

The Rose-breasted Grosbeak is among the regularly-occurring vagrants to the state. There are in excess of 50 records. Most are of the conspicuous adult males. Records are well scattered throughout the state. As with most other "eastern" vagrants, it is of most regular occurrence in Harney Co.

Spring records extend from mid-May to late June, but most are in the last week of May and the first week of June. There are also several records for various locations during the summer months, both inland and along the coast. A pair of Rose-breasted Grosbeaks built a nest at Cold Springs Campground, Deschutes Co., June 21 to July 3, 1976, but no eggs were laid. Fall birds are less frequently noted than they are in spring; records at that season are also well distributed throughout the state, and extend from August 31 to October 3. There are also three winter records: Woahink Lake, Lane Co. on Dec. 13, 1989; Lake Oswego, Clackamas Co., on Dec. 25-30, 1972; and at Salem, Marion Co., on Jan. 7-8, 1993. One at Tillamook from March 5-13, 1986, may have wintered.

Black-headed Grosbeak. *Pheucticus melanocephalus.*

Uncommon to common summer resident and migrant statewide.

The Black-headed Grosbeak breeds throughout Oregon in deciduous and mixed forests, usually with an understory of deciduous brush. It is a common summer resident in the interior valleys of western Oregon and the surrounding foothills,

273

inhabiting bottomland woods of cottonwood and willow, and forests dominated by maples. It also breeds in oak woodlands, where brushy understory or evergreens or other deciduous trees are also present. It is a fairly common summer resident in the Coast Range, the Siskiyou Mts., on the southern coast and on the west slope of the Cascade Mts., where it ascends locally to about 4,000 ft. in the north and occasionally higher in the south. Homogeneous stands of red alders are seldom inhabited. On the northern coast it is an uncommon summer resident.

On the east slope of the Cascades, Black-headed Grosbeaks are locally uncommon to 5,000 ft. in dense deciduous woods bordering lakes and watercourses. They are locally uncommon in deciduous bottomland woods bordering larger rivers of north-central and extreme eastern Oregon. In the Blue and Wallowa Mts. they are common in valley bottoms and locally fairly common to about 5,000 ft. where deciduous trees such as aspen are present. On desert mountains such as Steens Mt., Harney Co., and Hart Mt., Lake Co., they are fairly common in aspen groves to as high as 7,000 ft.

Migrants are uncommon to fairly common at lower elevations throughout the state, and regularly occur at oases in open country. Fall migration begins in early August, peaks in the latter half of August, and few birds are noted by mid-September. Extremely late individuals have been observed west of the Cascades into mid-October. A bird observed at Portland, Multnomah Co., Dec. 9, 1972 is the latest record. Spring migrants generally arrive west of the Cascades in late April (occasionally mid-April) and peak in early May. An exceptionally early record in March 30, 1980 at Philomath, Benton Co. East of the Cascades, migrants generally first arrive in early May and peak in mid-May.

Blue Grosbeak. *Guiraca caerulea.*

Vagrant.

The Blue Grosbeak has been recorded twice in Oregon: one at Corvallis, Benton Co., Jan. 4-17, 1975 (photographs); and one seen near Eugene, Lane Co., on Dec. 21, 1980.

Black-headed Grosbeak

Lazuli Bunting. *Passerina amoena.*

Uncommon to common summer resident and transient at lower elevations east of the Cascade Mts., in the interior valleys of western Oregon, and in coastal valleys of Curry Co. Rare on the coast north of Curry Co.

West of the Cascades, the Lazuli Bunting breeds throughout the interior valleys and the surrounding foothills. In the Rogue and Umpqua Valleys it is common. In the southern Willamette Valley it is fairly common, and in the northern Willamette Valley it is uncommon to locally fairly common. Breeding also occurs on the west slope of the Cascades, with decreasing abundance and range of elevation northward. It seems to be increasing in the north Cascades, where emergent clearcuts provide suitable habitat. On the coast, breeding occurs only in Curry Co. where it is locally fairly common at lower elevations in dry valleys. North of Curry Co. on the coast it is a rare spring transient, and very rare and local summer resident north to Cascade Head.

East of the Cascades, Lazuli Buntings are uncommon to common summer residents in valleys and on lower elevation brushy slopes of the Blue Mt. region, and locally common in willows bordering watercourses and on brushy slopes in juniper and sagebrush country. In late summer following breeding throughout the state, there is some dispersal to meadows at higher elevations.

Breeding habitats in Oregon include open wooded bottomlands, weedy fields with brushy margins, willows along watercourses, brushy slopes, chaparral, and open oak woodlands. In the Cascades and in the Siskiyou Mts. some years, breeders are locally fairly common in meadows containing willows within coniferous forests, occasionally as high as 6,500 ft. (e.g. Crater Lake and Mt. Hood).

Migrants are uncommon to common throughout the breeding range, and appear in a variety of sites in addition to the nesting habitats, including oases and dense sagebrush in open country. The fall migration peaks in the latter half of August. By September most have departed, but individuals are very uncommon into late September. Spring migrants west of the Cascades generally first arrive in the latter half of April and peak in mid-May. There are occasional observations in mid-April, especially in southwestern Oregon. One at Grants Pass, Josephine Co., March 25, 1977 provided an extremely early record. East of the Cascades migrants generally first arrive during the first week of May, and exceptionally as early as about the beginning of the last week of April.

Indigo Bunting. *Passerina cyanea.*

Vagrant, with occasional summering birds.

This species has been recorded about 28 times in Oregon, with most records from the last week of May and the first week of June. One at Brookings, May 8, 1991, is the earliest definite spring transient record. Sightings have been scattered widely around the state, including the coast, the inland valleys of western Oregon and their foothills, and at various locations east of the Cascades. Not surprisingly, the well-birded areas of Harney Co. produce sightings most consistently.

One male near Roseburg, Douglas Co., in early August 1986 was apparently mated with a female Lazuli Bunting. Singing territorial males have been also recorded into the summer in Harney, Grant, Josephine, and Lane Cos. Other than late May, June, July, and early August, records include one April 10-12, 1987 near Elsie, Clatsop Co.; one at Corvallis, Benton Co., on Nov. 2-7, 1979; and records at Eugene, Lane Co., Nov. 29 to Dec. 4, 1975, and Nov. 9, 1977.

Painted Bunting. *Passerina ciris.*

Vagrant.

There are four records of the Painted Bunting for Oregon: a male collected at Malheur N.W.R. on June 2, 1963; an immature at Tumalo S.P., Deschutes Co., on Oct. 4, 1981; a female at Frenchglen, Harney Co., on June 10, 1989; and an immature photographed at Harbor, Curry Co., Nov. 20-29, 1992.

Dickcissel. *Spiza americana.*

Vagrant.

There are six records of the Dickcissel for Oregon: May 20-28, 1959, at a feeder in Tillamook, Tillamook Co.; one at a feeder at Lakeside, Coos Co., Nov. 30, 1979, and for several days thereafter; again at Lakeside March 9-April 4, 1988; one at Astoria, Clatsop Co., from Dec. 10, 1988 to Jan. 19, 1989; one at Manzanita, Tillamook Co., from Jan. 27 to Feb. 25, 1989; and one at Eagle Point, Jackson Co., from Oct. 23-26, 1993.

Subfamily Emberizinae

Green-tailed Towhee. *Pipilo chlorurus.*

Locally fairly common to uncommon summer resident in south-central and south-eastern Oregon, in the central and south Cascades, and the Siskiyou Mts. Locally very uncommon summer resident in the Blue Mts. and rare on the east slope of the north Cascades and in north-central Oregon north of Jefferson Co.

The Green-tailed Towhee breeds widely east of the Cascades. In southeastern and south-central Oregon it is locally fairly common, north to northern Malheur Co., Long Creek in northern Grant Co., southern Crook Co. and through Deschutes Co. and southern Jefferson Co. on Green Ridge. North of Jefferson and Crook Cos. it is only known to breed in the White R. drainage, Hood River Co., but it probably occurs very locally in other areas of north-central Oregon. In the Blue Mt. region it is a locally very uncommon summer resident in dry foothills and canyons. Habitats utilized east of the Cascades include open slopes and ponderosa pine and juniper forests with a dense brush cover of manzanita, sagebrush, bitterbrush, buckbrush and mountain mahogany. Riparian areas in dry open country are also used. Flat, lower elevation expanses of sagebrush are not frequented. Desert mountains like Steens and Hart Mts. are inhabited to 7,000 ft. On the east slope of the central and southern Cascades breeders are locally fairly common in open ponderosa pine forests, and in Klamath Co. extend locally into higher-elevation forest types, occasionally to over 6,000 ft. There is some post-breeding movement to higher elevations in August and September, at which time birds may be noted at timberline.

On the west slope of the Cascades in Douglas and Jackson Cos., and in the Siskiyou Mts. west to Curry Co., Green-tailed Towhees are locally fairly common on brushy slopes. Breeding may also occur locally on the west slope of the

Cascades in southern Lane Co. They do not breed in the chaparral on lower foothills surrounding the Rogue and Umpqua Valleys.

Records outside of the breeding range include two sightings (one collected) from the west slope of the Cascades in Clackamas Co., one in Medford May 22, 1976, and an immature observed on Roxy Anne Butte, Jackson Co., Aug. 6, 1977.

Migrants are infrequently reported from outside of breeding areas. Spring migrants arrive in late April and early May and the fall departure peaks in late August and early September. By mid-September few remain, but stragglers are occasionally noted into early October.

Rufous-sided Towhee. *Pipilo erythrophthalmus.*

Common permanent resident west of the Cascade Mts. Common to uncommon summer resident and rare to uncommon winter resident and transient east of the Cascades.

The Rufous-sided Towhee is a common permanent resident west of the Cascade Mts., where it inhabits a wide variety of brushy habitats. Although it is most common in the valleys and coastal lowlands it also occurs in the foothills to middle elevations. Late summer and early fall records at high elevations indicate there is some upslope post-breeding dispersal.

This towhee is a common to uncommon summer resident in a variety of brushy situations east of the Cascade Mts. It is generally absent from unrelieved expanses of sagebrush and greasewood flats. Most breeding birds depart by late October, after which it is rare to locally uncommon in winter, with numbers fluctuating from year to year depending on the weather. In winter it is probably in greatest abundance east of the Cascades in southern Klamath Co. Returning migrants typically appear in the latter half of March (rarely in late February), and by late April they are back in their usual summer numbers. Transients are sometimes noticed outside normal breeding habitat.

California Towhee. *Pipilo crissalis.*

Uncommon to fairly common permanent resident of the Rogue Valley and lower Klamath R. canyon. Very local permanent resident in southern Douglas Co. Rare permanent resident near Klamath Falls.

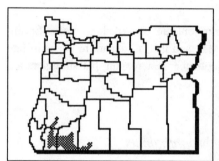

The California Towhee is an uncommon to fairly common permanent resident of the Rogue Valley and the lower Klamath R. canyon of southwestern Klamath Co. Within this range it is found in chaparral comprised mainly of buckbrush interspersed with oaks.

It is a very local permanent resident in similar chaparral in southern Douglas Co. near the town of Myrtle Creek. Gabrielson and Jewett (1940) list it generally from the Umpqua Valley, but cite no records. The A.O.U. Check-list of North American Birds, (1957) lists it from the Umpqua Valley and mentions the city of Roseburg. There have been several sight records in or near Roseburg in recent years, where it is apparently a rare visitant.

In recent years this bird has been found in all seasons in and near Klamath Falls, Klamath Co. The first record for this area was a bird near Keno on Oct. 25, 1972. Since that time this species has been seen several times at locally favored areas near Klamath Falls on sagebrush and bitterbrush covered hillsides, where nesting is suspected. There are several locations south of Klamath Falls on the California side of the basin where it occurs as a fairly common year-round resident.

There are a few unsubstantiated coastal reports of dubious authenticity. Old records from Corvallis, Benton Co., mentioned by Gabrielson and Jewett (1940) are also very doubtful.

American Tree Sparrow. *Spizella arborea.*

Uncommon winter visitant in northeast Oregon, and rare elsewhere east of the Cascade Mts. Very rare winter visitant to western Oregon.

The American Tree Sparrow occurs regularly only in northeast Oregon where it is an uncommon winter visitant in Baker, Morrow, Umatilla, Union, and Wallowa Cos. Elsewhere east of the Cascades it is a rare winter visitant. Wintering birds arrive from the north in late October and early November and usually depart by late March. Favored habitats are riparian growth and brush in grassy areas at lower elevations.

In western Oregon, American Tree Sparrows are very rare during winter, with approximately 30 records spanning the period from late October to mid-May. Four of these records are from the coast, including the latest in Oregon, May 11, 1985 at Bay City, Tillamook Co.

Chipping Sparrow. *Spizella passerina.*

Summer resident or transient in most of the state. Very rare in winter.

The Chipping Sparrow is one of the most widespread breeding birds in Oregon, occurring from the valley foothills to near timberline, most often where there are grassy clearings in forested areas. It is generally a common to uncommon summer resident, and fairly common transient.

It is rare or absent as a summer resident from the coast and northern Coast Range, and occurs there only very rarely as a transient. It occurs locally as a summer resident at high elevations in the Coast Range north at least to Polk Co. It is a local summer resident and a very uncommon transient in the northern Willamette Valley. Generally it is more common at mid- to high elevations.

The Chipping Sparrow is one of the earliest spring migrant passerines, with some birds often appearing in western Oregon by the last week of March, and east of the Cascades by early April. The major movement begins in mid-April west of the Cascades and late April to early May on the east side. West of the Cascades fall migration occurs mainly from August into early October, but a few birds linger through October and even into November.

The winter status of the species is clouded by the likelihood that some records are actually referable to the similar Clay-colored Sparrow, which, although

281

extremely rare, occurs in the state annually. Most experienced Oregon observers consider the Chipping Sparrow no more likely to occur in winter than the Clay-colored Sparrow. Chipping Sparrow is nonetheless probably annual in southwestern Oregon among wintering sparrow flocks.

Clay-colored Sparrow. *Spizella pallida.*

Very rare transient and winter visitant.

The Clay-colored Sparrow has proved to be a very rare transient and winter visitant as more observers have learned salient identification points. Records come from all parts of the state and times of year except mid-summer, with the latest June 15 and the earliest Sept. 20. It is most regular in fall, when it is most likely to occur on the coast. Most years, one or two are found to winter with other sparrows in the inland valleys of western Oregon or at coastal locations. Five of the six spring records (May 26 to June 15) are from scattered locations east of the Cascades. The only spring record for west of the Cascades was one at Toledo, Lincoln Co., on May 16, 1975. There are about 32 records for the state.

Brewer's Sparrow. *Spizella breweri.*

Common to uncommon summer resident east of the Cascade Mts. Vagrant to western Oregon.

The Brewer's Sparrow arrives in mid-April and departs by late September. During this time it is a common summer resident in much of the area east of the Cascade Mts., where it reaches its greatest abundance in the great expanses of sagebrush in the southeastern and central portions of the state. It is an uncommon summer resident in northeastern Oregon (Union and Wallowa Cos.).

Sagebrush is this sparrow's preferred habitat, including high on mountain slopes with warm southern exposures. It utilizes other similar habitats. In the large lodgepole pine areas of southern Deschutes and northern Klamath Cos. it occasionally can be found where there are open, sometimes rocky, breaks in the forest with an understory of bitterbrush. It is also found sparingly in greasewood flats.

Brewer's Sparrow is also likely to be found wherever there is a mixture of sagebrush and other similar shrubs and occasionally in grasslands interspersed with low shrubs.

In the western Oregon lowlands the Brewer's Sparrow is known mostly as a vagrant, though two adults and four immatures at Fern Ridge Res., Lane Co., in July and August of 1985 may indicate breeding. One or two transients are noted during some springs, usually in the last week of April or early May.

Other records are summer birds and may indicate nesting attempts: a singing pair in a logged-over area of the Upper Clackamas R. drainage, Clackamas Co., in June 1970; a singing individual in a burned area near Santiam Pass, Linn Co., also in June 1970; several individuals in burns at five different sites west of Fish L., Douglas Co., June 25 to July 15, 1974; several in a burn west of Fish L., Jackson Co., in June and July 1976; and June 20, 1976, near Emigrant L., Jackson Co. Four singing males and one incubating female were found in a clearcut west of the Cascade crest near Emigrant Pass, Lane Co., in June 1985. Additionally, an estimated seven pairs were found in stunted trees and shrubs at the Cascade crest (about 6,000 ft.) at Jefferson Park, Jefferson Co., during the summer of 1992. Young birds were banded and photographed. These summer records may represent an attempt by this species to expand and utilize habitat structurally similar to high-elevation areas used elsewhere in its range.

Black-chinned Sparrow. *Spizella atrogularis.*

Very rare summer visitant to Jackson and Klamath Cos.

There are five Oregon records, all from Jackson and Klamath Cos. Up to four birds were found at Roxy Ann Butte, Jackson Co., from June 7 to July 2, 1970, and nesting was suspected. A lone bird was found there on May 15, 1971. A pair was present on Roxy Ann Butte from late May to July 29, 1977, and nesting was again suspected. One was seen on Roxy Ann Butte in June 1979. Two singing males were found near Salt Creek, 10 miles northeast of Medford on May 23, and one was still present on June 11, 1979. A family group of two adults and as many as four juveniles were found July 17-22, 1990 on Stukel Mt., Klamath Co.

In Oregon the Black-chinned Sparrow has been found only in tracts of buckbrush in southern Oregon's chaparral country. There are large areas of this habitat in Jackson and Josephine Cos. where surveys might turn up more records.

Vesper Sparrow. *Pooecetes gramineus.*

Common summer resident east of Cascade Mts., locally uncommon to rare summer resident in Willamette and Umpqua Valleys, and locally uncommon summer resident in coastal Curry Co. Uncommon to common transient in Rogue Valley. Fairly common summer resident in the mountains surrounding the Rogue Valley. Very rare statewide in winter.

The Vesper Sparrow is a common summer resident and migrant over much of the grassland, agricultural land and sagebrush country east of the Cascades. It breeds from agricultural valley bottoms to over 7,000 ft. on desert mountains like Steens Mt., Harney Co. and Hart Mt., Lake Co. It is generally an uncommon summer resident in sagebrush country that is heavily grazed and has little grass cover. Transients are fairly common in many areas east of the Cascades where breeding does not occur.

Gabrielson and Jewett (1940) considered the Vesper Sparrow abundant during summer in the Willamette Valley and somewhat less common in other valleys west of the Cascades. Today it is a local, uncommon to rare summer resident in the Willamette and Umpqua Valleys, occurring primarily on drier, grassy hillsides. Recently, two were observed during June at 1,000 ft. in a fresh Coast Range clearcut above Scappoose, Columbia Co. It is widespread, although generally rare, in the Willamette and Umpqua Valleys during migration, and is also an uncommon to rare transient in the Rogue Valley. It occurs locally as a summer resident in Jackson Co. near Howard Prairie Res. and is a fairly common summer resident in the mountains surrounding the Rogue Valley (Browning 1975).

Gabrielson and Jewett (1940) reported the Vesper Sparrow occurred in coastal valleys, without presenting details of its breeding status or distribution. Currently on the coast, it is a locally uncommon summer resident only from Bandon, Coos Co., south through Curry Co. in grassy fields, agricultural land, and some grassy dune areas. It is a vagrant in spring and fall on the coast north of Coos Co.

284

In winter, Vesper Sparrows are very rare in the Willamette Valley and probably also very rare in the Umpqua and Rogue Valleys. There are several confirmed winter Willamette Valley records, but most reports lack verification. There is one winter record for Klamath Falls, one at a feeder Jan. 14, 1988. Elsewhere east of the Cascades, a Nov. 28, 1940 record, and recent CBC reports from Malheur N.W.R. and Wallowa Co. are the only winter records.

East of the Cascade Mts. spring migrants generally return in late March and early April. The earliest arrival date at Malheur N.W.R. is Feb. 28, 1975. By late September few remain east of the Cascades, but stragglers are occasionally noted into October. West of the Cascades migrants arrive in late February or early March, and depart by early October.

Lark Sparrow. *Chondestes grammacus.*

Uncommon to common summer resident east of the Cascade Mts. Fairly common permanent resident in Rogue Valley. Rare and local summer resident in the Umpqua Valley. Very rare visitant to coast and remainder of western Oregon.

The Lark Sparrow is an uncommon to locally common summer resident and transient east of the Cascades. Breeders inhabit grasslands with scattered bushes, agricultural land, open pine and juniper forests and sagebrush country. Nesting rarely occurs to over 6,000 ft. Migrating flocks are often encountered in areas where breeding does not occur. Spring migrants return as early as late March but the migration peaks from late April through mid-May. The fall migration east of the Cascades peaks in the latter half of August and early September, and by mid-September few remain. Individuals are rarely noted into early October. One was at La Grande, Union Co., Feb. 9, 1980.

West of the Cascades, Lark Sparrows are fairly common summer residents in the Rogue Valley and its surrounding foothills. Open woodlands and grassy terrain with scattered bushes are inhabited. They are fairly common to uncommon in the Rogue Valley in winter. Flocks of up to 40 can sometimes be found there at that season. In the Umpqua Valley they are very rare and local summer residents. They were formerly fairly common winterers in the Umpqua Valley, but are now very rare in the winter there (Matt Hunter, pers. com.). The decline appears to have begun in the late 1970s.

At the turn of the century Lark Sparrows were considered regular summer residents in the Willamette Valley. Today they are rare visitants in the Willamette Valley, where since 1972 there have been only about 10 records. Most of these records have been in the months March to June, but two are winter records from the Corvallis area. The species is a very rare spring (mostly early May) and fall (mostly in September) visitant on the coast.

Black-throated Sparrow. *Amphispiza bilineata.*

Uncommon to rare summer resident in southeast Oregon. Rare spring and summer visitant and possible occasional summer resident elsewhere east of the Cascade Mts. Spring and summer vagrant to western Oregon.

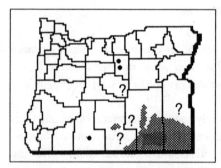

The Black-throated Sparrow is an uncommon to very uncommon summer resident in Harney, Lake, and Malheur Cos. In many areas populations are irregular, present some years and absent others. Breeders inhabit barren and grassy hillsides and the bases of hills with scattered sagebrush, rabbit-brush, and other shrubs, and also occasionally occur in flatlands with widely-spaced sagebrush and greasewood. In flat country with dense sage it is very rare. Black-throated Sparrows are very rare east of the Cascades outside of the above counties. Possible breeding records from outside those counties prior to 1994 include four birds, some carrying nesting material, during May and June 1968 on Nilakishi Ridge, Klamath Co. In the late 1970s and early 1980s a territorial pair, observed carrying nesting material, was seen during several summers in Wheeler Co. near Clarno. In 1983 three singing males were found near Bridge Creek, Wheeler Co. A territorial male was found in Deschutes Co., in 1994. Spring overshoots have been very rarely found at various locations east of the Cascades.

Black-throated Sparrows depart Oregon in late August and early September. There are no winter records. Spring migrants return from mid-April through early May.

West of the Cascades, there are at least 35 records ranging from late April to early June, and one fall record: a bird at Brookings, Curry Co., Sept. 26-28, 1985. Most records are for May. A major invasion in May of 1984 produced at least 13 reports from 10 counties. Another invasion occurred in many areas of the state in May 1994; that year the species was unusually numerous in southeast Oregon as well. At least three birds were present in potential breeding habitat on Roxy Anne Butte, Jackson Co., from May 30 to July 2, 1970.

Sage Sparrow. *Amphispiza belli.*

Locally uncommon to common summer resident and rare in winter east of the Cascade Mts. Vagrant in western Oregon.

The Sage Sparrow is a fairly common summer resident in the arid sagebrush and greasewood country of Harney, Lake, Malheur, and southeast Deschutes Cos. It rarely breeds above 5,500 ft. and is seldom found where junipers are plentiful. Elsewhere east of the Cascades including valleys of the Blue Mts., summer residents and transients are locally uncommon to fairly common in sagebrush and very rare in grasslands with scattered shrubs. Populations fluctuate from year to year and large areas of sagebrush are often uninhabited. During winter, small flocks and individuals have been recorded a few times in Lake and Harney Cos., and individuals have been recorded in several other counties east of the Cascades. Spring migrants usually first arrive in late February. The main spring migration is usually in the middle of March. The fall migration peaks in mid-September, and stragglers have been observed into mid-November (Littlefield 1990).

West of the Cascades there are about 14 records, including a territorial pair near Carlton, Yamhill Co., on June 8, 1976. Most records are from April, though some records correlate to the early normal arrival dates east of the Cascades, such as one at Portland on Feb. 18, 1914, and one at the Columbia R. mouth, Clatsop Co., on Feb. 22, 1981.

Lark Bunting. *Calamospiza melanocorys.*

Vagrant.

The Lark Bunting has been recorded in Oregon 16 times. Four are winter records, two from the Rogue Valley and two from the Willamette Valley. All of these birds were first located in January. The only one that was reported after January was one at a Portland feeder from early January to May 4, 1972. There are six spring records, three from east of the Cascades, one from the coast, and one each from the Umpqua Valley and the Willamette Valley. The extreme dates are May 14 and June 17. There are six fall records involving eight individuals, five from the coast and one from southeast Oregon. The extreme fall dates are August 26 and September 23. These observations reflect observer presence more than any particular pattern of occurrence.

Savannah Sparrow. *Passerculus sandwichensis.*

Common transient statewide. Common summer resident and uncommon to rare winter resident in the Willamette Valley, along the lower Columbia R., and along the coast. Very local summer resident and uncommon winter visitant in Rogue Valley. Common summer resident and rare to locally uncommon winter resident east of the Cascade Mts.

The Savannah Sparrow is a common transient statewide. During migration it can be found in almost any grassy habitat in the state, and in fall even occasionally high in the mountains. Nesting also occurs in grassy habitats.

It is a common summer resident throughout the Willamette Valley, along the lower Columbia R., and along the coast. It is typically uncommon in winter in the Willamette Valley, but may be locally common some years. It is very uncommon along the coast in winter.

The Savannah Sparrow is a common summer resident east of the Cascades, where it is typically rare in winter, but in at least some years has been found to be uncommon or even common at the lower elevations of northern Morrow and Umatilla Cos.

It is scarce and local as a summer resident in the Umpqua Valley. There is a small summer population of probable breeders near Howard Prairie, Jackson Co., which is the only known breeding area in Jackson or Josephine Cos. The Savannah Sparrow is an uncommon winter visitant in the Rogue and Umpqua Valleys. Spring transients sometimes linger into early June and fall transients arrive in August, sometimes giving the false impression of summer residency.

Grasshopper Sparrow. *Ammodramus savannarum.*

Rare and local summer resident. Breeds locally and irregularly, mainly in north-eastern and southwestern Oregon, mostly in small "colonies" that may exist for a few years and then move or disappear. Essentially invisible in migration; only three winter records.

The Grasshopper Sparrow is one of the most enigmatic summer residents in Oregon; it is difficult to describe a breeding "range" for this bird. Although the species breeds in the state every year, it does not always do so in the same places. In recent years these sparrows have been found regularly only in grasslands of Umatilla, Morrow, and Sherman Cos., where several sites have consistently supported birds. A thorough discussion of some of these sites can be found in Janes, 1983; see also Evanich (1990) and articles in *Oregon Birds* regarding various locales. The most important area is probably the Service Buttes of Umatilla Co., where at least 50 birds were seen on private land in May 1992.

Other breeding sites in use in the past 20 years have been near Fern Ridge Res., Lane Co.; central Jackson Co.; near Baker City, Baker Co.; near Buena Vista and at Baskett Slough N.W.R., Polk Co.; at Foster Flat, Harney Co.; in southern Gilliam Co.; and at a site at Dug Basin near the Snake R. in northeastern Wallowa Co. However, birds cannot be found at these sites every year. The status of most grasslands in western Oregon, heavily cultivated or grazed and seral, may render western Oregon Grasshopper Sparrow colonies equally short-lived.

Grasshopper Sparrows are essentially unreported in migration in Oregon. One was noted Aug. 25, 1987, at the Diamond Lake sewage ponds, Douglas Co., the only record for the Cascades. We are aware of three winter records, Dec. 29, 1991 and Jan. 2, 1993, both from the same area on the eastern edge of Fern Ridge Res., Lane Co., and one seen Jan. 4, 1982, at Eugene, Lane Co. and found dead two days later.

Le Conte's Sparrow. *Ammodramus leconteii.*

Vagrant.

This species has been recorded only twice in Oregon, an immature at Fields, Harney Co., on Sept. 27, 1983; and another there Oct. 12, 1991.

Fox Sparrow. *Passerella iliaca.*

Uncommon to fairly common breeder in dense brush in forested areas of the Siskiyou Mts., above 3,000 ft. on the west slope of the Cascades, and from the crest of the Cascades east. Fairly common summer resident in riparian thickets on desert mountains. Common transient and winter visitant west of the Cascades, and uncommon transient and rare winter visitant east of the Cascades.

Grey-headed forms (*P. i. schistacea, fulva, megarhyncha*) of the Fox Sparrow breed in eastern and southwestern Oregon and chocolate-brown forms (*P. i. sinuosa, annectens, townsendi, fuliginosa*) winter throughout the state. In forested regions on the east slope of the Cascades it is a fairly common summer resident in dense brush, including riparian thickets and especially buckbrush (*ceanothus*) and manzanita in open ponderosa pine forests. These habitats are more widespread from Deschutes Co. south, but occur locally north to the Columbia R. East of the Cascades it is a fairly common breeder in brushy habitats in forested regions. Near timberline in the Cascades and northeast Oregon mountains, breeders are locally uncommon. At higher elevations in isolated desert mountains of southeast Oregon it is a fairly common summer resident in waterside willow thickets. In the Siskiyou Mts. and on the west slope of the Cascades, Fox Sparrows are locally common summer residents at moderate and higher elevations.

Oregon summer residents depart the state in September and October, and return in April. Rusty-brown northern transients (probably mostly *P. i. altivagans*) are uncommon east of the Cascades in dense brush at lower elevations in September, October, April and early May, and are very rare west of the Cascades during these months and winter. A bird of the bright rufous form *iliaca* wintered in Eugene one year.

Chocolate-brown forms from the Pacific Coast region of Canada and Alaska are common transients and winter visitants west of the Cascades in dense brush at lower elevations and in the foothills. They generally are first noted in early September, are common by late September and increase through mid-October. Individuals have on several occasions been noted in June in possible breeding habitat in Clatsop Co. East of the Cascades they are rare to very uncommon transients and rare winter visitants at lower elevations. Spring migration occurs in March and April and they are rare into mid-May.

Song Sparrow. *Melospiza melodia.*

Common summer resident and migrant in dense brush statewide. Departs higher elevations in winter, when common west of the Cascade Mts. and uncommon to fairly common east of the Cascades.

The Song Sparrow is a common summer resident in deciduous brush in forests and open country from near timberline (less common and local at higher elevations) on the west slope of the Cascade Mts. west through the valleys and mountains to the coast. In southwest Oregon's dry chaparral country it occurs primarily near water or in other lush vegetation. During winter west of the Cascades it withdraws from the mountains and is common in the valleys and lower foothills. The Song Sparrow also occurs in marshy habitats provided some brush or trees are present. It has adapted well to residential areas in cities and suburbs.

East of the Cascade crest it is a common summer resident (less common at higher elevations) inhabiting dense deciduous brush, which in this region is primarily willows near water. During winter it is uncommon to fairly common in thickets at lower elevations and generally rare to uncommon above 4,000 ft. Numbers vary with winter severity.

Many local summer residents migrate southward out of Oregon, and Song Sparrows from the north pass through and also winter in the state. Migrating influxes are best observed at desert oases, where numbers increase in September and October, and in April and May.

Lincoln's Sparrow. *Melospiza lincolnii.*

Locally fairly common summer resident in the Cascade, Blue and Wallowa Mts. West of the Cascades, fairly common transient and uncommon winter visitant. East of the Cascades, common transient and rare in winter.

In forested regions in the Cascades and eastern Oregon mountain ranges, the Lincoln's Sparrow is a local, fairly common breeder. It inhabits wet meadows with willow patches and watercourses edged with marsh and deciduous brush.

Transient and wintering birds prefer tall grass and dense brush, often in wet areas. Transients are uncommon to fairly common at lower elevations east of the Cascades and generally uncommon in western interior valleys and along the coast. Local breeders depart the higher elevations by mid-September. Transients are generally first noted at lower elevations in late August (rarely mid-August), peak in number in the latter half of September and early October, and small numbers are noted through October. Some spring movement is noted as early as late March, but the migration peaks from mid-April to mid-May and small numbers remain in the lowlands into June. Breeders do not return to many high-elevation nesting areas until late June and early July, when these areas are clear of snow.

During winter, Lincoln's Sparrows are uncommon to locally common in the interior valleys of western Oregon, generally very uncommon along the coast, and rare (recorded most years) east of the Cascades. Wintering numbers vary from year to year.

Swamp Sparrow. *Melospiza georgiana.*

Rare transient and winter visitant west of the Cascade Mts. at lower elevations; locally fairly common on the coast. Very rare transient and winter visitant east of the Cascades.

The Swamp Sparrow is a rare but increasingly-located transient and winter visitant in western Oregon, both along the coast and in the interior valleys. It is very locally fairly common along the coast in winter, such as in the marshy areas near the mouths of the Wilson and Trask Rivers, Tillamook Co.; and near the Coquille R. estuary, Coos Co.

The first state record of this furtive species was in 1955. Beginning in the early 1970s one or more were located most winters. Several per year were typical in the early 1980s. In recent years there has been a sharp increase, and from fall 1987 through spring 1988 several dozen were located. Eighteen in a day by one group of birders near Tillamook on Dec. 19, 1987 was the highest one-day total to that date. In the winter of 1991-92 at least 60 were found in western Oregon. In all likelihood the increase of records, as with many other species, is attributable to more and better-prepared birders in the field. Greater familiarity with this secretive species' calls has certainly resulted in more birds being found.

The Swamp Sparrow occurs from early October to early April. There is an exceptional record of one singing at Salt Creek, Lane Co., in the summer of 1992. East of the Cascades, the species is known only as a rare transient and winter visitant.

In Oregon, this species is most frequently found in damp areas of canary grass and/or sedge, often with some small trees or brush present. They have also been found at the edges of cattail marshes, and in brushy habitats during migration.

White-throated Sparrow. *Zonotrichia albicollis.*

Statewide a very uncommon transient and winter visitant from late September to early May.

The White-throated Sparrow is a very uncommon transient throughout Oregon. Fall transients, which are noted more frequently than spring transients, first arrive in the latter half of September. The greatest numbers are reported in October and the first half of November.

In winter it is very uncommon at lower elevations west of the Cascades. East of the Cascades in winter it is rare and not recorded every year. Winterers depart, and spring transients pass through the state, in April and early May. There are a few late May records, and one was at Hunter Creek, Curry Co., on June 20, 1993.

White-throated Sparrows usually flock with other *Zonotrichia* species, but also occur singly. They more often inhabit woodlands than other *Zonotrichia*, but also inhabit brush patches in open country and visit feeders.

Golden-crowned Sparrow. *Zonotrichia atricapilla*.

West of the Cascade Mts., common winter visitant and transient from mid-September to mid-May. East of the Cascades in winter, uncommon in central Oregon and rare to the east. Transients east of the Cascades are rare in the northeast and uncommon to fairly common elsewhere.

During winter the Golden-crowned Sparrow is common in brush patches and brushy woodland edges at lower elevations west of the Cascades. East of the Cascades in winter it is very uncommon to locally fairly common (numbers vary greatly from year to year) in brush patches at lower elevations in central Oregon, extending south from Hood River, Wasco and Sherman Cos. to Klamath Co., and in northern Umatilla and Morrow Cos. East of central Oregon it is generally rare in winter.

Spring and fall transients utilize the same habitats as wintering birds and are common at lower elevations west of the Cascades and uncommon east of the Cascades, except in the mountainous northeast where they are generally rare. Transients are common in willows and at forest edges in the Cascades and other mountains of western Oregon, occurring to timberline in fall and locally to at least 5,500 ft. in spring.

Fall transients generally arrive in mid-September (late August occasionally) and peak in late September and October. The spring migration peaks from mid-April to mid-May. Small numbers are regularly noted through May, and occasionally into the first half of June, with the latest record June 19.

White-crowned Sparrow. *Zonotrichia leucophrys*.

Common summer resident in many areas. Uncommon to fairly common in winter locally. Common transient in spring and fall statewide.

The White-crowned Sparrow is one of the most ubiquitous birds in the state, highly visible (and audible) on the breeding grounds, and a fairly common member of winter sparrow flocks in the lowlands across the state. Three subspecies make up the Oregon population. Most breeders from the Cascades eastward are of the race *Z. l. oriantha*; most in western Oregon are *Z. l. pugetensis*. These races are distinguished most easily by differences in the head pattern: *oriantha* has black lores, *pugetensis* has white or pale lores. Most birds breed in shrubby areas with or without scattered trees; the species is most common as a breeder on the coast and in the mountains, and is less so in foothill and valley areas west of the Cascades.

In fall migration, when *oriantha* leaves the state to winter in the southwest, large numbers of *gambelii* (a white-lored subspecies) appear from breeding grounds in northwestern Canada and Alaska. Many of these pass through the state to winter in the southwest, but some remain in the valleys of eastern Oregon and, to a lesser extent, west of the Cascades. Some *pugetensis* move south for the winter, but others move in from mountain or northern populations. The nature and extent of these movements in western Oregon is not well understood. Migrants typically become noticeable in late March to early April, and again in late September to early October. The peak of the spring migration is usually noted in Portland in the last week of April. Great numbers are often noted in fall migration east of the Cascades.

White-crowned Sparrows remain uncommon to fairly common throughout the winter in lowland locations in western Oregon. At favored sites, flocks exceeding a hundred birds may be found, often in the company of Golden-crowned Sparrows and other seed-eating species.

Harris' Sparrow. *Zonotrichia querula*.

Rare transient and winter visitant from early October to mid-May.

The Harris' Sparrow is a rare transient and winter visitant at lower elevations throughout Oregon, with around five records annually. It is somewhat more regular in the northern and eastern parts of the state, and rare in the southwest. Fall transients generally arrive in late October and November (very rarely early October) and depart in April, with a few records extending into May. One collected near Nehalem, Tillamook Co., June 19, 1952, was probably a late, lost transient.

Harris' Sparrows inhabit brush patches in open country and flock with other *Zonotrichia* species or occur singly. Sometimes multiple birds are noted, and as many as six have been recorded together in Oregon.

Dark-eyed Junco. *Junco hyemalis.*

Common permanent resident.

In Oregon the Dark-eyed Junco is represented by four forms identifiable in the field, once considered separate species. Hybrids are occasionally noted.

The "Oregon" Junco is a common statewide breeder occurring from the coast to timberline in coniferous and deciduous forests. It is an uncommon summer resident in higher elevation riparian areas within open country, and in riparian areas within forests.

After nesting, flocks are common throughout the breeding range and in open country statewide. In winter, juncos are absent from higher elevations and common in brushy open country, towns, and forest edges at lower elevations throughout the state. The wintering population is probably augmented by birds that breed north of the state.

The "Slate-colored" Junco is an uncommon transient and winter visitant east of the Cascade Mts. and a rare transient and winter visitant west of the Cascades. It arrives in October (occasionally September) and departs by mid-April (exceptionally to late May).

There are two records of the "Gray-headed" Junco in Oregon: one at Malheur N.W.R., Harney Co., May 26, 1976; and one at Cottonwood Creek, Harney Co., on Nov. 14, 1987. This form breeds in southern Idaho and has been found in the Nevada portion of the Trout Creek Mts., just south of the Oregon border.

Most remarkable is the record of a "White-winged" Junco that was photographed at a Bend, Deschutes Co., feeding station, and stayed Feb. 25 to March 7, 1987.

McCown's Longspur. *Calcarius mccownii.*

Vagrant.

There are four Oregon records of this species. A breeding plumage male was observed east of Burns, Harney Co., Aug. 8, 1976; a male in winter plumage was seen in southern Klamath Co. Jan. 31, 1981; and another was there Nov. 26, 1986. One was at Lower Klamath N.W.R., Klamath Co., from Jan. 13-15, 1990.

Lapland Longspur. *Calcarius lapponicus.*

On the coast, uncommon fall transient, and rare in winter and spring. Inland, very rare transient and winter visitant in the interior valleys of western Oregon and over most of eastern Oregon, except in the Klamath Basin, where locally uncommon November to March.

The Lapland Longspur is an uncommon early September to early November fall transient in dunes and along estuary edges on the coast. After early November it is rare on the coast in winter and spring through April, and very rare in early May. An adult male at the S. Jetty of the Columbia R., Clatsop Co., on July 10, 1984 is the only summer record.

In the interior valleys of western Oregon and over most of eastern Oregon it is a very rare transient and winter visitant (September to early April), and is not recorded most years. In the Klamath Basin it is locally uncommon in winter, noted from November to March with flocks sometimes exceeding 100 birds. Inland, Lapland Longspurs usually occur in plowed or cut agricultural lands, often associating with Horned Larks.

Chestnut-collared Longspur. *Calcarius ornatus.*

Vagrant.

A male of this species was photographed at Fern Ridge Res., Lane Co., on May 1, 1976. Other sightings include one at Lower Klamath N.W.R. on Nov. 14, 1981;

one at the S. Jetty of the Columbia R., Clatsop Co., July 17, to Sept. 25, 1985; and individuals at the Diamond Lake sewage ponds, Douglas Co., on Oct. 2, 1987 and Sept. 13, 1989.

Rustic Bunting. *Emberiza rustica.*

Vagrant.

There are two records of this Asian species, both at feeders. One was in Portland, Multnomah Co., on Nov. 21, 1975, and one was at Eugene, Lane, Co., from April 2-17, 1994.

Snow Bunting. *Plectrophenax nivalis.*

Rare winter visitant to the coast and a very rare winter visitant to the interior valleys of western Oregon. Irruptive, fairly common to very uncommon winter visitant in northeast Oregon. Rare winter visitant elsewhere east of the Cascades.

Snow Buntings are occasionally reported from most open areas of Oregon, but by far the largest number occur in northern Wallowa Co. Flocks of several hundred birds are sometimes reported from this area. Numbers in Wallowa Co. and elsewhere in northeast Oregon are highly variable from year to year. In some winters the species is very uncommon there.

Small flocks are occasionally reported elsewhere in eastern Oregon, mainly in Union, Baker, and Harney Cos. There are records from Klamath, Lake, Malheur and Crook Cos, and it is likely that the species occurs irregularly in small numbers elsewhere east of the Cascades. The largest flock reported away from northeastern Oregon was a group of 60 birds seen Dec. 17, 1985 near Malheur N.W.R. headquarters. Littlefield (1990) notes that the species has increased markedly in its occurrence at Malheur N.W.R. in recent years, with an early arrival date there of October 27 and a late date of April 7.

The only other part of the state where the species occurs with some regularity is along the north coast, especially at the S. Jetty of the Columbia R. and the Bayocean Sand Spit, Tillamook Co. There are a few reports each year elsewhere on the coast, mainly from Yaquina Bay northward. There are records scattered the length of the coast, but it is very rare along the south coast. The earliest recorded arrival date in Lincoln Co. is October 1, the latest report is April 14.

Snow Buntings can occur almost anywhere where there is open ground. There are a number of records for the Willamette Valley and birds have even been reported from open areas (such as above timberline) in the Cascades. Even in the Willamette Valley, where there is plenty of apparently suitable habitat, the species is very rare and does not occur every year. We are not aware of any records from the Rogue Valley.

McKay's Bunting. *Plectrophenax hyperboreus.*

One Oregon record.

Two McKay's Buntings were observed and photographed with a flock of Snow Buntings at the S. Jetty of the Columbia R., Clatsop Co., from Feb. 23 to mid-March, 1980. This was the second record for the lower 48 states, and the most southerly record of this species.

Subfamily Icterinae

Bobolink. *Dolichonyx oryzivorus.*

Rare to locally uncommon summer resident and transient east of the Cascade Mts. Vagrant during migration west of the Cascades.

Bobolinks return to their very localized breeding colonies east of the Cascade Mts. in early and mid-May, with April 30 the earliest recorded. The largest of these loose colonies is located near the P Ranch at the south end of Malheur N.W.R., where in the mid-1970s 200 to 350 were estimated (Wittenberger 1978). The colony has remained approximately this size. Smaller numbers nest elsewhere in Harney Co. At the P Ranch grassy meadows interspersed with sedges and forbs are inhabited, but in other areas tall grass and hay fields are used.

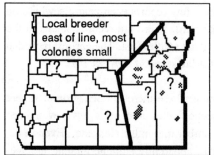

Local breeder east of line, most colonies small

In the Wallowa Valley, Wallowa Co., there are three colonies known, each with 10 to 15 breeding pairs. In Union Co. two to several pairs nest near La Grande, and in Baker Co. small numbers nest near Baker City and North Powder. Small colonies also exist near Prairie City and John Day, Grant Co., and Jordan Valley, Malheur Co. A singing male was observed near Paulina, Crook Co., in 1981. There are probably other colonies in eastern Oregon counties.

Bobolinks congregate in flocks of usually fewer than 20 birds during August, and migrate south in August and early September. It is during the spring and fall migration periods that vagrants appear in western Oregon. In fall it is vagrant to the coast in very small numbers, and is not recorded every year. Fall record are between late August and mid-October. Two were at Myrtle Point, Coos Co., on Dec. 10, 1979, a very odd date for this species to still be in Oregon.

There were three early summer records in valleys of western Oregon in the late 1970s: a singing male was observed on June 2, 1978 in a pea field east of Brooks, Marion Co.; an immature was seen on June 15, 1978 north of Brownsville, Linn Co.; and a male and female were near Ashland, Jackson Co., on June 26, 1978.

Red-winged Blackbird. *Agelaius phoeniceus.*

Common summer resident throughout the state. Common in winter west of the Cascade Mts. Locally uncommon to rare east of the Cascades.

The Red-winged Blackbird is a common summer resident throughout Oregon. Nearly all bodies of freshwater with standing aquatic vegetation for nesting are inhabited, including ditches and flooded fields. Occasionally it nests in bushes, trees, and tall grass. Breeding occurs from sea level to over 6,000 ft.

In July following nesting, flocks are formed which often include other blackbirds and starlings. The flocks forage over dry agricultural lands, and increase in size into September. Many birds leave the state, but large flocks often numbering into the thousands winter in the interior valleys west of the Cascades. Smaller flocks are found in coastal areas, especially on agricultural lands in Tillamook Co. Thousands occur in the Klamath Basin during mild winters, but in most areas east of the Cascades individuals and small flocks are uncommon in lowland agricultural areas. In severe winters they are rare in all areas east of the Cascades except the Klamath Basin, where they are typically uncommon. The species is generally rare at Malheur N.W.R. in winter. Spring migrants return to Malheur N.W.R. in mid-February (Littlefield 1990).

Tricolored Blackbird. *Agelaius tricolor.*

Breeds locally in the eastern Rogue Valley, southern Klamath Co., and at several isolated colonies, mainly in north-central Oregon.

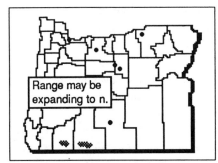

Range may be expanding to n.

The Tricolored Blackbird has been known as a local summer resident in southern Klamath Co. since the Newberry expedition report of 1857, and in Jackson Co. since at least 1958, with summering birds reported since 1956. For further information about the Jackson Co. records see Browning (1975). Gabrielson and Jewett (1940) considered all previous published reports from the state outside the Klamath Basin to be erroneous. Recent discoveries may render earlier reports worth re-examining.

In the 1980s and early 1990s several colonies of this species have been found at locales far removed from traditional sites. One colony uses small marshy ponds in northeast Portland, and may have been there since 1967, as there are sight records from that year and location. Most of the other colonies are in the Columbia R. Basin in north-central Oregon, with active sites reported in recent years near Clarno and Wamic, Wasco Co.; the Painted Hills unit of the John Day Fossil Beds National Monument, Wheeler Co.; and near Stanfield, Umatilla Co. Birds have also been found at Summer L., and there have been scattered summer reports elsewhere, including the Willamette Valley. Most birds leave the state in winter, although there are often a few remaining in the Rogue Valley and Klamath Basin. A few individuals have been reported from wintering blackbird flocks in central Oregon.

Observers should examine any apparent dense colony of nesting blackbirds, as Red-winged Blackbirds are territorial and Tricolored Blackbirds are colonial, breeding in marshes of any size. The true range of the species in Oregon needs further study.

Western Meadowlark. *Sturnella neglecta.*

Common summer resident in eastern Oregon, rare to fairly common summer resident of inland valleys of western Oregon. In winter fairly common in western Oregon, uncommon east of the Cascade Mts.

The Western Meadowlark is a common summer resident east of the Cascade Mts. in grasslands, agricultural lands, and sage country, where breeding occurs as high as 6,000 ft. The grazing, plowing, and spraying of sagebrush communities may benefit meadowlarks as nesting and foraging habitat is increased (Baker 1976).

In the Willamette Valley, it is a local and rare to uncommon summer resident in grassy habitats. Inland in the Umpqua Valley it is an uncommon summer resident, and a fairly common resident in the Rogue Valley.

From August to November migrating flocks, typically of a few birds but sometimes numbering over 100, are fairly common throughout the state. Many of these migrants may originate north of Oregon. Some flocks winter on grasslands and agricultural lands, especially in the interior valleys of western Oregon and less commonly on the coast. East of the Cascades numbers are greatly reduced in winter, but a few individuals and flocks, usually of fewer than 50 birds, do occur on agricultural lands at lower elevations. Migrant are first noted in late February, and summer residents are common by early April.

Yellow-headed Blackbird. *Xanthocephalus xanthocephalus.*

Locally abundant to uncommon summer resident east of the Cascade Mts. Locally uncommon summer resident west of the Cascades. Rare during winter in the Klamath Basin, Lake Co., and Harney Co. Very rare in winter west of the Cascades. Vagrant to the coast.

Colonies of Yellow-headed Blackbirds numbering in the thousands breed in the large marshes of Klamath, Lake, and Harney Cos. Smaller colonies occur in bulrush and cattail marshes in other counties east of the Cascades. Colonies occur at over 5,000 ft. in marshes bordering mountain lakes in western Deschutes, Lake, and Klamath Cos.

West of the Cascades, Yellow-headed Blackbirds are local and uncommon summer residents. In 1981 over 50 pairs nested at Fern Ridge Res., Lane Co., where the species breeds annually. The habitat of a colony of 25 to 50 pairs that occupied Smith L., Multnomah Co., in the 1950s has since disappeared. Other nesting marshes are utilized sporadically, breeding apparently being dependent on water depth and vegetative conditions. Areas where a few pairs have irregularly nested include Forest Grove and Gaston, Washington Co., Albany, Linn Co., White City and Hoover L., Jackson Co., and Corvallis, Benton Co.

In late July and August, Yellow-headed Blackbirds form flocks with other blackbird species, and these flocks usually feed in agricultural areas near the breeding colonies. By late September nearly all have left the state. During mild winters small numbers occur with other blackbirds in the Klamath Basin and at Summer L. It is rare in winter at Malheur N.W.R., and there are a few scattered winter records for other locations east of the Cascades. West of the Cascades they are very rare during winter in the interior valleys; and not recorded every year.

Spring migrants arrive from late March to mid-May. Individuals and small flocks are very rare on the coast during the spring and fall migratory periods.

Rusty Blackbird. *Euphagus carolinus.*

Vagrant.

The Rusty Blackbird has been recorded in Oregon nine times. A male was collected March 20, 1959 at Tillamook, Tillamook Co. Single males were observed on Nov. 13, 1977 at Baskett Slough N.W.R., Polk Co., with other blackbirds, and on Sept. 15, 1979 at Malheur N.W.R. Single females have been observed at Rose-burg, Douglas Co., on Jan. 24, 1981; near Nehalem, Tillamook Co., on Oct. 10, 1981; and at Sauvie I., Multnomah Co, from Feb. 14 to April 3, 1987; Dec. 17, 1987 to the end of the winter (two birds); Oct. 28, 1990; and Dec. 31, 1993 to late January 1994.

Brewer's Blackbird. *Euphagus cyanocephalus.*

Common permanent resident in inland valleys west of the Cascade Mts. Common permanent resident in coastal lowlands. Abundant summer resident and uncom-mon winter resident east of the Cascades.

The Brewer's Blackbird is a permanent resident statewide and one of the most conspicuous birds in Oregon. It is an abundant summer resident throughout the lowlands and nests regularly to over 6,000 ft.

Pairs nest singly or in loose colonies of usually fewer than 30 pairs. Open areas near water and agricultural lands are favored, but grasslands and sage and grease-wood deserts far from water are also inhabited. Nest sites range from the ground to high in conifers. This blackbird also frequents roadsides and suburbs through-out the year. Road-kill insects are frequent fare.

From July through winter most Brewer's Blackbirds occur in flocks, often mix-ing with other blackbirds and Starlings. Flocks commonly number into the thou-sands in agricultural areas west of the Cascades and in the Klamath Basin. Elsewhere east of the Cascades they are uncommon in agricultural areas in win-ter. From late February to May migrant flocks are common throughout the state.

Great-tailed Grackle. *Quiscalus mexicanus.*

Vagrant.

Oregon is on the front lines of this species' recent range expansion in the western United States. It first appeared at Malheur N.W.R. in 1980 and one to several have been seen there in most years since. In the spring and summer of 1993, as many as six birds were found in Harney Co., and one was at Umatilla N.W.R., Umatilla Co. Most records are from mid-May through the June 19. One at Malheur N.W.R. on April 25, 1994 is the earliest record. There are also three fall records: one at Fields, Harney Co, Sept. 27 to Oct. 3, 1993; one there Oct. 14, 1990; and one at Malheur N.W.R., Oct. 26, 1990.

Other sightings away from Harney Co. include one at Island City, Union Co., on June 5-6, 1980; one at Madras, Jefferson Co., May 23-25, 1992; and one on the coast at Port Orford, Curry Co., on June 1-4, 1992.

Common Grackle. *Quiscalus quiscula.*

Vagrant.

The Common Grackle has been recorded about 13 times in Oregon: one at Malheur N.W.R. on May 28, 1977; one at Hart Mt. N.W.R. Headquarters, Lake Co., May 9, 1981; one near Haines, Baker Co., on Sept. 20 and 23, 1982; one at Veneta, Lane Co., from May 1, 1987 and seen for several days after that; one at Port Orford, Curry Co., from June 23 to July 2, 1992; a male at Brothers, Deschutes Co., on May 2, 1992; males at Malheur N.W.R. May 30, 1992 and May 15, 1993; one at Coos Bay on May 31, 1993; three males at Fields, Harney Co., June 1, 1993; one, later joined by a second, at Port Orford, Curry Co., June 6-July 13, 1993; one and possibly a second at Port Orford, Curry Co., Aug. 13-19, 1993, and Sept. 3-14, 1993 (these may have been the same birds seen earlier in the year); and one at Silver Lake, Lake Co., May 8-14, 1994.

Brown-headed Cowbird. *Molothrus ater.*

Common summer resident and transient throughout the state. Uncommon in winter west of the Cascade Mts. and in the Klamath Basin. Rare in winter elsewhere east of the Cascade Mts.

During spring and early summer the Brown-headed Cowbird is common in a wide variety of habitats throughout Oregon, including arid sagebrush and juniper country, agricultural lands, marshes, grasslands, and coniferous and deciduous forests to at least 6,000 ft. As nest parasites of other passerine birds, breeding cowbirds invest no time in incubation or the raising of young, and so are not long tied to the habitats where their eggs are laid. Foraging is carried out primarily in open areas, often in association with livestock. Following breeding they gather in small flocks which often mix with other blackbirds.

Spring migrants first arrive in mid-April and by May breeders are common. The fall migration occurs in August and September, and by October most have left the state. During winter, flocks are uncommon in valleys west of the Cascades. As many as 400 have wintered at the racehorse stables in Portland. East of the Cascades flocks are uncommon during winter in the Klamath Basin, but elsewhere birds are rare or absent, and are typically found only in mild winters.

Brown-headed Cowbirds were first recorded breeding west of the Cascades in the early 1950s. Population growth was explosive, and by the early 1960s they were common in the valleys of western Oregon.

Orchard Oriole. *Icterus spurius.*

Vagrant.

There are four records of this species: an immature at South Beach, Lincoln Co., on Sept. 27, 1981; a female at Toketee, Douglas Co., on May 8-10, 1988; an immature at Brookings, Curry Co., from Nov. 12 to Dec. 12, 1990; and an adult male at Fields, Harney Co., on June 4-7, 1991.

Hooded Oriole. *Icterus cucullatus.*

Vagrant.

There are about 22 records of the Hooded Oriole for Oregon. Ten records are of spring birds that overshot their normal range. The spring records are between April 17 and June 7, and include Deschutes, Klamath, Harney, Jackson, Lane, Washington, and Clatsop Cos. There is one early autumn record, a female near South Slough, Coos Co., on Sept. 1, 1991.

There are at least five winter records, all of which have fed at hummingbird feeders. Most if not all of these birds survived the winter. Wintering birds have been found in Curry, Coos, and Lincoln Cos. and inland in Lane Co. The earliest any of these records have been detected was November 23, and the latest stayed into early April.

Streak-backed Oriole. *Icterus pustalutus.*

Vagrant.

The lone record for Oregon visited Malheur N.W.R. from Sept. 28 to Oct. 2, 1993. This is the northernmost record ever for this Middle American species.

Northern Oriole. *Icterus galbula.*

Common summer resident east of the Cascade Mts. and in the Rogue and Umpqua Valleys. Rare to locally fairly common summer resident in the Willamette Valley and the lower Columbia R. lowlands. In winter, very rare west of the Cascades. Very rare transient and winter visitant on the coast.

The western subspecies of the Northern Oriole, the "Bullock's" Oriole (*I. g. bullockii*), breeds in the lowlands of most of Oregon. East of the Cascade Mts., Northern Orioles are common summer residents, favoring cottonwoods and willows bordering watercourses as well as ranches and towns with large trees. Juniper forests are less commonly used.

In western Oregon, Northern Orioles are common summer residents in the Rogue and Umpqua Valleys, on Sauvie I., and along the Willamette and Columbia Rivers in Multnomah and Columbia Cos. Elsewhere in the Willamette Valley breeders are rare to uncommon. The only breeding record for the coast is that of a pair feeding two young barely old enough to fly at Hammond, Clatsop Co., on July 15, 1983. Western Oregon birds inhabit riparian areas, semi-open oak and madrone woodlands, woodlots in agricultural lands, and to a lesser extent trees near human habitations.

The fall migration peaks east of the Cascades in mid-August, and occasionally a few are seen into mid-September. In western Oregon, migrants are seldom noted, though few birds are observed after early September. Strays are very rare on the coast in fall and spring.

There are some 13 records since 1966 of individuals wintering in the state: three were in the Willamette Valley, five in the Rogue Valley, four on the coast, and one in Baker Co., the only winter record east of the Cascades. The earliest migrants in the Rogue Valley have arrived in very late March, but more typically arrive in mid-April. In the Willamette Valley the species usually is not present until the last days of April. At Malheur N.W.R. the earliest arrival dates are after the first third of April, but more typically near the end of the first week of May. The peak of migration there is around May 15 (Littlefield 1990).

There are about 25 records of the eastern subspecies of the Northern Oriole, the "Baltimore" Oriole (*I. g. galbula*), for Oregon. These are most regular in Harney Co. but have been seen at a variety of other locations including the coast. Most records are in the spring, but there have been fall and winter records on the coast.

Scott's Oriole. *Icterus parisorum.*

Vagrant.

There is one record for Oregon: a female photographed at Fields, Harney Co., on June 4-8, 1991.

Family Fringillidae
Subfamily Fringillinae

Brambling. *Fringilla montifringilla.*

Vagrant.

A male Brambling was a Portland from Nov. 22 to March 31, 1968 and was photographed. The record was the first of this Eurasian species on the mainland of North America. Another was in La Grande, Union Co., from Dec. 9, 1983, into

1984. During the 1983-84 winter, Bramblings also were found in several other western states. Additional records include one at Dallas, Polk Co., on Dec. 1, 1985; one at Florence, Lane Co., on Oct. 25-31, 1990; one at Umapine, Umatilla Co., Feb. 8, 1992; and one at Aloha, Washington Co., in February of 1992.

Subfamily Carduelinae

Gray-crowned Rosy-Finch. *Leucosticte tephrocotis.*

Uncommon to locally fairly common summer resident above timberline in Cascade and Wallowa Mts.and on Steens Mt. Generally an uncommon winter visitant east of the Cascades (sometimes in large flocks). Rare visitant west of Cascades.

From April to October the Gray-crowned Rosy-Finch is found near summer snowfields, alpine glaciers and barren rocky areas above timberline in the Cascade and Wallowa Mts. and on Steens Mt. It is an uncommon to fairly common summer resident.

The winter status of this species on their breeding areas is poorly known. There are only a few records, but these suggest that it may in at least some winters be common. One hundred to 1,000 were at Timberline Lodge, Mt. Hood, Clackamas Co., from Dec. 10, 1962 to Jan. 26, 1963, and 50 were there Dec. 27, 1968.

In winter it descends to lower elevations east of the Cascades, where it is most often encountered in north-central and northeastern counties in open fields and on exposed hillsides. Here they are rare to locally fairly common and are highly unpredictable from year to year. Flocks can number in the thousands. Elsewhere east of the Cascades they are much less common and more erratic.

The Gray-crowned Rosy-Finch is generally a vagrant west of the Cascades in winter and early spring, not recorded most years away from Mary's Peak. At Mary's Peak, Benton Co., the species is a regular winter visitant, usually in small numbers. Forty there on Feb. 17, 1974 is the highest count for the location.

Three subspecies occur in Oregon. The "Wallowa" Rosy Finch (*L. t. wallowa*) is the breeding form of the higher peaks in the Wallowa Mts. This race, along with the winter-occurring "Gray-crowned" Rosy Finch (*L. t. tephrocotis*), is the form with the gray of the head restricted to the crown. "Hepburn's" Rosy Finch (*L. t. littoralis*), the breeding form of the Cascade Mts., has the gray of the crown spreading over the head to give this bird a gray-hooded appearance.

Black Rosy-Finch. *Leucosticte atrata.*

Uncommon summer resident on Steens Mt., Harney Co.

The Black Rosy-Finch was recently again designated as a distinct species by the American Ornithologist's Union. It occurs as an uncommon summer resident above timberline on Steens Mt., Harney Co. The Gray-crowned Rosy-Finch also occurs as a summer resident there.

Black Rosy-Finch remains on Steens Mt. until at least mid-October; and where these birds winter is not certain. Littlefield (1990) indicates that there are no records for the nearby Malheur N.W.R., and he suggests that they may descend to the Alvord Basin.

The species' status in the Wallowa Mts. is not resolved. Two specimens were collected at the head of Big Sheep Creek on July 22 and 23, 1923. Those dates imply possible nesting. These Black Rosy-Finches were with Gray-crowned Rosy-Finches when collected (Gabrielson and Jewett 1940). Evanich (1992) indicates that the Black Rosy-Finch has been found only two or three times in Wallowa and Union Cos. Autumn flocks of rosy-finches have reportedly contained Blacks as well. A flock of 500 in the Wallowas in November 1967 contained an estimated 10 percent Black Rosy-Finches. It would come as little surprise if small numbers of Black Rosy-Finches were found to breed in the Wallowa Mts.

There are no winter records for the Black Rosy-Finch in Oregon. The approachable flock of Gray-crowned Rosy-Finches that sometimes winters near Zumwalt, Wallowa, Co., has not produced any records of Blacks. Black Rosy-Finch should be looked for in winter whenever flocks of rosy-finches are encountered.

Pine Grosbeak. *Pinicola enucleator.*

Uncommon to rare throughout the year in the mountains of northeast Oregon; very rare in winter elsewhere east of the Cascade Mts. Very rare year round in the Cascades.

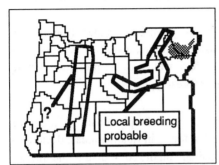

Local breeding probable

The Pine Grosbeak is an uncommon to rare summer resident in the Blue and Wallowa Mts. in Union, Wallowa, Baker, and Grant Cos., where it inhabits coniferous forests above the ponderosa pine zone. It is most regular in the Wallowa Mts.

In winter its occurrence in Wallowa, Union, and Baker Cos. is irregular, ranging from absent to uncommon. Winter birds and the irregular spring and fall migrants occur in coniferous and deciduous woods at lower elevations, and have also been found in the mountains when conditions have allowed birders access. Other portions of the Blue Mts. also occasionally harbor small winter populations. Elsewhere east of the Cascades it is very rare and irregular in wooded areas and in towns; sightings are often separated by several years.

The Pine Grosbeak is rare and irregular in the Cascades and has been reported in those mountains from north to south. There are more than 20 records spanning the months December to August, and it is probably also present at least occasionally in autumn. Breeding has not been recorded but may occur. Spring and summer records, which have involved flocks of up to 15 birds, are primarily from higher elevation coniferous forests. Winter observations, which include a flock of 30, have been made in low and high elevation coniferous forests.

West of the Cascades, there are three records: one at Sutherlin, Douglas Co., on May 17, 1968; three on the Alma-Upper Siuslaw R. CBC, Lane Co. on Dec. 19, 1977; and one in Roseburg, Douglas Co., from April 29 into May 1993.

Purple Finch. *Carpodacus purpureus.*

Fairly common to common permanent resident from the western slope of the Cascades westward. Rare to locally fairly common permanent resident on the eastern slope of the Cascades in Klamath Co. Uncommon summer resident in Lake Co. Very rare transient and winter visitant elsewhere east of the Cascade summit.

The Purple Finch is a fairly common to common permanent resident from middle elevations on the western slope of the Cascade Mts. westward. It is most common from April through September in conifers, which are its preferred nesting habitat. Nesting occasionally occurs in other forest types.

In winter its numbers may decline slightly or even sharply locally as it can be erratic at this season. At this season it is often found in riparian areas, deciduous forests and in towns. Generally it is less common on the coast than in the interior during the winter.

The Purple Finch is a permanent resident on the eastern slope of the Cascades in Klamath Co., where it is generally rare but locally fairly common around Klamath Falls and upper Klamath L. It becomes more scarce in winter. It is an uncommon summer resident in northern Lake Co. A few also breed east of the Cascade crest in Deschutes and Jefferson Cos. Elsewhere east of the Cascades it is a rare transient and winter visitant. The approximately 25 records for this area extend from late September to early June.

Cassin's Finch. *Carpodacus cassinii.*

Fairly common to common permanent resident of the Cascade Mts. eastward throughout all mountainous and forested regions of eastern Oregon. Uncommon transient and winter visitant to lower elevations east of the Cascades. Very uncommon permanent resident of Siskiyou Mts. Very rare winter visitant to western Oregon.

The Cassin's Finch is the typical *Carpodacus* finch of middle to high elevation forests of the Cascades and eastward. It is most abundant in ponderosa and lodgepole pine forests but is commonly found throughout all coniferous forests up to timberline. It is also found in aspen groves, especially if conifers are nearby, such as on Hart and Steens Mts. In winter there is some downslope movement into lower foothills and valleys. Away from forested regions this species is found as an uncommon transient and winter visitant (for example, Malheur N.W.R.).

In the Siskiyou Mts. of southwestern Oregon this finch is a rare to very uncommon permanent resident of at least Jackson and Josephine Cos. It probably occurs in eastern Curry and possibly southern Douglas Cos. It is regularly found on King Mt. on the Josephine/Jackson Co. line in May and June. In the Siskiyous all records are from high elevations, usually in very open Jeffrey pine forests. Its status and habitat requirements are still very unclear there.

In western Oregon knowledge of the status of the Cassin's Finch is somewhat muddled. It is often reported on Christmas Bird Counts, usually without substantiating details. Distinguishing this species from the Purple Finch can be difficult and it is suspected that many of these records may pertain to Purple Finches. There are a few valid records, though, which can give a selected representation of its occurrence in western Oregon: Jan. 1, 1980, at Cottage Grove, Lane Co.; Jan. 11, 1981, Beaverton, Washington Co.; Feb. 5, 1976, at Corvallis, Benton Co.; March 9, 1973, (three banded) at Medford, Jackson Co.; and May 31, 1979, at Cape Blanco, Curry Co. At best this species is a rare winter visitant and transient to western Oregon.

House Finch. *Carpodacus mexicanus.*

Fairly common to common permanent resident at lower elevations throughout the state.

Gabrielson and Jewett (1940) described the House Finch as a common permanent resident in all of the valleys east of the Cascade Mts. and of Jackson, Josephine, Curry, and Douglas Cos. It remains a common permanent resident in these areas today. They mentioned it as being only "casual elsewhere in western Oregon" and cited only one record, a specimen from Forest Grove, Washington Co.

Since that time the House Finch has become a common permanent resident throughout all of the valleys west of the Cascades and a fairly common permanent resident in the coastal lowlands. This range expansion is undoubtedly due to this species' preference for habitats created by human disturbance.

Throughout the state it is found mainly around farms, ranches, towns, residential areas, and open fields and woodlands. It is absent from high elevations, heavily forested and wooded areas, and the great expanses of eastern Oregon sagebrush deserts (except where interrupted by human influences).

Red Crossbill. *Loxia curvirostra.*

Common to rare erratic permanent resident of coniferous forests statewide.

The Red Crossbill occurs throughout Oregon from sea level to timberline. Its erratic seasonal and regional distribution appears to be largely dependent on local cone crops. Nesting may occur at any time of year. Although populations in all areas vary widely, it is generally a fairly common permanent resident in conifers along the coast and in ponderosa pines on the east slope of the Cascade and Blue Mts. In high elevation coniferous forests throughout the state, it is more erratic, but usually is uncommon to common and occasionally abundant in summer and fall. It occurs less frequently at higher elevations in winter and spring. Summer residents are generally rare in conifers in the interior valleys of western Oregon and in the surrounding foothills, but some years they are locally uncommon. In all seasons, non-breeders occasionally appear in deciduous trees far from coniferous forests.

In winter Red Crossbills generally descend to lower-elevation coniferous forests. In the Blue Mt. region deciduous woods and towns in valleys are also regularly inhabited in winter.

White-winged Crossbill. *Loxia leucoptera.*

Very rare and irregular visitant.

This species had been found in Oregon only 11 different years from 1933 to 1981, but has been found in at least six of the 12 years since. Most records come from the Cascade Mts. and northeastern Oregon (Umatilla, Wallowa and Union Cos.). It has occurred in all seasons but most records are from late summer through winter. Thin observer presence in this species' preferred habitat means that only the most significant invasions are well-documented.

The biggest invasion years on record are 1978, 1981, and 1985. There are five records from 1978 starting in March when two were found on the coast in Tillamook Co. and ending in late November with one found in Bend, Deschutes Co. The five records in that year came from five counties (Clackamas, Clatsop, Deschutes, Tillamook and Wallowa) and the largest concentration was 20 or more in Clatsop Co. on May 14. In 1981 there were multiple records. The first was a single bird with Red Crossbills in Eugene, Lane Co., May 15-22, the first western Oregon record away from the coast. The other six records are from the central Cascades, where between July 25 and November 13 more than 40 birds were found at six different locations in Deschutes, northern Klamath and eastern Lane Cos. In 1985, birds were found at many of the same locations as 1981.

An interesting summer record is of a small flock during the summer of 1977 near Enterprise, Wallowa Co. The members built nests but no young were raised.

Common Redpoll. *Carduelis flammea.*

Rare to uncommon and highly irregular winter visitant to northeastern Oregon. Very rare to uncommon winter visitant elsewhere east of the Cascades. Very rare winter visitant to western Oregon.

The Common Redpoll is a highly erratic species. In recent years it has been found mainly in the northeastern section of the state from late November through February, where it is most often reported from Umatilla, Union, Wallowa, and Baker Cos. There are usually fewer than 100 birds in any year and often less than 20. In exceptional years, flocks in excess of 100 birds have been noted. Elsewhere east of the Cascades, it is a very uncommon to rare and irregular winter visitant, with records south to Klamath and Lake Cos.

West of the Cascades, it is a very rare winter visitant, not recorded most years. Records west of the Cascades typically are individual birds, often noted with related finches at bird feeders. Exceptional was a flock of about 150 birds on Jan. 20, 1900, near Corvallis, Benton Co., from which specimens were obtained. A record from Nehalem, Tillamook Co., on May 12, 1991 is the latest for the state.

In Oregon the Common Redpoll is found around fields, farmlands, conifer forests, forest edges, and open brushy country.

Hoary Redpoll. *Carduelis hornemanni.*

Vagrant.

This species has been found among flocks of Common Redpolls on two occasions: one to three birds near Milton-Freewater, Umatilla Co., Jan. 21 to Feb. 5, 1986, and one near Bates, Grant Co., on Jan. 14, 1990.

Pine Siskin. *Carduelis pinus.*

Fairly common to common permanent resident of coniferous forests statewide. Fairly common to common, but erratic, transient and winter visitant throughout the rest of the state.

In coniferous forests the Pine Siskin is a fairly common resident. As a summer resident it is perhaps the least common in open pine forests, preferring firs, spruces, and hemlocks. It is an erratic and unpredictable species often occurring in large numbers in a particular area one year and in small numbers the next.

At least a few are usually present year round. In most coniferous forests there is a downslope movement during the winter which increases numbers at lower elevations. This species is occasionally found in flocks of several hundred birds during the fall and winter.

As a transient and winter visitant it is likely to be found anywhere, even in the open sagebrush country of eastern Oregon where it is rare to uncommon. Throughout Oregon, transients and wintering birds can be found in residential areas and in a variety of woodlands. During the winter it is generally more abundant in western Oregon valleys and foothills than in eastern Oregon or the mountains, but its unpredictable and erratic wanderings mean numbers fluctuate. It often remains in the lowlands away from breeding habitat until mid-June.

Lawrence's Goldfinch. *Carduelis lawrencei*

Vagrant.

A male frequented a Florence, Lane Co., feeder from Dec. 24, 1991 to Jan. 11, 1992 for the only Oregon record.

Lesser Goldfinch. *Carduelis psaltria.*

Fairly common to common permanent resident of the southwestern interior valleys north to the southern Willamette Valley. Fairly common to rare permanent resident northward in the Willamette Valley. Very uncommon visitant along the coast and uncommon in Coast Range valleys from Lincoln Co., south. Fairly common permanent resident of southern Klamath Co. Uncommon summer resident of Lake, Harney, and Malheur Co.

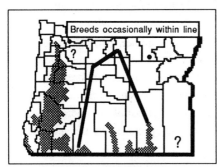

The Lesser Goldfinch reaches its greatest abundance in Oregon in the Rogue Valley. It is common there all year, but can be particularly conspicuous in winter when flocks of up to 100 or more birds can be found roaming around the oak foothills, riparian woods, and brushy areas of the valley floor. It is also commonly found around residential areas. During the nesting season it is more scattered through much the same habitat and occasionally occurs in the surrounding mountains to elevations of at least 2,500 ft. It is also a common permanent resident in the Umpqua Valley.

This goldfinch is a fairly common permanent resident in the southern Willamette Valley. It is generally more scarce northward in that valley, being locally fairly

317

common to rare. It is rare or absent throughout much of the more humid north-eastern part of the Valley, while it is fairly common on the drier western edge of the valley even as far north as Yamhill and Washington Cos. There may be some withdrawal from the Willamette Valley in winter.

This species is an uncommon visitant along the coast in Coos and Curry Cos., and an uncommon summer resident in the small valleys of the Coast Range from Lincoln Co. south.

East of the Cascade Mts. the Lesser Goldfinch is a fairly common permanent resident in southern Klamath Co., with numbers somewhat lower during the winter. It is a locally uncommon but increasing summer resident in southeastern Oregon.

Nesting has occurred in junipers at 7,000 ft. on Steens Mt., adjacent to the Blitzen Valley. It has also nested near Prineville, Crook Co. Other summer records are from Hood River, Wasco, Gilliam, Jefferson, Deschutes, Wheeler, and Grant Cos., where it may be a local and rare summer resident.

American Goldfinch. *Carduelis tristis.*

Fairly common to common permanent resident throughout the state; smaller numbers in winter east of the Cascade Mts. and most of western Oregon.

In western Oregon the American Goldfinch is a common permanent resident. Numbers typically decrease in winter in northwestern Oregon and along the entire coast, and there is much local movement and dispersal from breeding areas from fall through spring. It is a bird of open lowland areas being particularly fond of weedy fields. Whatever nest site is chosen, close proximity to open country is essential for the ground and low vegetation foraging preferred by the species.

East of the Cascade Mts. it is also mainly a permanent resident, although its distribution is more scattered due to large areas of unsuitable habitat. It is fairly common to common from spring through early fall, and uncommon to occasionally common through winter.

318

Evening Grosbeak. *Coccothraustes vespertinus.*

Uncommon to common permanent resident with much local movement.

In general the Evening Grosbeak is a common to uncommon summer resident in coniferous forests statewide from middle to high elevations and a transient and winter visitant throughout the lowlands. It occurs rarely at lower elevations after mid-July.

The Evening Grosbeak is least common as a summer resident in the Coast Range. On a statewide basis it is least common on the coast where it is typically an uncommon spring visitant but occurs occasionally at other seasons.

In western Oregon it is most conspicuous in spring when large lowland incursions occur from March into June. It is not unusual at this season to find very large numbers around towns and cities of the inland valleys where they are especially attracted to bigleaf maples. The Evening Grosbeak is an uncommon to common winter visitant throughout the western lowlands, up to middle elevations, but is not as abundant as during the spring incursions. It is very scarce some winters.

There are also spring incursions to the lowlands east of the Cascades, but the numbers involved are not as great. It becomes common in towns and lowland areas where suitable trees provide foraging. It can also be found in desert oases far from coniferous forests during fall and spring.

Family Passeridae

House Sparrow. *Passer domesticus.*

Common permanent resident near human settlement throughout Oregon.

The House Sparrow is a common permanent resident from sea level to at least 5,000 ft. throughout the state. It occurs mostly near human settlements, and large concentrations often gather where grain is stored. Outside of the breeding season small flocks are formed, usually containing fewer than 100 birds.

The combined depredations of two introduced Eurasian species, the House Sparrow and the Starling, through their effective competition for available nesting cavities, are believed to have resulted in a severe reduction in the populations of a number of cavity-nesting native species.

Bibliography

Many records in the text reflect personal communication to the authors and reports to seasonal reports in *Oregon Birds, American Birds* (or *Audubon Field Notes*) and other publications. To cite such records individually would have severely affected the length of the book.

Ainley, D. 1976. Occurrence of seabirds in the coastal region of California. Western Birds 7:33

Bayer, R. and Booth, S. 1977. Birds of Lincoln County, Oregon. Sea Grant Advisory Program, Oregon State University Marine Science Center.

Bellrose, F. 1976. Ducks, geese and swans of North America. Stackpole, Harrisburg.

Bendell, J and P. Elliott. 1966. Habitat selection of Blue Grouse. Condor 68:431-446

Browning, M. and English, W. 1972. Breeding birds of selected coastal islands. Murrelet 53(1):1

Browning, M. 1966. Additional records on the birds of southwestern Oregon. Murrelet 47:76

Browning, M. 1973. Nonbreeding birds observed at Goat Island, Oregon. Murrelet 54(3): 31.

Browning, M. 1975. Distribution and Occurrence of the Birds of Jackson County and Surrounding Areas. US Museum of Natural History, Washington DC.

Bull, E. 1978. Notes on the Flammulated Owl in northeast Oregon. Murrelet 59:26

Buss, I. and E. Dziedzic. 1955. Relation of cultivation to the disappearance of the Columbian Sharp-tailed Grouse from southeastern Washington. Condor 57:185-187.

Crawford, J. 1980. The quail of Oregon. Oregon Wildlife 35(6):3-7.

Davis, D.E. 1950. The growth of Starling (*Sturnus vulgaris*) populations. Auk 67:460-465

Devillers, P. 1970. Identification and Distribution in California of the *Sphyrapicus varius* group of Sapsuckers. California Birds 1 (2):47-76

Dzubin, A. 1979. in Management and Biology of Pacific Flyway Geese (R. L. Jarvis and J. C. Bartonek, eds.) Oregon State University.

Evanich, J. 1980. The status of White-tailed Ptarmigan in Oregon. Oregon Birds 6:98-100.

Evanich, J. 1992. Birds of Northeast Oregon. Oregon Field Ornithologists Special Publication No. 6.

Farner, S. S. 1952. The Birds of Crater Lake National Park. University of Kansas Press, Lawrence, Kansas.

Forsman, E. 1976. A preliminary investigation of the Spotted Owl in Oregon. MS Thesis, Oregon State University.

Forsman, E. and Maser, C. 1969. Saw-whet Owl preys on red tree mice. Murrelet (51(1): 10.

Gabrielson, I. and Jewett, S. 1940. Birds of Oregon. Oregon State College.

Griffee, W. 1944. First Oregon nest of the Yellow Rail. Murrelet 25:29.

Griffee, W. 1954. Some Oregon nesting records. Murrelet 35(3): 48.

Griffee, W. 1960. Bohemian Waxwing nests in Oregon. Murrelet 41(3): 44

Grinnell, J. and Miller, A. 1944. The distribution of the Birds of California. Pacific Coast Avifauna 27.

Gullion, G. 1951 Birds of the Southern Willamette Valley, Oregon. Condor 53: 129-149

Hand, R. 1960. A sight record of the Brown Towhee in northwestern Oregon. Murrelet 41(3): 40

Henny, C. and Kaiser, T. 1977. Organochlorine and mercury residues in hawk eggs from the Pacific northwest. Murrelet 60:2.

Hoffmann, W. and Elliott, W. 1974. Occurrence of intergrade brant in Oregon. Western Birds 5(3): 91

Hoffmann, W., Elliott, W. and Scott, J. 1975. Occurrence and status of the Horned Puffin in the western United States. Western Birds 6(3): 87.

Horn, K. and Marshall, D. 1975. Status of Poorwill in Oregon and possible extension due to clearcut timber harvest methods. Murrelet 56(1): 4

Jackman, S. 1974. Woodpeckers of the Pacific Northwest: Their Characteristics and Their Role in the Forests. M.S. Thesis. Oregon State University. 147 pp.

Janes, S. W. 1983. Status, distribution, and habitat selection of the Grasshopper Sparrow in Morrow County, Oregon. Murrelet 64: 51-54.

Janes, S. 1987. Status and decline of Swainson's Hawk in Oregon: the role of habitat and interspecific competition. OB 13(2): 165

Jewett, S. 1942. Some new bird records from Oregon. Condor 44: 36

Jewett. S. G. 1946. The Starling in Oregon. Condor 53: 245

Kridler, E. 1965. Records, obtained while banding, of birds unusual in southeastern Oregon. Auk 82: 496-497.

Kridler, E. and D. B. Marshall. 1962. Additional bird records from southeastern Oregon. Condor 64: 162-164.

322

Littlefield, C. 1990. Birds of Malheur National Wildlife Refuge. Oregon State University Press.

Marshall, D. 1992. Sensitive vertebrates of Oregon. Oregon Department of Fish and Wildlife.

McLandress, M. 1979. Status of Ross' Goose in California, in Management and Biology of Pacific Flyway Geese (R. L. Jarvis and J. C. Bartonek, eds.) Oregon State University.

Morrison, Michael and Sherry W. Morrison. 1983. Population trends of Woodpeckers in the Pacific coast region of the United States. Am. Birds 37:361.

Paulson, D. 1993. Shorebirds of the Pacific Northwest. University of Washington Press and Seattle Audubon Society.

Pyle, P. Spear, D. & Ainley, S. 1993. Western Birds 24 (2):110.

Richardson, C. and Sturges, F. 1964. Bird records from southern Oregon. Condor 66(6): 514.

Sanger, G. 1970. The seasonal distribution of some seabirds off Washington and Oregon, with notes on their ecology and behavior. Condor 72(3): 339

Sawyer, M. and Hunter, M. 1988. Checklist: Douglas County Coast. Oregon Birds 14(1): 93.

Schmidt, O., ed. 1989. Rare Birds of Oregon. Oregon Field Ornithologists Special Publication Number 5.

Shelton, A. 1917. A distributional list of the land birds of west-central Oregon. University of Oregon Bulletin (new series) Vol. XIV, No. 4.

Short. L. 1965. Specimens of Nuttall Woodpecker from Oregon. Condor 67:269.

Short, L. 1982. Woodpeckers of the World. Delaware Museum of Natural History.

Stern, M., C.D. Littlefield, & G. Pampush. 1987. The status and distribution of Greater Sandhill Cranes in Oregon, 1986. Unpublished final report to ODFW, Portland, OR. 18 pp.

Stern, M., J. F. Morawski, & G.A. Rosenburg. 1993. Rediscovery and status of a disjunct population of breeding Yellow Rails in southern Oregon. Condor 95:1024-1027.

Taylor, A and Forsman, E. 1978. Recent range extensions of the Barred Owl in western North America, including the first records for Oregon. Condor 78: 560

Townsend, J. K. 1839. Narrative of a journey across the Rocky Mountains, to the Columbia River, and a visit to the Sandwich Islands, Chili, &c.; with a scientific appendix.

Varoujean, D. and Pitman, R. 1979. Oregon seabird survey 1979. U.S. Fish and

Wildlife Service, Portland, Oregon [unpublished report]

Wahl, T. 1975. Seabirds in Washington's offshore zone. Western Birds 6(4): 117

Wilbur, S. 1973. California Condor in the Pacific Northwest. Auk 90(1): 196

Wilson, Ruth. 1980. Western Snowy Plover Workshop Summary. Oregon Cooperative Wildlife Research Unit, Oregon State University.

Winter, J. 1974. The distribution of the Flammulated Owl in California. Western Birds 5:25

Wittenberger, J. 1978. The breeding biology of an isolated Bobolink population in Oregon. Condor 80:355

Woodcock, A. R. 1902. Annotated List of the Birds of Oregon. Oregon Agricultural Experiment Station.

Woolington, D.; Springer, P; and Yparraguire, D. 1979. Migration and wintering distribution of Aleutian Canada Geese, in Jarvis, R and Bartonek, J. Management and biology of Pacific flyway geese: a symposium.

Yocom, C. 1947. Observations on bird life in the Pacific ocean off the North American shores. Condor 49(5): 204.

324

Index